ABSURD MEANING
Love pursuit

Philippe Gregoire

Publisher: BoD – Books on Demand, info@bod.fr
Printing: BoD – Books on Demand,
In de Tarpen 42, Norderstedt (Germany)
Print on demand

ISBN: 978-2-3220-9208-6
Legal deposit : February 2023

PREFACE

I allow myself, from time to time in this book, to deliver my deep feelings and a more subtle vision, 30 years after this epic, with my current eyes and heart, in order to analyze and deconstruct my impulses of the time, virgin of spirituality that I was at that time.

This story will therefore be frequently interspersed with texts in italics which are my current notes and points of view, concerning the person I was at the time, after I had met - and sometimes married - precious women on my way, after training courses and seminars of personal development, after many Essene cures received with the blessing of the divine light, and especially after more maturity and physical experimentations of certain laws of the Universe, on Earth.

I wish, without pretension, to popularize concepts that are difficult or complex to grasp, such as reincarnation, our past lives, astral travel, and others that are simpler *(although)* such as dogmas and religions on Earth, our health, food, or our mental hygiene.

I like to exchange on themes such as unconscious patterns that repeat themselves without our knowledge, to deconstruct emotions that everyone feels without being able to find a deep meaning, in relation or not to our early youth.

All this in the end to try to better understand who we are and what we came to do in our present incarnation, because after all, aren't we all similar, with our emotions? We all live more or less the same traumas, setbacks and accidents of life from personal angles, but aren't these experiences intended to make us grow, until our final judgment, back in the light, when the time of the assessment of our life will have sounded?

These are my beliefs anyway.

Enjoy your reading.

TABLE OF CONTENTS

1	Start, first laps of the wheel...	1
2	End of the spaghetti, the wind is blowing to Greece	19
3	Free and happy in Greece	25
4	The Gods of Olympia	32
5	The Cyclades, Ios, and life in white and blue	36
6	Mykonos, and the sale of the bike	44
7	Winter is coming to the islands	57
8	Strong as a Turk!	63
9	The Valley of the Smurfs	77
10	Istanbul	90
11	Destination Orient, Bangkok	98
12	The Golden Triangle	117
13	A descent into hell in Koh-Samui, I hit rock bottom.	126
14	Sex, alcohol and rock & roll	137
15	End of the holidays	155
16	Back to school : Thai massages	163

17	End of Thai massages	174
18	Discomfort in Malaysia	180
19	Monastery Retreat	192
20	Buddhist teachings	206
21	Dancing with the cobras	218
22	End of the monastic retreat, a new man	229
23	The dream island : Koh Pee Pee	235
24	Adam and Eve in Paradise	252
25	Krabi, Bangkok, and goodbye Thailand	260
26	The Burmese: People with a pure heart	270
27	The face of Myanmar	282

1. Start, first laps of the wheel...

1st day : woke up super sleazy. Slept for an hour and a half in Helena's arms after a great party with my friends.

I have to say that I've been preparing myself for this departure for more than a year and that, of course, the last evening was quite intense.

I invited all my friends, and especially all my ex-girlfriends, like the guy who wants to show off and have fun... Yep, my last seven girlfriends with whom I lived something like love, for a few nights or a few weeks, just to have a little fun and choose the one I want to spend the last crazy night of my old life with.

It will be memorable and I don't want to miss it.

Play it up a bit too. Who's going to deserve me one last time? Proud young man that I am.

We had a great time, lots of noise, music, weed and booze, and I sorted them out one last time to see which one I wanted to cum in again. Helena won the jackpot, a package of meat soaked in alcohol, half dead. The lucky girl...

I feel fragile, like I don't really know what I'm going to do. My heart and my mind are a bit panicky. Even if all this has been carefully thought out, it's not a small thing to decide to leave everything, to go far away, to close the door of your apartment one last time, knowing that you'll never come back, and not knowing where you're going.

No more job, no more reassuring routines, no more friends nearby, end of contract at work, break of lease for my studio, announcements to the family. Tough last few weeks...

It's crumbling in my weakened brain, but it's getting through...it's holding, I have to do it and I will do it.

I'm made for it.

I close the door to my house, put the keys in the mailbox for good, and walk out onto the sidewalk with my bike and its baggage. I impress myself with what I'm doing.

I snort, squeak, unravel my skeleton, almost force myself to start the first turns of the wheels that take me away from what used to be my home, and this life so reassuring...

To understand the path that led me to accomplish this initiatory journey, you have to know where I come from.

I was born into a poor family of farmers from the Haute-Savoie region.

My mother, as a teenager, kept cows, she was a simple farmer with too little intellectual baggage to be confronted later with the vices and predation of men. She was beautiful, and what had to happen, happened. When she was twenty, she met a handsome man from the south of France who made her dream and hypnotized her. And he swept her off her feet, much to the chagrin of her parents, who had seen the predator coming and warned her off. But doesn't love make you blind? So she left her green Savoyard meadows for a small village in the south of France. There she saw the true face of her new lover and got to know the sidewalks. Not to stroll, but to work... For her boyfriend was a pimp, and through his schemes she found herself a whore. But the little country girl that she was, was good for nothing. So they broke her in, as they used to say in the trade. Rape, punishment, humiliation, abuse, the brutal panoply of pimp exactions to shape her docile and malleable. But nothing worked. The new little whore of the neighborhood did not bring back anything flashy and stumbling at night. So she got herself knocked up, between two exits from prison, by her lousy guy, my biological father.

And I was born a little later, a year after my sister. Nice to meet you. I quickly discovered the pleasures of crying, abuse, humiliation, and the early loneliness of the child.

My sister and I sometimes ate from the dogs' bowls, we sometimes slept in the cellar, we were useless in this family eager for easy money, and everyone was happy that my sister would at least be good for something later, in 17 years, on the sidewalk. Meanwhile, my mother was sent to Switzerland to work. Since she was useless outside, she might as well go work there and bring back some money...

The in-laws kept us prisoners in their house, just to put pressure on my mother, so that she wouldn't screw up, and especially that she would send her salary at the end of the month.

That was the plan, and it lasted three years.

The first years without love, without a cuddly mother, without affection. Moreover, since the grandfather, who also lived under our roof, fell seriously ill with tuberculosis, we threw our young bodies into this disease... And here we were, tuberculosis patients.

And off to a preventorium 50 km from any habitation, inland, as this deadly disease was very transmissible at that time. We were five and three and a half years old respectively. My sister and I were there for 18 months. Daily injections into our flesh, all the children lined up in rows facing the wall, with the nuns coming up behind us, poking our butts like barflies playing darts. Bad memories, all that...

In short, our small and ungainly duo will have spent almost the most beautiful first years of their childhood without hugs, tenderness, kisses and love. When we know that almost the whole psyche of the child is built during this period, we can't say that we missed to have a damn beginning of incarnation in this life.

3

Let's continue...

When I was about five years old, my mother came to visit us at the preventorium on a beautiful summer Saturday with a man and a blue car, a beetle. And they kidnapped us. Come on, no more children! We were taken from the clutches of these in-laws and this inhospitable hospital environment to sneak back to Switzerland and start a more normal life again, all together.

The end is much happier for her because she dared to ask for a divorce and obtained it five years later.
My sister and I never knew the son of a bitch of a biological father who passed on his genetics to us.

I told you this for the following reason: to demonstrate how powerful negative emotions experienced can be transformed into a positive force for the individual.
I have always been a stutterer. I didn't start talking until I was about 21-22 years old. Deep traumas prevented me from speaking normally. Too many emotions were blocking my throat. Unless I also brought up emotional slag from a previous life in which I would have, why not, died hanging or strangled in a situation of injustice... This is a possible way to explain my problems of verbalization. Anyway, since I can't really express myself like everyone else without attracting mockery and hurtful taunts, I have developed a sense that allows me to read bodies. Yes, I read bodies as openly as I read a book. Nothing can be hidden in a moving body. It has allowed me all my life to see the truth behind words and actions, or the tricksters who try to cheat behind gestures. I love it, it's an infallible gift.
This beginning of life also allowed me to develop a huge compassion for all living things, and in particular for animals, as we will see later on.

It was therefore strong and fragile at the same time, from these deep wounds and invisible traumas that I decided to brave destiny, to get

4

the lead out, to whip myself to find myself, to meet myself, to flush out deep inside who I really was.
And there was work to do!

But what few people know and have known - even my childhood friends didn't know it at the time when I left them - is that I basically left Geneva-the-Swiss-well-too-smooth for a more intimate reason than simply going on an adventure.

I wanted to go and find the one who would become my wife.

Yeah... I know, it's crazy.
I felt it unconsciously deep inside me, I was getting ready, I felt that it was time, at 29 years old, I knew I was strong enough to build something with my partner of heart. The desire to seriously get involved with a woman, and why not have a child with her, to get married, was now pressing. This destiny was calling me. The Gods were impatient to see me vegetate as I had done for too long. Unconditional dreamer that I am, I had just spent over ten years of nightlife in all the local nightlife circles, and I had not found the one who could become my wife. I thought then, rightly, that she was certainly not here, not in this city.
So I had to go and look for her, even if I had to go to the farthest reaches of Australia...
And so I went.

But the Gods were always very playful and teasing with me...

Hard day. Train to Toulon, waiting half awake on a bench in zombie mode, getting the bike back. Great !
Installation of the bags and luggage on the bike. The front must weigh about fifteen kilos and the back about twenty. A few clothes, tools for the bike, spare parts, patches, tubes, some special light camping gear, enough to heat water, two or three

kitchen utensils, not much in fact, the minimum. The bags are hanging on each side of the wheels, it's a great look! "Expedition" look, but without stickers and sponsors.
All on a quay.
Photo that smells like the departure...
A little proud man.
Then get in the huge steel boat. Not many people, nice staff, I have a private cabin and it's good for my luggage. I'm lame, it's 9pm and I go to bed when the bow starts to split the water.

The next day, strong swell on waking, it is the delirium at the bow of the boat! The waves exceed the deck of the ship by three to five meters. It's pitching! Most of the passengers offer their dinner to Neptune from the deck... the fish are happy.

Arrival at Porto Torres. I touch the ground of Sardinia. First contact. It's ok, the language is not too lost, you have to shake your brain a bit to get out the Italian knowledge from school. I manage.
I found a pension with a typical mamma. Or a typical boarding house with a mamma. Wandered around. Nothing to see but steep and calm cliffs. The sea is beautiful. I am relaxed.
Tomorrow, first real ride to Alghero, about 30 km south.
I take deep breaths, I'm far from home and I'm starting to realize what I'm doing.

My calves still remember the Tour of Corsica two years ago. Once you've done that, you can do anything! In Corsica, fifteen meters from the seaside, the slope is still crazy! It's a real mental feat of strength to keep going! Not to mention the number of punctures because of those little thorns on the side of the road, typical of Corsica.
So I'm happy to be on flat ground compared to Corsica.

The same goes for the first mountain pass. When you've done it, something gets loose in your head. Because the climb is never-ending, it is a succession of upward bends, wheel turns, pedal strokes, hard work, a way of the cross for a non-Catholic, strewn with "I've got to go" in the head, a real test. A test that lasts three or four hours. Yes, the first pass puts you to the test. A lot happens in your head when you pedal so hard for so long.
A bit like when you get a big tattoo... you travel through pain! You don't know if your thighs are going to give out first or if your head is going to say: "Stop, stop! I can't take it anymore, stop Phil, I don't even know what you're doing, are you crazy or what? Do you really enjoy being in pain and suffering that much? And by persevering, once at the top, at the pass, so satisfying! What a long struggle! And you tell yourself that after having done that, you can do anything! The world is mine!

But for the moment I'm getting stronger, I need to sleep a lot, eat, be cool. Recover from this last week with its succession of emotional goodbyes and wild parties.
I've been preparing for this departure for over a year.
Every evening I would come home from work focused on the calm and peace I needed to find in my heart, I would lie on the couch for about an hour and a half and meditate, repeating to myself mantras I had created with short and strong phrases, like "my physical body is indestructible", "my force of action is dynamic", "my energy is unlimited", "my creativity is infinite", "my will is steel", "my mind is powerful", etc...
I repeated them over and over again, just to silence all the fears naturally lurking in my brain, which kept popping up again and again. Because it's easy to think about a huge project like this one, and even easier to give it up, beset as we can be by all sorts of negative questions.
First, think about it mentally. Will I be able to do it?
It's a long way around the world, full of unknowns, unforeseen

events, surprises, fears, and perhaps terrors...
Aren't you a bit crazy Phil? Well, yes, precisely, I've always liked
crazy projects. And all my friends, my family, who said to me:
"Yes, yes, of course..." with a kindly look, thinking that the sweet
dreamer wouldn't do it.
Well, yes, he's on the road, Phil...

All those financial sacrifices to get there. A year ago I didn't have
a penny, I blew all my wages on stupid things and motorbikes,
because I was aimless. God, if I could go back... so much money
spent unnecessarily!

I was able to put aside 15,000 euros for this trip.
Knowing me, that'll keep me going for a long time. I don't need
much, I know that. I don't mind sleeping on a straw mattress and
having very little. I've already sold everything I had to go to Ibiza
seven years ago, I know I don't need much. I know I don't need
much of anything, but I can't touch food. My palate is delicate
and I'm a lover of the senses. So I'll never go without good food,
that's impossible.

My bike is an old, strong and heavy nail, declared stolen by a
friend who gave it to me. It's nothing exceptional and that's good
because in my case it's better not to attract any covetousness and
to be discreet. At least I'll have less to worry about when I leave it
somewhere. I tinkered with it to strengthen it a bit, installed a
rack on the front and back, bought some repair tools, a patch kit,
one or two wrenches, it should be fine. That's all I need.
A week before I left, I tried to sell everything. Everything I had.
Clothes, household accessories, motorbike and bike
stuff, in short, all of it in a big pile in the middle of my living
room, and the friends who sometimes came to see if they could
find something they liked. All for 10 euros.
Well, I didn't sell much, but it's still a good way of clearing out

the clutter.

It's quite something to sell everything you've got!

Day by day, the apartment empties and the feeling of freedom grows in my heart. It's an intimate feeling and it's linked to fear, itself mixed with excitement and anxiety. It's very weakening to part with everything you've acquired, to feel empty, as if impoverished. But so much freer.

Fear too, because I am not like everyone else. The duality in me is changing day by day and I always have this little guy on my right shoulder who tells me: "That's good Philippe, go for it without knowing where you're going, be cool, we're here to help you, trust us", and the other one on my left shoulder: "Aren't you a little crazy! Where are you going like that? That's not the way we should live! And your job that you quit, such a great career *(you sound like my mother)*".

Well yes, because I had to quit. I had a great job, very well paid, the equivalent of 6,000 euros in salary, a lot of diplomas obtained in the last few years, everything I needed materially.

But nobody understood me...

My life didn't really make sense.

I was surviving more than I was living, through routines, motorcycles and women.

I was missing something...

I longed for the intangible, the non-palpable, to feel the breath of a new wind on my face, smells, to be surprised, not knowing what will happen the next day, the unknown.

Go explain that to the rational and fearful people, those who talk about retirement and have a short vision of their future...

But I am Philippe.

And I left everything.

Following my heart and its surprising aspirations.

Believe in your dreams, have faith in yourself and keep going.
It's hard to keep believing in your dreams when you grow up, when
you become an adult, when you get married, when you take on
responsibilities at work.
Add to that the big slaps of Life...
There are not many people out there who talk to us about this, who
push us on this path, who teach us.
So what? We must forget everything and bend to the System, to the
Matrix? Even if it means getting lost in it? Erase the joy of the child,
the excitement of the new?
The problem is that the System doesn't care about dreamers.
We must produce and consume. Not dream and be happy. The
Matrix has no interest in this. It doesn't bring happiness. It doesn't
sustain the hospital and drug system for example.
So how can we find in ourselves this different energy to dream of
something else, to believe in ourselves again, in the power of the
invisible, and in the little child who always sleeps in our heart?

Personally I have my method : when I fall asleep, or just before I
wake up, there is always this moment when I am not yet totally in my
body, when my etheric body floats above my physical body, and I
become conscious again with the world. This moment is precious, it
is the alpha wave of sleep/wake. We can self-program ourselves in
this phase, all by ourselves.
Just imagine, for example, that the little child I once was is still
there, curled up in a cozy little cave in my heart, and I can talk to
him. To ask him what he wants to do, what he would like to be
happy. For that little boy is me. He knows what is good for me. He
will always tell me what to do to make me happy in my everyday life.
As soon as I start talking to him, I believe that I can achieve
anything, that anything is possible. He knows that. He just asks that
I face my fears, that I take them on the chin, that I find the courage
and take the first step. Boldness, courage and temerity, he expects
from me. He also knows that the Universe will react with

*benevolence from my first move, to show me the signs and
synchronicities that I can continue.
That's how it works for me. When I get a crazy urge, when I feel
something crazy in my heart and my rational mind starts fighting it,
I know I'm holding a great idea...
Like the day I entered a dive shop in Thailand on a dream island,
and, without ever thinking about it, came out as an instructor a year
later.
A sick story that I will tell you later...
And on this adventure born from a crazy idea, the sweet madness's
only followed...
From a professional diver I became an underwater photographer
and made great pictures during two years. Then I went back to
France - with a baby in my wife's trunk - and decided to scan them
because, on the one hand, there were strange square boxes
containing Windows 3.1 on the desks, and on the other hand, the
Internet was developing and one started to find on the web tutorials
to create one's own animated website with lots of tips and tricks
which seriously excited me.
So I wrote my first website filled with pictures that made me dream...
And guess what? I won the 'Nets d'Or' of Wanadoo in 2000!
Crazy, my ideas as a kid, my happy child's ideas! That's where they
led me... People needed to dream at that time, I guess, and I was
providing them with that through my site and these pictures.
As you can see, nothing was decided in advance when I was
shooting fish underwater, but from joyful perseverance to
methodical tenacity, everything happened, and even more than I
could have imagined.
These are examples that show that by listening to yourself, by
trusting your sweet madness, by listening to your kind and
sometimes crazy little inner voice, it can give birth to a new life full
of joy and love...*

*Believe in your dreams, act, and above all take the first steps,
continue to have faith in yourself, and the doors of the Universe will
open on your way!*

Isn't it said in all the great dogmatic books that: "Help yourself, and heaven will help you..."?
Go forward, and trust!
The heavens and the Gods love the bold!

And I find myself at the beginning of my road that should lead me... I don't know where.
I don't really realize what is happening to me, how lucky I am to be free and at the beginning of a great adventure that many will envy me later and that should lead me to the east, several thousand kilometers away. I'm heading towards the unknown, I've already been in this situation several times and I must say I love it. I'm a discoverer. It excites me. It frightens me. It scares me and it makes me powerful.
And on the bike I must say that the feeling is even more intense. Because you only need good calves and energy. Then comes the crazy question that we never ask ourselves in our society, when we go from point A to point B: am I going south, north or east? The first time I asked myself this question, I never in my life felt so light and free, it's so exhilarating it makes you dizzy.

But for the moment I'm going to try and ride the 30 km to today's stage without blowing my legs off.
I feel a great calm in my head. That's it! I have begun the transmutation of my soul. The one I was waiting for all those times when, lying in the sofa of my living room, I meditated after work by visualizing this adventure.
Provided that the Gods help me, that the good spirits are with me, that I only meet interesting people. I'll take care of the rest!

I have always loved living with the invisible, the immaterial world, spirits, ghosts and entities imperceptible to our human eyes. It is part of me, I often talk to them, to the Gods.

Although I am sure that it is my energy that generates everything that happens to me, and that there is no point in relying on something else, or someone else, I like to imagine powerful spirits in the ether who watch over me, whom I can ask for help or protection. Like in those mythological stories that made me dream so much. I feel that I am helped in this life.

As a teenager, I was already attracted to books about aliens and UFOs in libraries. Then, about paranormal experiences, out of body experiences, astral travel, past lives... Thanks to Lobsang Rampa and his many paperback books which made me dream so much by his spiritual adventures in his Tibetan monastery. Thanks to you, Edgar Cayce, for all these testimonies on the former lives that I devoured in your books.

I have always been attracted by this world, always known that it exists, that it is really true, that crop circles are not created by young people who play with wooden boards, that other civilizations are quietly observing us and see us with the eyes of parents amused by these different children's groups who inhabit this beautiful planet and do not even know how to control their demography, and take almost all its resources. Such children! Dirty kids, yes, wrapped up in their egos...

This earth is an intermediate planet to strip the souls, to descale the egos, to allow the entities to refine their essence in order to progress in the higher and luminous floors of the higher consciousness, and to continue their adventures. In the 3D, the density. To experience what this dimension can bring as trials for the consciousness.

So yes, I talk to the Gods, as in ancient mythology, I imagine them playing from their clouds with humans, on the great chessboard of Life, sometimes laughing at our setbacks and always having fun with us. It makes me smile and sometimes I resent them, or I thank them, depending on what I am experiencing...

In reality I know that it is rather me that I thank. For I am part of the Whole. I am merged with everything and everyone. And it is my soul that I congratulate, as if I were giving myself a big pat on the back. "Bravo Phil, well done!".

Sunday 26 September: this morning I set sail quickly. Can't wait to start pedaling.

40 km stage. About two hours at an average of 20 km. Not bad for a start. I arrive in Alghero. I find a campsite. This time, I'm there! Unpack my stuff, beach not bad, not very interesting town but I don't care. Pitch the tent under some curious looks... Who's that guy ? Where does he come from ? I don't mind this feeling... Always this duality in me. I like to go unnoticed - with the bike loaded as it is, it's impossible - but also to be looked at, admired. Aaahhh... this eternal need of consideration because of this shitty childhood ! Thanks mom.

It's in my interest to pedal as much as possible because the hours are long alone. At least when I pedal I'm doing something.

It's amazing how the Italians show off. It's in their blood. In the evening, the cars drive at a pace, one behind the other, there are crazy traffic jams, and I go round the center three times to show off my shiny Fiat and to make sure people see me. It's a ritual, a cult! They're all groomed, the lira is down, they eat potatoes but there's always enough to buy hair gel.

I met a Moroccan guy working in Italy, nice but contaminated by the show-off. Getting in the car to get a pack of cigarettes across the street, music blasting, windows open. Damn it, it's small things, but it bugs me!

On the other hand, Italian women.... "bellissime"!

27 Sept: Monday. Quite a stage!
I set off, true to myself - that is, optimistic - on the road to Bosa,
about 40 km away. I make 15 km, but it starts to fucking climb!
My providence was a trucker who took me on his initiative, bike
in his tipper, and I realized what my ordeal could have been: 20
good kilometers of beautiful climbing! He took me to Bosa, a
small town that doesn't break anything, the most beautiful city in
the world according to him. I go on, having bought some food,
and I stop at the top of a hill, in a shack under construction but
abandoned for a long time. I am stiff!
I'm still very lucky! And thanks to all those who love and protect
me! Let me explain: before the hill, the trucker stops, that's lucky,
isn't it? Then, completely exhausted, my eyes dripping with salt
and my shirt soaked, I stop in front of this house under
construction, it's still lucky. And do you know why? Because right
now there is a huge storm! And lightning, and thunder, and rain.
The deluge...
Impossible to unpack the tent and settle down.
I'm on the first floor, on the sheltered terrace, there are no walls,
no balcony, no windows, everything is open and the view on the
small hillside with its pueblo in front of me is delightful. The
hammock is set up in the supposed living room and my stuff is
unpacked in the dining room, or what should be because there is
nothing but a big can and some bricks, the walls are bare and
nails are everywhere. My palace for a night!

On the menu: starter - tomato mozzarella, no oil or vinegar, salt,
pepper, fork, plate. A delight! Then, for the main course, we have
a good loaf of local bread, exquisite! For dessert, supreme
refinement, a raw velvety banana or a crushed pear coulis.
Humm... I will come back to this relay!
 And outside, it falls. I'm going to have an incredible night if it
rains like this all the time!
Look, I can see my breakfast for tomorrow morning: grapes from

a vineyard fifty feet away.

Tuesday, mountain stage, 30 km. Hard!
Early wake up, coffee in my special camper stove that I use for
the first time, and departure to a village located at 500 meters of
altitude. On the map it looks cool, on the bike it's a pain. My first
pass.
Well, it's not that much, you just have to be on the right gear and
push, relentlessly, without stopping...
I arrived at the top soaked. And then the descent. It's all about
not getting cold. I know that my weak point is the top of my
lungs. I was raised with tuberculosis. Always have the sweater
around my waist and listen to my body.
It's a bad day today. I'm doing a few more kilometers but I'm fed
up, I feel the rain, I'm swimming in my filthy clothes, I'll take the
first hotel I find.
Empty, mortified, I found it, with a superb view on a deserted
and romantic bay, and this deep blue sea. From my room I can
see the whole village and the bay with its cliffs torn and molded
by thousands of years of erosion.

I love this feeling of peace that is starting to settle in me. Peace,
or serenity. Something has calmed down. I feel settled.
I like to feel this peace, this inner calm. My mind has been
nagging me less since I started pedaling.
I am on my way.

But there is something wrong with the beginning of this journey.
Or maybe I'm not in the right place. Something that I feel is
wrong, out of place... I still wanted to have some entertainment,
to be able to stop in small bars along the road, to go from
campsite to campsite... But here, everything is closed or closed
down, a desolate image, the small bars hardly exist. The season is
over. There are no more tourists except me, and some Germans

on motorbikes, the campsites are closed.
I hadn't thought of that! I'm looking for peace and quiet but it makes me melancholic and puts pressure on me. I didn't want this. I'm wondering if I'm going to reconsider my plans for Greece. I wouldn't like the absolute solitude either.
Besides, the sun is shy!
I have to think about it, it's upsetting, it's not what I imagined...

Wednesday 29 Sept: Origiano. 30 km stage, quite long and, under the full moon, it seemed even longer... its influence I guess. I've decided that tomorrow I'll go to Cagliari by bus because the route leaves the seaside and I only feel good on my bike by the sea.
I find a quiet spot on a small beach, far enough away from the road not to be disturbed and I set up my tent. My own little trick: I put four sticks around the tent, three meters apart, and joined them with fishing line to create an invisible line around the tent. The alarm will be triggered as soon as an animal or someone approaches the tent, the wire will act as a stop and it should ring and wake me up.
I fall asleep serenely.
It's not much to do with peace of mind. A wire half a millimeter thick...

It's amazing how crazy Italians are about glasses! They all wear them. Women, girls, men, on their noses, in their hair, in their sweaters, whether it's sunny or not, inside or outside. Only me, a tourist passing through, doesn't wear one. I am quickly spotted...

1er October: two days that I am in Cagliari. I arrived by bus from Origiano directly to the tourist office which indicated me a cheap pension. I go there, it's nice. Then I visited the city, first by bike, then on foot. It's superb. Cagliari is on a mound where the old town is nestled, with its narrow, sinister alleys, but where all the artists have their shops. Sculptors, painters, welders. It is very impressive to see. And nobody in these alleys. Another striking fact is the lack of terraces outside. While the streets are teeming with people, not a single terrace. One person tells me that it is the Sardinians who prefer to gather in taverns.

 The evening "passegiatta" is very colorful, people are all dressed up and stroll around quietly, passing and passing again up to five times in a quarter of an hour! The girls are all very cute, they look with insistence but they are also rather short on legs, too small for my meter eighty-eight, small cubes on legs what!

I went to get my ticket for the ship to Italy, thinking I would go through Naples, but departures to that destination are only on Wednesdays. Tonight there is a ship leaving for Civittaveccia. So, although I've never heard that name before, I take it. It's above Naples and on the other side is Ancona, the naval base for departures to Greece.

My thighs are taking shape. I never really cared about them - I always thought my legs were flabby, even skinny - but I find them beautiful! They're gaining muscle, they're getting a nice shape, I'm even finding them sexy and showing them off, like shorts that are a bit too high, sitting on a café terrace, like: "Hey, look at the work of the hamstrings and the calves, not bad eh! Look at that little ball, there, sticking out of the bone, go on... see and admire what was for too long one of my intimate contrition's, one of my big weaknesses, those little flabby legs...".

In short, I am in good shape.

I must say that, as a teenager, I was always self-conscious. I was skinny. Far too disembodied, not "down to earth" enough, not grounded enough in matter. More like a head in the air, in the stars. Joe-the-dreamer. I used to tread lightly and regularly on my ankles, so little attached to the ground, to the earth. They called me Iron wire-Phil because I was so skinny. The guy who hesitates to go out when there are big gusts of wind... So when I did, it was often with a

pair of jogging pants under my jeans, just to furnish the container a bit.
I know, it's sad... I don't want to tell you the trouble when I was in a nightclub and I had to pee, all those layers to take out and put back on, the heat while dancing, the sweat, in short... Not cool the teenager struggles that weigh down his life and complicate it.
Once again, thank you mom.

It took me about twenty years to get rid of these complexes, to start loving myself truly, to see myself in the mirror without seeing only flaws.

By the way, do a nice and funny test: try to kiss yourself in a mirror. In an elevator for example. You'll see, it's not as easy as you think, especially if you put your heart into it!
It took me a long time to get there.

2. End of the spaghetti, the wind is blowing to Greece

Saturday, October 2: It's amazing how sometimes our destiny -
by not controlling it exactly but by staying on the highway of our
birth path - can lead us to what is good for us!
I've been wanting to go to Rome for a long time, and now I'm
here, for the sake of a braised octopus!
How the hell did I get there, for the sake of a fried squid?
No boat to Naples, so I took the one that went to Civitacitta.
Then, after an epic crossing where I was thrown out twice from
the place where I was sleeping by guys who were in the right, I
ended up sleeping outside on the deck, alone. I wasn't cold, with
the full moon reflecting off the calm sea. It was great! Especially
with good music in my ears.
Freshly disembarked, I jumped on a bus going to Rome, I was
too eager to be there. A child's dream at two and a half hours by
bus. The bike lying in the luggage compartment.

Arriving in Rome, the first hotel we found asked for the
equivalent of $150! GASP! The next one, 250 $... Ouch! Finally,
not wanting to go all over the city with a bag, which was itself on
this pile of bones that had become Philip, which was itself on the
bike, exhausted, I ask a guy to meet me and I had the best
hideout in all of Rome. In this case, just at the beginning of the

"big tourist crowd" center, where the pedestrian area starts, a pension on the third floor, in the kind of impressive building with its ten meters high floors and its 120 steps stairs between floors. Imagine, on the roof... a view of all Rome!

I'm currently living in a tiny room measuring three by two meters, with a small skylight made from a piece of plexiglass placed over the opening.
Result of the races: 25 $ for two or three days, it is perfect! The pension is huge, there must be about twenty rooms and the owner, very nice, is painting in his living room. Leonardo da Vinci atmosphere... There's really a little air of Rome's fine arts from the beginning.

Armed with a map that turned out to be too small, I walked only a small part of the city, about 10 km², not much on the map, to check the bus schedules to Ancona, Bari or Brindisi.
I walked around, got lost, bought a more detailed map, stopped on terraces and finally saw what Rome was, and its ultimate symbol: the Trevi Fountain. This great fountain with these gods trying to tame powerful horses, all on a waterfall of marble and water. Gosh, it's beautiful, dazzling!
Of course, all these alleys are full of tourists, and I take a bath in the crowd, breaststroke in one direction, crawl in the other, I like it, being social incognito soothes me.

I need to do some laundry, I'm so dirty.

It's funny, I'm starting to dream in Italian...

Last night, I went out through the skylight of my room to take a walk on the roofs. Feline and muffled atmosphere in exploration mode.
Rome, there is so much to say! It is so beautiful! And funny in

this season. All these tourists, with a map in their hands, coming towards me, who don't have one, to ask me where this monument or that street is. Many weddings are held in front of all the major monuments. In front of almost all the buildings I visited, a large limousine stopped to let down the bride and groom who were going up the stairs on which dozens of tourists in search of a rest were crowded. Unusual and beautiful at the same time.

The Trevi Fountain is for me the must, I am attracted by these sculptures of strong men, with perfect bodies, pulling their horses, I could stay there for hours, spellbound.
In front of it is an esplanade with a basin of water containing thousands of coins at the bottom, the tradition being that you have to make a wish, with your back to the fountain, and throw the coin over your shoulder. Then it was a parade of people, tourists and locals, having their picture taken while performing this mythical gesture.
I witnessed an amusing
scene in which a man in rags, or almost, asked a group of tourists for a coin. The tourists could not refuse because they were about to make a wish and could not throw it away because it would jeopardize their gesture of kindness. Once he had the coin in his hand, he stepped aside to let them think he was going to make his wish and do his business too, but snuck away once their backs were turned. It was only a small coin, but the way it was done taught me a lot about human cunning.

This afternoon, a visit to the Vatican.
In my humble opinion, it is the eighth wonder of the world. I climbed to the top of the dome through a maze of stairs as wide as my shoulders and never ending, to get out at the top after a quarter of an hour, exhausted like everyone else, but even more stunned by the beauty of the panorama. All of Rome at my feet.

This is the kind of sentence that Caesar must have often said to himself!

Back from the peaks, visit the Sistine Chapel, which is nothing but grandeur, marble, dazzling earthenware, grandiose sculptures, gilding, silver. What magnitude, this vault! There is not a place, not a wall that is not decorated, adorned. An atmosphere of respect, admiration, humility among everyone, all these ants walking with their noses raised on this painted or sculpted marble floor. I was amazed!

I met two interesting couples. The first had spent two weeks cycling in Italy, and I was able to speak French again, and the second were Canadian and had visited Paris and Rome before returning home. It's good to talk to people!

The next day, I took my stuff and my bike, direction the east coast. And Brindisi, goal Greece.
Cool ride, flat road, lots of traffic, I don't care, I'm going to change country soon and I'm excited about it.
Camping in the evening where I find a place.

Wednesday 6: Brindisi, located on the heel of Italy, almost in the south. Found an ordinary hotel. Nothing to see except that all the tourists, with their backpacks, are jostling for a deal with the travel agencies for Greece. In fact, in the street where I am, there is only that. Every ten meters there's an office where you can buy boat tickets to Greece.
I'm leaving for Patras tomorrow at 2pm.

I met a nice guy at the hotel, a Colombian chico and we spent the evening laughing in Spanish. What folklore to juggle with languages, I love it.

Today, with Pablo, we talked with Czechs who had nothing to eat. Czechs with no provisions.

They came here and got a job in a circus to pay for a boat ticket to Haifa, Israel. There they can work the land and earn between $1,000 and $1,200 a month. In their country, they earn the equivalent of $200! I really realized that I was lucky, that I shouldn't show that I have more money than them or that I'm going very far. It's all about philanthropy and respect for others.

Took the boat to Greece. Met two Germans travelling with their dogs. They are cool, the new "grunge" generation, they live from everything and nothing, especially from nothing, they make braids or tattoos to live. They must be 20 or 25 years old and have left for "they-don't-know-how-long". Just like me. Cool attitude.

I'll have to learn the Greek alphabet, because so far and pretty much everywhere in the world, the alphabet is the one we know. But Greece has its own alphabet. The "R" becomes the "P", another letter forms the sound "PH", etc...

To the Gods of Olympus, I am coming!

To imagine and begin such an adventure, you have to surrender to a special state of mind: letting go.
Very difficult for most of us.
Certain astrological signs are favored for this: Pisces, because they are wanderers, dreamers and wanderers in the soul, some Scorpios, kings of I don't care, because it helps to relativize and to let oneself live according to the winds, Aquarians also. The earth signs are not really willing to let themselves be guided by the Gods, too fixed to the ground that they are, and the fire signs are more the type to provoke the elements and to put their foot in the door rather than kneel down in front of the invisible and let themselves be carried away...

Letting go, the basic ingredient of this adventure.
Indispensable for any aspiring adventurer. So difficult to create in our brains, so structured, from civilized and material societies, used as we are to our lives of routine, stubborn habits, routines that lead us and keep us in comfort.
A sacred word that not many people talk about outside. Our comfort! Too precious that it is for all of us. Except that by basing our lives and decisions on the concern for comfort, letting go is likely to be missing. It's hard to let go of everything and open yourself to the unknown when you're swimming in comfort. Because letting go is daring to say: "Screw you all!", but also "Let it be so!" and "I open myself to the universe and to what it will bring me". To surrender to the Gods, to God, to the Creative Forces of the Universe, or to simply surrender to others, is a real personal challenge. To be able to surrender everything, or ourselves, to the All.
I even dare to claim that it is too difficult for a majority of people. You have to have a lot of confidence in yourself or in your values to give up everything and go into the unknown.
And maybe that's the biggest obstacle for everyone: believing in yourself. Because with nothing left to hold on to, we must at least have a good, healthy and strong Self that we can rely on, right?

Letting go is also about following your instincts and therefore listening to your inner feelings, to the messages that the Over self sends you.
I must say that in thirty years of travel, every time I am on the road, out of my bearings, I have only my instinct to guard me and advise me, and every time I decide to follow it, I find interesting paths, great walks, events or people that I would never have met without the sweet folly of listening to myself.

Trust the Universe.
Three magic words! Impossible to achieve without being a yogi or an ultra-transcended being? Well no, in fact, it is very easy. All we have to do is silence the fears created by our mind and act. The key

25

*word. **Act**. Take the first step. Once on the road, in the action, it is impossible to lie or cheat. Each step, each gesture, each turn of the pedal in my case, comes from this confidence in ourselves, to lead us to our goal. And synchronicities happen, messages that the Universe or the Gods send us from their pedestal to show us that we are on the right track, that we can continue.*

Letting go therefore contains words that are not for everyone, it is born with words like "adventure", "surprise", "unknown", "I don't know", and even "I don't care" or "whatever".
I've known people who couldn't smoke a joint or have a drink for fear of falling into that world, an unknown world that often contains and brings beautiful surprises.

3. Free and happy in Greece

Blessed be this evening when I am in Greece. I am happy. New country, new people, new language, new alphabet, new currency and new mentality. It's a country I feel good in because I've been to the Cyclades several times camping, with a girl or by myself.

The last time I was in the Cyclades was a few years ago; I had met a beautiful young Brazilian girl in Switzerland who I liked a lot. A gazelle's body that inflamed my pupils, I wanted to eat her, to devour her quietly as any hungry predator would do. So I invited her to go to the beaches in Greece with me, to the Cyclades. And off we went. But she didn't speak French, and I didn't speak Portuguese. I can't tell you how long some hours can be at the beach when we have nothing to say to each other... We were going to spend a week there, but four days later I brought her back to Geneva because we couldn't go on looking at each other for hours.
Ahhh la la... when your brain goes down between your legs, what doesn't it make you do, my Philou!

Everyone left when the boat arrived, the two Germans with their dogs, Pablo, my Colombian friend, I hope we will see each other again soon.

I take my bike and start my first rides. I have to get out of Patras, which is the very type of ugly industrial city. After 8 km I see a campsite. I stop on a terrace. A woman, in her forties, sits down next to me. We start a conversation. She comes from Los Angeles and is touring the European capitals. Two days here, one day there. We talk a bit about the California fault line that causes earthquakes. "Oh, now I'm used to it," she tells me. She's been through four of them and doesn't think she'll move. What she babbles to me for two hours! A real gramophone! Very kindly, she makes me a sandwich with what she has, and it's a good thing!

I take the road again. After 30 km, another campsite. I enter. No one there. Waiting. A young woman with a baby welcomes me. We don't speak any common language. She offers me a beer, some food, without asking me anything. Warm in the heart!

I'm all alone in this campsite. The hammock is up, the tent too. I'm at the seaside, it's 6:30 pm. The sky is completely clear, a lot of wind, peace, royal.
At the end of a wooden promontory, I look at the water, it is crystal clear. A wonder. Several schools of fish, it's fantastic. I am amazed as a child would be! My heart is happy to see all these fish. I have a real weakness for them.

Former Atlantean, I have a real urge towards fish, if possible very big, I feel close to them...
Here is a nice story :
A grey and ugly Thursday during the monsoon. I am on one of the most beautiful beaches in Thailand, I walk slowly on the sand because I have the blues, I am sad. I've just been thrown out of the office of a hotel owner who was looking for a guy who spoke several languages to welcome tourists. I liked this job because I'm in Koh

Pee Pee, a real paradise on Earth, and I want to stay there. A little before Di Caprio came to play his famous movie "The Beach". The island is so beautiful. I walk with my shoulders down, hunched over, looking at the ground and railing against fate and the Gods who didn't give me what I wanted. Suddenly, I look up by a chance that doesn't exist and see a dive shop. I've never been interested in it in the past, because whenever I've been in a pool, I've always had an earache two or three meters underwater, so I've never thought that diving could be for me. But today is special, I'm sad, and this mood rekindles an instinct that I really want to listen to. It's called "sweet madness"...

So I walk into the shop and go straight to the boss: "Hello, I'd like to learn everything I need to know so I can work for you later... Teach me! The guy can't believe it. A guy as naive as that? I see his pupils turn into dollars and the cash register that is his brain tells me what to do. It will cost me $2,000 and I start tomorrow. "Banco!".

So I learned the basics of diving, and I loved it. No worries, sitting on the bottom of the water I was breathing normally, I was at home. Strange... I passed all the certificates, advanced level, "Rescue" level, and then the instructor level. A year later, I easily passed my instructorate in Phuket and I came back to the island proudly wearing the big professional watch on my wrist and my Padi instructor diploma.

I could then show off, and I didn't mind!

How about this, if I hadn't followed my instinct by walking on that beach and pushing the door of that store, the Universe wouldn't have offered me this sublime part of my life which was this one. Following our innermost aspirations and instincts, even in an absolutely unknown field, can sometimes magically open the doors to a new life...

The next day: I'm in a hell of a mood right now. I don't know if it's the fact of being in Greece but my energy curve is at its

highest. I left the campsite and hit the road again. Great! For 40 km I drove along the coast. The road is practically flat, it rolls itself. Great. Stop to buy food, picnic with my ass in the air on a beach, just to let my old fella breathe, alone, next to a fisherman's boat. At the end of the afternoon, I find a nice campsite. The boss is a backpacker on a bike who found a job for a month here. He's from Holland and sold everything before leaving. He's been riding his bike for four and a half months and has crossed the whole of Eastern Europe. Hats off to him! For the moment, I'm still very small compared to him.
Tonight, I have to eat well.
You bet your ass I do! There was nothing but canned corned beef and some leftover bread I had, plus two tomatoes. But I don't have to be picky, those are calories, so they're energy.

I left this morning, Thursday, October 8, after having met my camping neighbors who were going home, and after having been invited by a German couple to have coffee. They stayed three weeks in this campsite, relaxed, maybe too relaxed for my taste. But they had a baby, so... While
my neighbors, a couple of young Dutch people, whose daughter had a pair of amazing boobs (I'm obsessed with that at the moment), travelled more than 5,000 km in one month, and they were on the knees! What a beautiful kaleidoscope of humanity!
No one is alike, everyone has their own way of life. We tolerate each other, we love each other sometimes. It's rich, I think.

Then I set off for the longest stage so far, 55 km. No camping by then... But I knew that, I had seen it on the map. So I went shopping. Water, canned sardines, tomatoes and bread.
It was long, with a headwind all the way, bent over the handlebars. But always with the sun, my faithful friend. And the clanking of the chain links and wheel hubs as music.
Stop in a small restaurant around 1pm, family food, beef stew

with chips, all quite fatty, but once again, energy, energy! By the end of the afternoon, I was fed up. Sick of pedaling, sick of this wind. I was starting to complain out loud, a warning sign of physical and moral fatigue.

You have to have experienced it to realize how painful it can be to be alone, always alone, in the action. Getting up in the morning alone and unpacking my tent, packing everything up and getting back on the bike, alone. Ride alone, stop to eat alone, get back on the road alone, ride all afternoon without talking, alone in my head, then find a place to rest, unpack and reassemble everything, and settle down alone for dinner and the evening. That's the routine of the guy who leaves alone to go around the world. Sometimes it's heavy. I think it's starting to be. It's not the body that gives up or wants to, it's the mind. In any case, that's what's happening to me. And I didn't know it, I didn't think about it, I'm discovering it. Some hours are just too long and heavy...

Stop between two villages, behind a hedge of reeds. There was already a tent. A father and his son, German. I settled down quietly and discreetly so as not to intrigue the people passing by. "To be happy, let's be discreet" my mother kept telling me.

Tonight, night under the stars, under the mosquito net. The sky here is incredibly clear. That's the word that comes to my mind. Usually we say that water is clear, but here the sky is clear too. It's a pity I don't know more about astronomy, because I can see everything: several Milky Ways and absolutely all the stars, even the small ones. It seems to me that one of them is missing... in the background on the right... The photo poster that I always dreamed of putting on the ceiling of my room. Tonight, it's life-size!

31

Saturday 9 : departure towards the Corinth Canal. Ordinary road. I didn't sleep well. Especially a bit cold in the morning. My sleeping bag is not adapted to what I do. I took the lightest one, less than 3 kg, and it's not the best. No hood, a zipper only up to the middle, and I'm tall...
A baby cat made meow-meow last night. Just in time, I had some leftover corned beef that I wanted to throw away. He took a bite out of it. Then he licked the two cans of sardines I had finished. A king's feast for a junior cat. But too wild, impossible to touch. He hung around me all night. In the morning, he loved the Nutella, and he let himself be tamed like that. Well done multinationals, your junk food even pleases animals!

After a tearful and mewling departure, I head for Corinth. Apparently a big industrial city. Great! Hum... The road goes up and there is a lot of traffic.
From a level crossing, I managed to hang on to the back of a truck that was slowly going up, and this truck pulled me at 60-70 km/h to the canal. It was great. Hello adrenaline. The roadsides were broken, I was afraid my luggage would fly off the bumps, with one hand I held onto the truck and with the other I tried to control the bike as best I could. There was nothing I could do if anything fell off! Some people honked at me, but I was Belmondo in his early days! And then, you've already tried to climb a big hill while being overtaken by hundreds of trucks whose wheels are sometimes as high as you are, it's really scary. So even if you're scared, it's better to climb this hill easily, like Bébel...

It must be the elections. There seems to be a lot of political propaganda going on at the moment, because they all have flags and all the cars, buses and trucks are flying their colors.
The flags are flapping in the wind as the cars honk their horns. There is green, blue. I read in the guidebook that Greeks are

passionate about two things: football and politics. And apparently for politics, it's true!

The Corinth Canal is really impressive. At a height of about 200 meters, the mountain is cut in two, with a laser. The walls are steep and straight as if a giant hand had cut its piece of the cake with a knife. The width: 40 meters. And where I am now, that is, in Isthmia, one of the mouths of the strait, on a tourist terrace, there is a steel bridge that goes up and down with each passing boat. It's nice to see. But the best part is on the banks, just below, in the clear turquoise water, where hundreds of fishes are swimming. There are the feeders, these schools of very small fish, and under them, at a depth of two meters, there are the biggest ones. I'm not lying, it's a real vivarium down there! It's fabulous to see. I want to dive down and join them. I can't wait to go diving in Turkey or Asia.

In the evening, I'm a bit bored. I never manage to fall asleep quickly. In the campsites, there's nothing to do, so I go to bed saying to myself that I have to rest, and I turn around and around in my tent with only one thing on my mind: that tomorrow will come soon. How I wish I had a lady with me... I'm starting to miss that too...

Tonight, for food, nothing! The campsite cafeteria is empty, so the old caretaker warmed up some bread for me, and I spread two slices of Nutella on it. I'm not happy about that either, I didn't pay for it! And I'm afraid it's the same on the islands towards Turkey. The end of the tourist season also means the end of the abundance and a kind of sadness. And on the bike, I'm a bit annoyed to be walking around with five kilos of food from the supermarket in the morning. But I'll have to do it.
It's a good thing I ate well at lunchtime. I'm not too hungry yet. I can't wait for tomorrow because I'm coming to Piraeus.

Animation, youth, noise, food, try to find a pension not too expensive, because I will stay there for several days.

4. The Gods of Olympia

Arrival in Athens, in Piraeus. After having taken a ferry twice to cut through an island near Athens *(saving 40 km)* and after having eaten my breakfast in a tavern on the road, where I made friends with the owner who spoke to me about the politics of his country in a passionate and original way, I found a hotel not too expensive, thanks to the Hitchhikers Guide.

Had a good meal at 3pm and slept.

In the evening, prepared the day of the following day and... the first tile! I forgot my address book at the campsite! And shit! I made a call, and I forgot it on the counter.

Well, let's think. My motto: "There are no problems in life, only solutions!" So I have to rent a scooter to go back and get it. In this notebook, all the addresses for postcards to be sent, the bank or phone numbers if my credit card is lost or stolen, lots of important or vital information in case of problems. It's one of my most important organs when I travel, along with my money, my passport, my keys if I have them, my head and my purses.

And maybe also my stomach... because, and this is another of my sacred principles, I can sleep on the floor *(it already happened to me several times)* or in a dirty place, I don't care, but I'll always spoil myself when it comes to food, there's no question. On a full stomach, everything is OK, anything can happen to me, it's always fine.

The day after, October 11: I first have to find the metro, then I have to go near the Acropolis, because I read that there are two scooter rental shops. I find one. We agree on the price. Not too expensive, about $12 a day. And off I go. I don't know where I'm going, but I'm going. In fact, I'm completely lost! I have to use the compass, and one thing is for sure, the further west I go, the closer I'll get to the right exit in Athens. Well, after twenty minutes of terrible traffic and breathing in stinky gases, I'm heading straight for my old campsite. That's it, I'm there. The problem is that the owner doesn't understand anything other than Greek. So I wave at him, putting a block near the phone, etc. Nothing. The bastard was pulling my leg all along, he had it under the counter, and gave it to me after a few minutes. I breathe...

Phew, happy and clear heart, I take the road back to Athens, but all cool this time. Stop in a restaurant, Greek salad + fried fish. It's cool, the weather is nice and I have all my vital organs back. I can now think about leaving Athens.

It's not the first time I've been there and every time, this kind of megalopolis puts my nerves on edge and I'm revived when I find space and nature again.

A short stop for swimming and sunbathing, and I go back home. The horror. As soon as I get back to the outskirts, and with the help of a great plan, I get lost again.

I'll show you this alley, and then this district. Lost. An hour to find my way back. Fortunately I was on a scooter. On a bike, it would have been suicide. I ride along holding my map in my hands, and there it goes. I had to stop in a hurry between the lines of cars coming out at full speed, all in a noise of fury and an opaque and brown fog of gas, diesel, and big spits of smoke. In short, I had to return the scooter at 6pm, I was there at minus ten!

Cooool! It's over. What a day! Food, phone, postcards and climbing on the terrace of the building to watch "Athens by night".
I get tired of big cities. This one must be 20 km long! The boulevards are like motorways, and I'm not talking about the state of the asphalt... corrugated iron.
Athens, you are not a beautiful city.
Moreover, when you come from the island opposite, you see a layer of brown fog, the whole city lying under this toxic slick. From the outside, it is scary to even think of entering. From the inside, you get used to it and no longer see the noxious fog.
The Athenians are all quite fat. They are not very beautiful either.
Such a city, such a people! Paf, take that Athens!

Tuesday 12: I took my boat ticket for an island that I chose for its animation. According to the Hitchhiker's Guide, 80% of the visitors are under 20 years old, 40 discos, noise all night long, the party. Its name : Ios.
That's what I need now. Action!
Sorted out a few things. Bank, phones in Switzerland, buy food because the boat arrives at midnight and as I see it, I'll sleep outside.

Spent any day waiting for the boat, which will be here at 4pm.

At 5pm, I embark, after having put the bike, a frail skiff next to the monsters that rush into the hold, full of trucks with several axles. In a big blackish spit of smoke, the ship shakes.

5. The Cyclades, Ios, and life in white and blue

On board, on deck, indeed, many young people. That's good. I wonder what their story is. Are they coming for a week or two or are they on a trip? A lot of Americans, I think. It's a long trip for them, one or two weeks!
The boat is moving away. Farewell Athens, I won't miss you.

The ballet of the seagulls and gulls at the back is superb. They let themselves be lulled by the heat of the engine and the air spat out by the huge boilers on the deck, ten or twenty meters high, without making any effort.
It's six o'clock in the evening, the sun is setting, I've got my walkman in my ears, cool music, it's great, terribly romantic, exhilarating, my heart swells with joy. The wind in my hair, the wind in my head, the adventure ahead, I feel good, happy.
From the back of the boat, I am more aware of the immensity of the city. Not a square meter of free space, no green, no trees. Concrete piled up all along the coast.
How happy I am to leave this place!
I will definitely never live in a megalopolis, the ultimate concentration of all the nuisances that man can create: smells,

noises, fury, darkness, aggressiveness, toxicity, junk food.

I bought some fishing gear from an old man on the harbor. Hooks, weights and nylon line. He wouldn't sell me ten meters of fishing line! Not profitable enough for him. I called him an old fart, but he didn't get it.

I'd like to stay three or four weeks on the islands, Ios, Mykonos, and then head off to Turkey.

I'm going to take my time, party a bit, tan my little ass, fish if I'm lucky and if I find a good spot, maybe prepare the fish and stuff my face! I'd like to learn more about fishing, find fishermen who will take me on their boats. This life attracts me. Simplicity. I love the sea so much, and fish fascinate me.
Speaking of fishing, I should not forget the beautiful mermaids either: I'm starting to miss their song and their vaporous spells...

I especially like the fact that I can support myself by my own means. I already get around by muscle power. There is still food, and logic pushes me towards fishing. Hunting is not the same. Killing a poor hare that brings food to his female hase... and then taking her doggy style, ha ha ha! In short, I can't. Same for the birds, so beautiful to see flying. They are free. I don't know why, but fish are different. They are there to feed us, I feel it. And the sea is so big. There are many more fish than land animals. And when a fish gives birth, it releases at least 10,000 babies at once! What rabbit, even the most obsessed one, can say that much, right?

Sometimes I wonder if I'm the one with a problem with others. Maybe it is, maybe it isn't. I am often alone, surrounded by people who are not. Discrepancy. Who is normal and who is not? So, in these cases, my conscience starts talking to me, my Jasper on my shoulder saying, "See how you are, standing alone in your corner, waiting for others to come to you..." He's not really wrong, Jasper. And that sometimes scares me because I know I should be reaching out to people more, but I can't, or not often. I express myself in action. Not in a living room. Besides, I'm not so bad on my own. Okay, when I see all these people laughing, pretty girls together, my little Jasper puts on a show and starts nagging me again. But as much as I can be ecstatic about a landscape, a beach, a sunset against the backdrop of a ballet of gulls, I don't know what. I'm not really a communicative person, I'm more of a sensitive person. Each to his own. If someone asks me how a ride was, it's almost impossible for me to describe it in words, you had to be there to feel it...

And sometimes talking pisses me off! That's it, it's clear.

I prefer the company of animals, it's easier, and at least they understand me right away.

What about jerks? Are we talking about idiots? We shouldn't take the idiots for people, should we?

They don't even know that they are, but we have to deal with them, don't we? They pollute our days with their stupid behaviors, they throw their mental quagmires in our faces and prevent them from being good and accomplished human beings, and their stupidity or vacuity never ceases to contaminate my more haughty vision of Man living on Earth with animals and spirits.

Too heavy, jerks just make me want to disappear or have huge palms to hand out pies in the streets all day long and do housework. Fantasies, fantasies... Where are you Hulk ?

I believe that in life, everyone has their own area of expertise. There are the communicative ones who are in their element among the crowd, the party men who talk nonsense while partying and make the blondes laugh, the lymphatic ones who are more receptive to their feelings, the sanguine ones, the down-to-earth ones who live only for material goods, although they are good-natured and a bit rude *(spiritually speaking, of course)*, and the action men who live and fulfill themselves only in action. When I have nothing to do, I do ab-so-lu-te-ly nothing. I sleep. I put my body in lethargy. And as soon as I have to move, I explode. So, you think if in a trip like this, I realize fully. And again, I'm only at the beginning, I don't know some of my limits yet. On the other hand, if I don't talk, it's probably because I'm comfortable with myself, that I assume myself, and I think that the talkers are trying to fill their fears, or an inner void, and are looking for support, comfort, or even fleeing a solitude that they don't dare to face in their stripped shell.

Tonight I'm getting drunk, I'm letting go! Yepeeee...

Arrival on the first island. Paros.
To go to Ios, you have to pass by two other islands.
This is the Greece of postcards! I love it...
Small whitewashed houses, beautiful harbors where brightly painted boats rest.
It's 11pm, and at night I feel like I'm disembarking in a country of peace and quiet, where life is sweet and good. Some of the passengers have disembarked. I'm relaxed, a bit cheerful with the three beers drunk and the music in my ears. Not at all tired.
Tonight I'm not planning anything and that's good; if I end up drunk on the cobblestones or the beach, it's well deserved. After all these litres of sweat, I can make up for it in beer and have fun.

I got out of the boat by pushing the bike. It is 2:30 in the morning. The air is soft, almost no noise, people are talking quietly. I'm a little drunk, I waited for everyone to leave, for the village to be asleep, to go outside the village, on the beach, with just enough light to install the hammock and unpack the sleeping bag.

First night in Ios, in the hammock on the beach. Not bad...

I slept quite well, despite a cat *(another one)* noisily looting a garbage bag. I realized that in the morning, the tree under which I was sitting was beaded with dewdrops mixed with a brownish and syrupy liquid, sticky. When I woke up, I was covered with brown drops. Nothing too dramatic, but everything sticks.

Then I found a room in the middle of the village, half the price of the one on the mainland.

A postcard village, white houses and shutters, balconies and doors painted in azure blue. Beautiful!

The island seems to me rather rocky, little greenery, few trees.

In the afternoon, on a beach, one of the most beautiful in the Aegean Sea according to the guide. And it seems to be true, just the right amount of people... but no single girl...

Small repairs to the bike, installation of a new front rack bought in the capital.

Next day: I meet two Swiss Germans, slightly punky, living on the beach. Nice. There is a pub here in the center of the village that shows several movies every night. We get to know each other.

After having eaten spaghetti carbonara, just to have a little cement in the belly, we go to have a drink in the center, with the two punkies. The village square is delicious. Narrow alleys to reach it. Everything is white. Houses without a well-defined architecture, a mixture of curves, squares, peaks and rotunda roofs that are a feast for the eyes. And two charming naiads are there, playing backgammon. I happen to be a beast at this game *(which I learned from one of the Argentine champions in Ibiza during my year there)* and I'm also an opportunist... so I invited myself to play against the winner. It's ok. Come my turn. I settle down and we play. And we get to know each other. Two Australian girls, a little bit crazy, in permanent fun. I love that. We spend the evening laughing, drinking and playing. The kind of threesome where the one who loses gets a dare. So the girls do the little dog on all fours in the street or put a table in the middle and dance on it, I drink my beer straight down and walk across the village square full of people, hopping on one leg like the village simpleton, and so much other nonsense for two hours.

Then we dance. Around four o'clock in the morning, I'm as round as a propeller, one of the girls goes home, and only the pretty one is left... We end up in my room, not without having copulated like two dogs in an alley, under the tender and benevolent eye of the neighborhood cats. We spend one of the most orgiastic nights of my life, or what's left of it. Screaming, moaning, laughing, clucking and groaning, how much she wants it and how happy I am to give it to her... How good it feels! The vampire that I am has had his fill of fresh blood...

The next day I meet them on the beach. Hmmm... I got up at two o'clock. They are really nice. Unfortunately they are leaving tonight. We eat together and I accompany them to the boat, still rubbing my last night's sweetheart a little, my shorts still taut with desire and my heart a little tight. The goodbyes are touching. I go back to the village sadly.

And I find myself alone again. A big blow to my morale. I have the blues, my heart aches... Emotional waves... Up, down...

I hate it when others leave. I prefer it to be me, it hurts less.

Friday 15: I left the room. The old woman who rented this room had wickedly demanded 1,000 drachmas from each of the girls for taking a shower before taking the boat. I felt like tearing something down or putting rocks in the drain of the washing machine!

To make matters worse, the first glitch: some kids from the village stole the odometer of the bike parked at the back of the house. It was a mistake to have left it there! It was useful...

Grimacing and grumbling, I go to the beach campground two kilometers away. I set up my bivouac by the water and spend the afternoon on the sand, meditating in front of the waves.

Tomorrow I buy a mask, a snorkel and some fins.

To keep myself busy.

Crazy wake-up call: wrapped up in my sleeping bag, I open one eye in the morning and see three kids between fifteen and eighteen years old, sitting five meters away from me. They look like Spaniards. They seem to have slept there and wake up too. Seeing that I am moving, one of them, all mocking and laughing, comes to me, and with very explicit gestures of his hand towards his wide open mouth, seems to offer to suck my cock for some money. I'm not sure, but it sounds like it...

Holy shit, I wasn't expecting this! I'm flabbergasted, shocked, and

I manage to answer a "no thank you" in English, and the guy quietly walks away laughing to his buddies. I still can't believe it, and it takes me a while to digest it. Not because of the blowjob that passes me under the nose, but because of the nerve of these guys who don't seem to care, without any scruples and without any shame, and who propose this to pay for their holidays or to extend them. I'm falling off the wagon this morning...

Saturday: I reconnect with the beauty that the sea offers to the eye.
I go to a small remote beach and dive. I see some beautiful fish but I can't catch them with a line and a hook. I open two sea urchins hoping to eat their genitals as I had done in Corsica, but either they are males, or it is not the season because the shells are almost empty. Poor guys, I don't know what sexuality they have but seeing what's in their entrails, it must not be crazy!

What peace and quiet!
The campground closes in four or five days. Then I'll go to Mykonos.

6. Mykonos, and the sale of the bike

The days pass, peaceful, calm. Time lets itself be forgotten. It's good.

I met a guy who got hit by a car and he doesn't remember anything. It was one night, he was drunk, and he woke up in the hospital covered in stitches. On top of that, he's broken all over, he can hardly walk. Anyway, it's an unbelievable story. He's alone with me in the campsite.

Yesterday evening, big party, with the program: "Jurassic Park". It was good, in the pub, but I didn't understand anything because it was a bad copy with horrible sound.

Today I bought fins to go further and faster. But after ten minutes the water is getting cold...

Still no clouds on the horizon! For three weeks now! I've got quite a tan. I even got a sunburn on my buttocks, they're candy pink. They're like a little pig's buttocks!

My equipment is starting to deteriorate. My knives are rusting. I give them a new lease on life with canned sardine oil. Well, they've got their youth back, but now they stink a bit!

I like to tinker and fiddle with things. And above all, I like to work with what I've got. I already have the beginnings of deconsumerism in me.

Materials, consumption, recycling for the Earth.
Even as a child it was important to me not to throw anything away.
Maybe because I came from a poor family. So we didn't throw
anything away, we recycled, in the sense that we gave another life, a
second life. A bit like the cars and trucks that go to Africa to finish
their lives and then travel another million kilometers. Or like the
knife sharpener who used to pass under the windows of our building
when I was a child to give a new life to dull blades.

Nowadays and in my daily life it is almost a duty of an awakened
citizen. It touches an unknown fiber in me, and I suffer thinking of
the Earth, which I consider a benevolent Mother for all of us.

By recycling - whether it is plastic, glass or paper - we allow the
earth to breathe, or at least not to be drained of its raw materials, its
soil, its trees or its water.

But also, and above all, by not buying new stuff, so somewhere by
recycling used stuff, we can push for the closure of polluting
factories because sales can decrease to put them in difficulties, we
can stop deforestation or the spreading of toxic products, we can
also put an end to the unique cultivation of a plant or a tree for a
valley or an island (such as palm oil plantations) which will kill all
the flora and fauna of the area by impoverishing the living places.

We can see how important it is now for every awakened person not
to buy new, but to recycle, or think "second hand".

As I said above, I had this concept in me when I was a kid, and I see
that 40 years later, I still have friends of varying ages who don't

think about it at all, and do it even less. Water flows abundantly in their homes, electricity is used to the full even when they are not at home (the air conditioning for example), things that make my heart ache, and it makes me sad to see that people's consciences are not opening up more quickly!

Tonight in the pub, it's "Avatar" and "Bodyguard". Another great movie night ahead.

Today, rest. Yesterday I cycled, did a lot of karate, did a repetition training, swam, dived, in short, I didn't stop. Today, not one, I won't do one!
Yesterday evening at the terrace of the beach, I met two French nurses, very nice who play backgammon very well.
But not enough to panic my greedy lobster, the excitement was not there.

Another day gone. Last night, video night at the fun pub. Talked with a beautiful girl, but she's leaving tomorrow. Chatted with some Canadians, some very nice Germans from Munich who left me their address.
I'm building a crazy physic because it climbs a lot to go to the village located at 350 meters from the campsite located at the edge of the beach. There is only one road. To reach my little beach, you have to go down to the port on the other side of the mountain, walk along the sea for a while, then go up another hill to get to the other side, and then go back down. Of course, you can do the opposite in the late afternoon. Count on 45 minutes.

On the way back, in the middle of the road, I find a baby cat covered in flies, one eye closed with pus. I had already seen it on the way there and had given it some water. Now, my heart could not bear to see such distress. So I put him in my backpack and went back to the village to buy some milk. But he didn't want it. Maybe he didn't even know what it was. So I took him to the beach bar, where many cats live who look fat compared to my skinny kitten. Maybe he'll find food and human warmth there. If I see him again tomorrow, if he makes it through the night, I'll be really happy.

I haven't seen him again and, according to the rumors, he was taken in by a drunken Englishman who was passing by and took him with him.

I left Ios on Thursday the 21st.
By the boat that takes me to Mykonos.
Again full of backpackers, tourists and travelers.
It's good for morale.
I sold my fins, mask and snorkel back to some Quebecers, as I feel the water is getting colder and I don't want to lug this equipment all the way to Asia.

Departure for Mykonos on the "Mykonos Express", which has only its name. Apparently, the slowest boat in Greece! Six hours of crossing...
Arrival in Mykonos, an island that carries with it a reputation for homosexuality...

I have nothing against gays, I think I'm a pure straight guy, nothing about me attracts me to a man. I can't see myself kissing one and rubbing against his irritating beard, I can't see myself caressing hairy arms or legs, and I love hairless asses! The same goes for my most intimate fantasies, I've never imagined myself with a man. A "trans", why not? I've already had experiences with male-female surgeries and I'm fine with that, as long as it's a female body. Maybe I have a problem with someone else's dick, or my own... or maybe I just don't. I feel manly, fairly male. I'm gentle, calm and pleasant on the surface, which is what gay men must feel and they like it. But I don't like the ones who are mannered and goofy! It irritates me straight away and makes me go up in towers... And there were a lot of them in Mykonos. They like me. That's my problem here...

We're talking about virility and men...
I've noticed a lot of beards among young people since the 2000s. It's as if they have to show their virility on their face, for lack of knowing what it is, or not knowing what a man is.
How to be masculine?
What is the sacred masculine?
When I was a kid, we lived in a patriarchal society and the father ruled everything in the house, everything went through him. The pyramid model. Children shuddered at the thought that huge fatherly hands might come down on their little pink butts if they got into mischief. And it worked pretty well at home. Respect was instilled, learned, and kids respected authority, teachers or cops. Thanks to the father who taught his children that. The father also taught respect for women, good manners, and how to be a gentleman. At least, I had that chance.
And I see that 30 years later, the pyramid model has flattened, and at home, for example, when the child first goes to his mother to ask if he can go out, she replies: "Go and ask your father". The father replies: "Go and ask your mother". Everything is flat, there is no more authority. Similarly, children can no longer be hit. I grew up

with a slap, and once being a father, I thought that a little slap from time to time would have calmed the world down, or a good kick in the ass. But we don't have the right to do that anymore, ok... So, young teenage males who don't have these reference points anymore are looking for how to imbibe the attitude of a man, how to be one, and what virility is. So the beard arrived on faces around the year 2000, the first times on TV, in commercials with bearded models, and little by little on TV sets, with three or four day beards. Before, it looked dirty, and now it was okay! Go figure...

I did not understand. And you have to explain something to me: since when do women like hair on men's faces?

From my female experience, I know that women don't really like it. However, they do like manly, masculine men. But hair? On the face? I don't get it...

I don't think this beard thing is going to last long, because it's kind of bringing us down to the level of the hairy apes of yore, who were in the process of emerging from that and moving into the new Aquarian Age, into a new humanity in which hair - a hallmark of the primary animal world - would tend to disappear.

Have you ever seen science fiction movies with bearded characters? No, and neither have I. Hair, the hair, seems not to exist in the galaxy.

Except for Chewbacca in Stars wars... Laughs.

Have you ever seen non-hairy, non-bearded imams? No, I haven't either, and that's normal because they are still in the Stone Age! Laughs again.

Just kidding. Not so much...

I've been noticing for a long time that women no longer have (or want) hair under their arms. The same goes for men. Why is that? Nobody knows, but it's a fact now, big tufts of hair under the arms remind us of monkeys, and it's time to get out of them, to move away from them.

It's the same for the sexes, they're getting naked, they're wearing their summer finery. It's hot in the underpants. Even men are getting into it, and I personally vote for it.

The hair is dying, and soon has no place...

Another observation seems to prove me right: the disappearance of the hair (body) goes hand in hand with hair loss. More and more young men are losing their hair. It didn't happen much in the 60's, but now it's normal and commonplace to see young men of 25 bald or becoming bald. This is proof that humanity is growing, taking us with it in its evolution and, in the future, I do not see the bearded and hairy man. On the contrary.

I think we are at a turning point in our history and it is time to leave the category of the great apes.

For me, the man of the future is slim, because he is careful about what he eats, has perfectly integrated the mechanisms of good health, and has no hair. As a result, he lives to .... point of age.

Just like the aliens and extraterrestrials we've always seen, right? They're thin and they seem to feed on ether.

A theory that may not be so far-fetched...

Ah, and long live Jason Statham too! He helped me out when my hair started to grow out of my head and turned it into an airport for flies...

I arrived with two Australians, a couple who had already cycled 13,000 km in nine months! Very nice. We head to the village to find a room not too expensive.

Ouaaahhh... the scam! It is true that this is the most expensive island of the Cyclades!
But I find a roof to sleep, style "terrace on the roof", for 1000 dr (about 6 $).
Installation of my stuff, mosquito net, etc... Night falls on Mykonos, I just arrived and I find myself on the roof of one of the houses in the city center, alone, dominating the crowd.
Once my things are settled, I go down to the street and I meet a young American girl of 21 years old spending her holidays alone. We wander the streets together for a while. Apparently there are quite a few gay men here! And they seem to like me, damn...

Friday 22 : I slept very well on my small roof, protected from the wind and without humidity. Perfect wake up call! Go to "Paradise beach", the most famous beach. Took a bungalow because I don't want to set up my tent and it doesn't cost much more. Bamboo, sun and sand atmosphere. I don't think I'll stay long on the island, there are really too many guys staring at me. But if my sister sends me the book on Asia I asked her for in Istanbul, it should be there in ten days. So where to stay in the meantime? That's the question!

Two days I'm here, it's cool. The beach is really beautiful. Nudists at the end let themselves be admired a little bit by a few people, relaxing music in the bars along the beach, trees - rather rare in Greece - it's a little piece of paradise!
Hence the name of this beach!

Last night I met a very nice American woman, she's been going around the world for six months. She has to go home for a wedding and she doesn't really want to. She's accompanied by an

Australian woman, who's also been on the road for a while. It's really crazy this world of travelers. I didn't think there would be so many of them, and especially that they were travelling so far and for so long. Mary is really the prototype of the American woman. Tall, strong character, incredible accent, long blond hair, a little strong too. Too much for me. She travels alone. We spent a great evening talking, drinking, in the center of Mykonos, where only Greeks go, and then we danced in a kind of club where the DJ was really bad. She wanted us to finish the night together, but she's a little too chubby, the girl. She must have grown up on soda and junk food, and there's still a lot of extra weight on the scale. Even drunk, there's too much for my criteria, which are, all in all, quite tight on the figure! And without climbing equipment, I don't go for it.

Let's see... how can I talk about such a simple and complex subject without being lynched by the madding crowd, or being called macho-misogynist? It's
true that the world population is becoming more and more obese, that people are getting fatter by the minute, and that the subject is a bit of a taboo among women. Society has accepted mediocrity and sometimes holds it up as an example. Yes, being fat now is simply normal. We can't do anything about it, or almost nothing... Blame it on sodas and junk food!
We mustn't criticize these poor obese women...

It's forgetting that the lobbies are there to make us buy their industrial crap, and that we're no longer children to absorb everything that television spouts! You still need to have a brain and know how to use it.

So I say here that I only like thin women. I've already put fat women in my bed, often under the influence of alcohol, and the next day, I had to get out of there fast. Well, I can't help it, I have an Oedipal complex, my mother was tall and thin with long hair, and between the ages of 8 and 10 I had this image of the perfect woman. The one I would look for all my life. From then on, it was my first aesthetic criterion. I always need to sensually desire my partner, and my very first glance analyzes the silhouette.

This has often played tricks on me and I have sometimes been called a superficial man. Okay, no worries, I can take it. I don't care.

Actually, it goes even further. Because a woman who doesn't pay attention to what she eats or drinks is not for me. It is not up to me, at her level of evolution, to educate her about food. I am only looking for women who are at least at my level of knowledge in this area, or even higher. Otherwise what? I'm going to wait and take a break from my own evolution because my partner is stagnant and needs years to learn the proper basics? Because she still eats McDonald's and drinks Sprite without question?

To me - and I see it in futuristic movies where there are no obese people - evolved people pay attention to their bodies - the temple of their souls and the only vehicle they have at their disposal - and to the food they put in them. I think it's rude to ignore the composition of Coca-Cola, to eat a lot of meat or cheese, or to do so to appease your inner demons.

Or you shouldn't complain, and especially not about men who don't like fat girls...

A young girl who knows nothing about food is fine, but a mature or adult woman who eats anything won't be able to go with me, I'd be wasting my time with her.

Note that I know this is a sensitive subject and that women don't like

to be criticized about their weight. Immaturity. Or hypocrisy.
I'm not trying to create a buzz by writing this, I have nothing to hide
and I'm trying to be honest. And it seems to me that a vegetarian,
yoga-practicing woman isn't going to hook up with a guy who hunts
on the weekends to kill time and adorable little animals with his
buddies, right?
Is a top athlete going to hook up with a belly fatty who eats anything
all day long because he doesn't care about his hygiene? Love can be
blind, but frankly I doubt it will last.
There, we should all agree on that a little bit...

Since I like to look first, what I see has to appeal to me, make me
want to know what's behind the woman's plastic. And that will
necessarily involve the horizontal position later on. I don't see
myself as the pure and simple friend of an atomic bomb.
Impossible... Too many fantasies and attractions...

Therefore, for me, fat women are almost invisible.
And I am quite bored nowadays, from an aesthetic and sensual point
of view, in the streets of our big cities...

Well, let's change the subject, otherwise I'll get formic acid thrown
at me - and not to fuck me - when I leave my house...

Anyway, I came home drunk, having spent a ton of money,
smoked a lot, and my pockets are still full...
I don't like the aftermath of a party. I feel like my body is
intoxicated, super relaxed but dismantled. Afterwards, I have to
exercise, sweat to eliminate. The days after are usually bland and
insipid, to be forgotten very quickly.

I feel like selling the bike. I don't have the blues, but almost... Big questioning.
What to do? Where to go? And how?
Grey day today. The skies have clung to my morale, the Gods are titillating me and testing me...

From the beginning, I felt a weight over my head. It took me weeks to figure out what it was.
I've thought about everything, for months and months, but not about one ultra-important detail: the time of departure, in the year.
And I did the worst! Leaving in autumn, for a long time, by bike, in Europe. What a nonsense! What an idiot...
So, everything closes, it's cool or cold at night, few people everywhere because everyone is working or has finished their holidays, in short, it's not a party in neu-neu. I screwed up, I must say. I should have left much earlier.
So I have to change my plans.
And sell the bike.

I think that being on foot, with light equipment, I will feel freer. And above all, I'm SICK OF BEING ALONE! So I start dreaming of getting on a coach, taking a bus, being surrounded by people who speak loudly, I want campsites full of people, crowded streets. From now on, it will be buses, planes, crowds, etc...
It's crazy all these paradoxes in me. As much as I love being alone, I love being in a crowd, the noise against the silence.
It's a complex thing to be me sometimes.

Since I don't want to be alone anymore, I will have to sell the bike. My mind is made up.

It would be too stupid to leave it there somewhere, I can still get something out of it. And then... it was a part of me for three long months! I owe it some respect, I can't just abandon it.

One client. Then two. Maybe I'll sell it faster than I thought...

Today, Sunday, big arrival of American tourists.

Typical cliché: the well-to-do American on holiday, old and fat, with a hat on his head, a cocktail in one hand, under a wicker parasol, in a deckchair. Black people, quite opulent in appearance. They are very happy, very happy to be here. They take pictures of anything, they all have a camera in their hand, they are being photographed with their underpants on their feet, all proud to show off their tiny sex disappearing under their fat mass.

Yuck. This is Mykonos, the depraved one.

I met a more than very charming 21-year-old from Chicago. Hmm.... Maybe....

That's it, my bike is sold! For the sum of 70 000 dr, about 420 $.
 Now I have to realize that I am on foot and that it is another way to travel. Just with my backpack. More free, but more dependent too. No big deal. This is what I wanted, to travel in another way.

7. Winter is coming to the islands

Yesterday evening, we had a meal on the beach with a whole group, then I played Rummy. As there were no more buses, everyone took the road for a 45 minute walk to the village. I was very excited about the evening with Missy, the more than very charming girl. We spent the equivalent of eight or ten beers - that's three hours - dancing in a bar, and then this little bitch gave me the girl-is-seduiced-too-fast-and-is-seeking-to-make-the-guy-jealous trick. In other words, this young slut, who was too playful, threw herself into the arms of another man, after we had danced together, kissed, etc... It made me mad and I drank even more. How stupid we men can be! How fucking fragile we are in the hands of manipulative or playful women. Or drunk. And me especially.
I spent my sleep calling her names, and in the end it played a bad trick on me because I didn't sleep well, of course...

I lost a shirt. I had two, now I only have one.
The choice in my wardrobe is decreasing... It will be faster to get dressed in the morning.

The days pass, quiet.

Every day is different here. Today, not many people, the sea is very calm, there is not much excitement. Compared to yesterday, it's really another beach.

I still haven't said a word to the other man-eating bitch. I think she's gone by now, which is good. It seems to me that women have a lot of trouble apologizing, whereas a man needs to have his honor and esteem restored by an apology, while a woman needs or prefers to be comforted and reassured. Quite a difference. But this little minx is too young to understand that.

This morning, an hour of tai chi in the hills to help me rebalance myself after the bender and my emotional setbacks. Then, shower + breakfast on one of the terraces of the beach, with classical music in the background. A true happiness.

Studied the map of Turkey because something tells me I'm leaving soon. Destination Samos, the closest island to Turkey. Then it will be over with the beach for a while.

The next beautiful beaches should be in Thailand, in about three months.

This morning, a few clouds and I get a drop of water. The first one in a month.

Last night, I met a very nice Argentinean chico with whom I spent the evening in town, and we ended up at the "Down Under", the only bar where you can dance. It was a farewell evening because three people, a German girl - the little mermaid of the beach - and two cool Israeli girls were leaving the next day. Once again, a farewell full of emotions where everyone left with a heavy heart. It's silly to say but when you travel alone, you quickly get attached to the people you meet and with whom you sympathize. And when you're alone, it's hard to cheat, you always try to be as correct as possible with others and you meet beautiful people, beautiful spirits, and even more...

I slept in town, in Gaston the Argentine's room, because the walk back from Paradise Beach was too long.
This morning he rented a moped to visit the island and we crashed twice. No seriousness or material damage, and a few good laughs because these motorcycles run so slowly that you have to calculate the curves well when climbing and especially not cut the gas. We hit a wall twice!
The Guide du Routard is right, a lot of people get hurt because of the state of the roads and the motorcycles.

Every day brings new acquaintances. Yesterday, two girls arrived, young, Australian and South African. Evening at the beach canteen to discuss. Yumm, my canines are growing and asking for fresh blood...

Friday 29: Yesterday, not a very important day, stayed at the campsite, a lot of wind, nothing done. Sport in the morning on the hill, food, reading. In the evening, discussion in the canteen and sleep.

Today, last day in Mykonos.
Put my things away. This afternoon I'm going to the city to get the ticket for my boat which leaves at midnight. I will be able to drink a few beers in town, and then, far away!

Friday, October 30: Well, here I am in Samos. It's nine in the morning, it's been an hour since the boat arrived. I found a room thanks to a guy on a motorbike who offered it to me as soon as I disembarked. The people are very friendly, very nice.

I'm going to rent a scooter because it's the cheapest way.

The island at first sight is very green. Trees! It's been two weeks since I saw any. Everything was rocky there.

You can feel the change. The Turkish coast is only 20 km away. I have my moped for $6 a day, and I drove a few miles out of the village. It's mountainous and green. But the good weather is over, the sun shining against the infinite blue sky. I'm almost cold. Clouds. Winter is at the door of the islands.

In the evening, nothing to do. A few inanimate terraces. I eat. I go home. Sleep.

This morning, Sunday, jogging on the port at seven o'clock. With dogs. Cold shower. I'm in good shape.

Then I left for the Turkish border. Took the moped to go... I don't know where...

In search of a café, I find a small village by the sea. I find one. I go in. Only little old men who are fiddling with their pearl necklaces in their hands. Time stretches...

I feel sympathy for this young man who is honoring them with a visit. We don't understand each other but there is respect. I believe that all men have a dream or a journey in their eyes. Especially on an island. Their horizon is not only material. The sea gives them such a powerful immaterial gift that they seem to need nothing else. Just to contemplate it. All the fishermen's gazes carry the dreamed infinite. And from this dream in their eyes are born certain principles and qualities not to be outraged. One of which is respect. A bit like the Tuareg people have the desert as their mistress and kill for honor or lack of respect. Here the mistress is the sea. And you can do or say what you want, it teaches that you should never disrespect anyone. And beyond the differences between these old men and me, we have in common the dream and the respect. And that's why nothing will ever happen to me because I have so much respect for people and their lives.

I hear so many stories of tourists being molested in bars because they didn't want to drink, for example...

People are fundamentally disrespectful. There is too much levity in morals, less and less real values, like honor, loyalty, courage, honesty, frankness, dignity.

Too many vices in the hearts of men, and it is true that it is sometimes difficult to fight them. We must draw strength from within ourselves, and meditate, or pray, or do exercises like tai chi to rebalance ourselves.

Some days I succeed, others not.

I realize that in a short period of time, in just two generations, honor and dignity are terms that few people understand anymore. As if they had disappeared...

In the 1980s, at the end of the patriarchal society, these notions still carried weight. Men could die for honor. For a woman, for their own name, or for their nation. In Japan, the samurai had elevated this value to the rank of their most precious possession, for which death was of little importance in the face of humiliation, as long as their honor was safe.

So many rulers try to evacuate the notion of human dignity into the sewers of society, so that the people do not care about it or even forget it forever. So humans are crushed, they are allowed, they are even pushed to trample on others, they are asked to banish fraternity, their dignity, for the benefit of others, the powerful.

Yet it would be the function of the powerful and the rulers to set an example.
Couldn't we imagine a council of great sages, the most educated by heart, and the most empathetic, who would govern the planet with dignity?
Ahhhh, God... it is clear that I was incarnated way too early, in a society of baby players who give so little value to Life and to the dignity of the Human...

Tonight, I leave Greece at 4pm. Another country is coming. I like it.
Three weeks that, despite the clouds *(insistent gays in Mykonos, wind in Ios, sadness to see friends leave, chicks tackling me, etc.),* will remain a memory of quietness, of the beauty of the white villages on blue skies, of the elegance of the sea and its azure tints, of a people a bit rough but deeply generous, of the separation from my bike, and of all the really beautiful and nice people I met.

Costs and expenses so far (for these last three months):
Sardinia: $400
Rome and Italy: $250
Greece: $1,000

Now it's Turkey's turn!

8. Strong as a Turk!

Well, two days later, it's Tuesday, November 2, 1993, and it's a giant foot!
Why? Because I am now travelling with three people, two guys and a girl, Argentinians. I had already seen them several times on the beach of Ios, "hi - hi", and here they are again in Samos, waiting for the boat. We got to know each other and they are really nice. Always laughing. They have adopted me. Each one of them brings his contribution in knowledge to the others.

Turkey, the people, the life, everything is pleasant, and incredibly cheap. Tonight's pension is the equivalent of $2. It's really the first time I can spend money with a smile and without counting. But be careful, without falling into stupid tourism.
It is also a Muslim country and that changes a lot.
We feel here that the man is king.

I didn't realize at the time how much religion shapes people. How much it can change from one border to another.
In the south of Thailand, for example, everyone smiles, has a childlike, laughing face, few wrinkles, carefree faces. Once you

cross the border into Penang, Malaysia, things change. The faces are closed, and almost all of them have a big wrinkle between their eyes, the wrinkle of concentration, the one of careful-we-no-longer-laugh-life-is-heavy. In the space of 200 meters, people are no longer the same.

Thai Buddhism makes people happy and joyful, and Malay Muslims seem closed, serious, concentrated. You can feel the heaviness, something that weighs down.

Personally, after having visited more than 45 countries now, I only go to Buddhist or Christian countries, just to have some fun in the evening. Go to the Seychelles for example, a real paradise, but a Muslim postcard where in the evening, from 9pm, everything closes, no more music, no more noise, no more fun. It's just boring.

I have nothing against Muslims, everyone has the right to follow the dogma they want, if they have little character and prefer to have their life dictated to them, but I like too much to see a woman's hair waving when she walks, to admire her figure without my senses failing or it driving me crazy; I have far too much respect for the free woman to adhere to such a limiting and depriving dogma. And when they ask their wives to cover their skin, it would be according to them, because seeing some of it might divert them from the path, put them in danger, make them faint, poor little virgins... And then, how do we, Christian men, look at all those naked women on the beaches without getting a hard-on or fainting immediately? It doesn't make sense, unless all Muslims turned into premature ejaculators at the mere sight of a piece of female flesh... It's a shame, a lame excuse covered with a layer of virtue to pass the pill. I think it's rather to lock them up, to assign them to a reduced place in society, so that they don't show themselves, what! That's already more logical and coherent. Stop lying to yourself/us!

So yes, I tend to shun Muslims, who are far too inquisitive by nature and doctrine.

I had a Christian friend who fell in love with a beautiful Muslim woman. He was forced to convert in order to marry her, to relieve the weight of his sex by some 20 grams, and to learn the Koran. What other religion forces this?
Their conquest of the world is based on this, among other things. They continue to conquer.
My relationship with my friend got worse every time we saw each other. He would tell me that I was a lost sheep, that I had to join the flock, that I was going to get lost... We could no longer exchange and share our views freely and in tolerance.

Who was the sheep? Who was lost? Who was no longer thinking freely?
The worst thing is when someone tells you this in such a conviction-filled way... that I doubted it a few times... in my normal pseudo-freedom of thought.

From Kusadasi, an uninteresting city formatted for tourism, we took the bus to Denizli, 150 km to the east, going inland.
But I have to tell the story of last night's episode at the casino in Kusadasi.
I go there with Beto, one of the Argentinians, 36 years old, but he doesn't know much about it. He agrees to go there for a drink.
We go in. Metal detector out of order, I go in with my big knife on my belt, which will make the doorman laugh at the exit!
Drinks and food in abundance, and it falls damn well because we have an empty stomach. I play poker, slot machines, I lose 20

dollars. Then I go to the blackjack table and win 50! That's great! I'm not going home empty-handed! They call me. "Philippe, Philippe!". I look up and see Beto waving at me. I run to him and he shows me his machine. Jackpot! Unbelievable! With his last chip, he won about $200, a huge amount here! And he couldn't even buy me a drink because everything was free!
We left the casino like kings.

The next day, Tuesday, we set sail for Efes, a tourist attraction for its remains of a city built in the year 1000 BC. About 200 000 people lived here, and the ruins are in good condition. But for those who don't know the history, they are just old stones. Afterwards, we will go to Denizli and from there, Pamukkale, another great tourist place, famous for its natural terms in the mountain; springs of boiling water come out of the ground and have drawn on the slopes, for centuries, natural white pools of limestone.

A fifth person joined us, a 36 year old French woman, very nice who travels alone for a few more weeks. The "family" is growing. We have a good time.
 Only problem here, now it's cold. Really cold. I have to buy socks. And we're going to go to Cappadocia where it's freezing cold. Ouch, yikes, and quack!
We try the hammam, a great national institution reserved for men, and we are pampered like kings. They massage you while climbing on top your body, you are washed with a scrubbing sponge like a mother would do to her baby, washed with foam, purified with big buckets of water, and rest. Ouuaaahhhhh! What a great feeling! A new skin!
You can hear the muezzin and his Muslim chant from the top of the minarets five times a day.
Frankly, I could do without that...

We leave at midnight of our pension because there is no cover, no water, disgusting toilets, in short, too much is too much! And we really have the impression that the young people of this boarding house do not care about us. It's a bit annoying this pressure that we are constantly under since we arrived in Turkey. They don't give us time to breathe. So I'm a bit dry, I raise my voice; like when this guy jumps on us when we get off the bus in Denizli, I tell him to fuck off and explain that we're not stupid tourists, and he finally comes back to us in the evening in a bar, to apologize. It's tiring for everyone. And it's only the third day!

Wednesday, November 3rd: the shit! To start with, I forgot a pair of sneakers in Kusadasi. But that's nothing. In the first boarding house yesterday, while we went to eat, those bastard sons of bitches from the boarding house stole my money from my satchel in my backpack. I was like crazy, I almost broke their heads, especially that fat pig's head who really looks like an idiot. Police, statement, then everyone at the police station, where of course I understood nothing. The impression is that you're being gently mocked, that the party is for the local guys. Then city hall where the fuckers are brought before a judge. Verdict in three weeks or a month. But I don't really get it. Maybe they're getting off scot-free. It pisses me off.
Abused, denigrated, denied my honesty, I am upset all day.
I don't want to be looked at the wrong way today!
In all, there was $100 + the equivalent of $200 in Turkish liras + the $30 I won at the casino.
That's a lot of money right there! I curse the money they took from me, hoping it will bring them bad luck.
And well... since I'm not a Christian to turn the other cheek, I have my own rules. I leave in the morning, leaving them several small gifts: liquid glue *(bought the day before)* in the locks I meet on the way out. It should really annoy them because it's impossible

to remove, you have to dismantle and replace the lock. Paf in your face! The same goes for the front door of the guy's car. Gently lift up the little protective pull tab that gives access to the lock itself, and PAF, take this asshole, go try to open your door now. Your car sucks.

I'm telling you, it's a hell of a thing to really piss someone off *(who deserves it of course)*.

I left having also graffitied their front door and boarding house sign with a "thieves" in French and English, with a big black marker I bought specially.

It is with a heavy heart and full of anger, but with a little smile on my face, thinking about the biased justice of the System and that of men: when one does not satisfy you, there remains the other, more fair sometimes.

I'm like that, always nice and with my heart on my sleeve, but you mustn't fuck with me, my dark side is terrible, I know it, sometimes I'm afraid of it; and sometimes I like to stay there for a while and feed the monster ...

There, we can approach the concept of reincarnation and karmas. I know that what I have done is not good, that I should not have done it. I will certainly have to pay for it later, in this life or in another. Everything has to be paid for, right? Sooner or later... Personally I believe in the principle of reincarnation, that I have already had hundreds of past lives. I have felt several in this life, I know that I have already lived several other lives before this one. Or at the same time, in another dimension, depending on whether you prefer to think of it on a non-linear level.

When I die, I will return to the light, to the astral, which is made up of an infinite number of vibratory light levels and, depending on the quality of my energy obtained at the end of this life, I will join the dimension that most closely corresponds to my new vibrations. I will

return to real life. After this short passage on Earth, once again.
And again and again, my soul, my essence, will seek to evolve
constantly, to vibrate ever higher. As long as my soul needs
material and density to learn and experience - and our dear planet
is perfect for that - then I will come back to Earth to absorb more
and more experiences. So that one day I won't need this dense
dimension for a certain type of learning and I will be reincarnated
in another dimension, another world, more etheric than our good
old Earth.
These are my beliefs, and I like them.

So if my consciousness absorbs strong emotions in this life, and all
my actions are recorded in the akashic records (or akashic
memories), I will inevitably have to pay in one way or another for
what I did when I acted wrong. The good will come back to me as
well as the bad, which will have to be paid. So be it.
But did we not incarnate imperfectly in unfinished
bodies to grow and learn?

That's why in this life I like to experience all kinds of emotions, good
and not so good, and anger is one of the feelings that we imperfect
humans have.

So yes, sometimes I screw up, in good conscience, knowing that
there will have to be reparation. I'm ready, I'll pay...

The next day, I climbed the mountain overlooking the city of
Egridir. I am at about 400 meters of altitude, one hour of
climbing, and I see everything. It is magnificent. The noise of the
city rises to me. The lake is turquoise *(which comes from the word*
"Turkish") because the bottom is made of special plants that give
it this color.
We start to enter the real Turkey.
After a few setbacks in the tourist corners and a few bad

pensions, here is finally the Turkey of every day under its true nature. One word comes to mind: strong. Strong like a Turk! Strong like coffee, strong like those looks that are deep, dark, powerful, strong like those 8 or 10 year old children who walk the streets with their shoe polish box to shine the shoes of the gentlemen, strong like this omnipresent religion that oozes from the minaret from which come, five times a day, those haunting calls, to the mosques filled with serenity, faith, forgiveness, repentance, fervor. Strong as the images of little girls in traditional costume playing in the alleys. Powerful and abundant moustache, the Turkish seems to me curious and playful in front of the foreigner. They are not afraid. Not even the children, not frightened when they approach you first.

I'm always with my four companions. We get along well. There is Beto, the restless one who has a fantastic sense of humor, with whom I share rooms in the guesthouses, Jorge, alias "the Dalai Lama", very mystical and meditating every day. There is Laura, his wife, simple, kind, and Maryse the Frenchwoman, a lively person, curious about everything. We form a happy team, and everywhere we go, laughter and good mood are part of the story.

We leave Pamukkale and its white limestone mountains. It is an incredible sight to see this water running down the mountain, covering it with white and digging basins, small pools in the wall. We bathe under the waterfall, by 12° outside, in the basins, and one hour later, the skin is dry, white... the hair, we do not speak about it! Shower with fresh water obligatory then.

I started to cut my hair. A more and more pressing need is born in me. Need to clean myself from my appearance probably... Today, it's the back of my neck and I cut my long hair behind. Goodbye mullet. In about a week, I'll be shearing my head. I've decided to do so. It's a step in my inner transmutation. I want to change my image, to lose those reflex movements I've been doing with my hair for so long, all those gestures we all unconsciously make to sweep a strand, touch our hair back, comb our hair, etc. I don't want them anymore. I don't want it anymore. I'll gain freedom from it. I've been wanting to do it for a long time. Here I can and will do it. But of course, being the precursor that I am, absolutely nobody has a shaved head, here or elsewhere. Only the legionnaires and the military are like that. But what do you want, I always liked to provoke a little, or to be ahead of the game...

It reminds me of the last slap I received during my adolescence. The emancipation of the teenager, and the necessary rejection of the parents.

I put it here because we are in a bit of the same attitude, a need for detachment to be stronger, an emancipation from the System, of which parents are part.
I had a not so great childhood, as I explained earlier, and a not so great teenage years either.

Mom was depressed and emotionally unstable. A woman who had trouble managing her emotions between the outside world and her inner world. At home, there was more than laughter and joy. Her emotional instability meant that at the slightest annoyance, things would go haywire under her skull and slaps would rain down. Or not. It was like the weather. Uncertain, every day...
Like when she came home from work, opened the door and immediately looked at the kitchen table. If she didn't like what she saw - my sister and I were instructed to prepare the dining table before she arrived - she would cheerfully give us a volley of phalanges back and forth, which would revive our somewhat pallid complexion and give us nice red cheeks.

I was growing quietly, and every year my head was getting closer to its one meter seventy. And the slaps didn't help, I kept growing. Until the last slap. As usual, something would set off her moods and she would unload on us. And I still remember her surprise when the slap hit my cheek, my face expressed no emotion and I continued to look at her impassively. There she knew that this was the end of her way of doing things, that she could never again use it to let off steam and control me.

That said, I think that these power struggles between parents and teenagers are necessary to prepare the growing child for the future "No! I even believe that it is an essential step to confront the parents, this process is essential. The emancipation of the teenager and the rejection of the parents.
Well, without violence it's even better...
This is a particularly difficult period for parents if they are not prepared for it. We know that after two or three years, everything calms down, the period of rebellion is over, the wind goes down, and the parents find their child more calm and serene.
Well, in families that talk to each other of course, when there is love...
Which was not my case.
This period will have put on the market a young guy who was unstructured, unbalanced and rebellious to the core, and who took about ten years to rebuild his psyche.

Thank you to my dear limited parents, for using my sister and me to eliminate your tensions, empty your emotional overflow, and drown your fears by torturing us gently, without knowing what you were doing... You are going to leave without even being aware of all the harm you have done to us, ignorant as you are.

My nostrils have been dry for about ten days now. I don't know if it's the weather that's cooled down. Maybe it is. Because it's cold in the evening. And in Cappadocia, where we are going, it's even colder! Cold and dry. I think at this moment that I am rather made for a warm and tropical climate, with more humidity. I feel it in my body.

I start to do a little meditation every day again, because of course a day without television is long and therefore I have a lot of time on my hands. Especially in the late afternoon. Once the day's activities are over, once I've taken a shower, there are always two or three hours free to sleep, read, meditate, tidy up, sew, wash, in short, any relatively quiet and more or less obligatory act. At the moment I'm reading a book by Saint-Exupéry, bought in Mykonos, in French, written very small and full of poetry. Each sentence has a deep and hidden meaning. The pages don't scroll very fast and that's good. It is always a pleasure to read a little poetry, one or two pages.

All day long I speak in Spanish. I make huge mistakes, which makes my companions laugh, because when I don't know a word, I say it in Fren-nish. They laugh at my mistakes.
I thank God for having given me the possibility and the ability to learn several languages.
I get by in Italian, but it's such an easy language. I also learned German for nine years, but this language doesn't pass, something blocks in the back of my throat, as if I had been on the other side in a past war and kept a bad memory of it, in a previous life not so far away. It doesn't pass.
My Spanish is getting better every day and my English is pretty good, and I feel I'll be greatly improving it in Asia soon.
Add to that the six computer languages I've mastered as well, and it all suggests that I'm pretty good at languages.
I was born a stutterer... it's a wonder, isn't it?

Here in Egridir, when people look at you, you don't feel that bad gleam in their eyes as I felt it at the beginning of Turkey. It must be said that in the tourist places, we are meat. Sometimes they look at us with a contemptuous look. Because we are seen as a wallet on legs who comes to conquer a country with dollars as weapon. But from Denizli, as we go deeper into the land, the eyes become friendly, curious, almost helping...
We feel respect. We respect the other, because we are not at home, they respect these foreigners who visit their country. The main thing is to never shock or shock the mentality.

It's crazy here how men are pampered. I could almost say that this is a country of men. I believe - of course after only one week in this country - that women are in the minority. We have seen this in the hammams of course - because there are no hammams for women - but there are also barbers, lots of little salons, as big as trailers, set up anywhere, and men come to have their faces pampered. Barbers too. I've never seen a hairdresser for women. But there's a barber for men on almost every street! It must be a country of big macho men if I'm to judge by the super stupid soap operas that are on TV. There's always the mustachioed hero who kills everyone with a gun. It's half drama, half spaghetti western, and of course, no important role for women.

Macho: term from the 1980s-1990s. Later, it broke down into "machounet", and then disappeared into the lesser-used words of the French language.
Term from the patriarchal society in which the father was king. Children and women bowed their heads to the lord at home. Fathers were therefore the patriarchs, and were naturally macho, issuing

instructions and various orders in the homes. The macho was also created by very/too protective mothers who idolized their sons. In the media, the macho man was portrayed with attributes that marked virility, leather, a good big moustache, dressed in masculine materials.

So, growing up in that society, with those insensitive and uncommunicative fathers, how could you not get a big head and be just a basic macho teenager, the one who shows off, insensitive in front of women and who puts them down naturally. The macho man was no pushover, he didn't show his feelings, he preferred to play with women's feelings. Give nothing and just take. Some women loved it... and the era wanted it.

I was one of them. And it suited me because it allowed me to hide what was wrong in my head. Under the guise of a proud male, I could hide my fears and flaws, I didn't even have to question myself, I just had to assume the posture of the misogynist and without saying anything, it passed.

The macho was also respected. Charles Bronson, Delon, the cowboys in the westerns, even that gay guy in the Magnum series was one, pretty much validated by society, a macho man on screen... Now when you see a macho man on TV, you just feel sorry for him, you laugh...

What an extraordinary turn of events for the man! He has fallen from his pedestal and is now forced to give of himself to a woman. Otherwise she leaves him. I don't know many who stay with a man who doesn't reveal and offer his feelings or emotions. Fortunately, women have learned, evolved, and now ask men for more sensitivity, dialogue, balance and equity.
It took a long time and a lot of divorces.

Sunday: a real biblical Sunday. No sign of life. Today is election day. Which means that everyone is obliged to stay at home, and people are going to come by to count the number of people per

house, for the next elections. So there's no one outside! No cars, no noise, and of course, everything is closed!
We went shopping for food today.

Yesterday on the mountain, I scared myself. I wanted to go down the other side, and after 200 meters of vertical, I found myself facing a precipice shortly before daybreak- if not me - and I had to climb back up to go down the other side. This was no small hill but rock, high mountain. I felt like I was trapped. I really felt the survival instinct inside me. Two hours later, I reached the village, a tea, a cigarette, which I enjoyed!

In the evening, after dinner, we play cards in one of the rooms. It is always a moment of laughter and relaxation. We make up rules for Jas, Chinchon, a Spanish game, or other games.

Now I am on the peninsula of Egridir... so calm!

I've been waking up to sunshine every day for the past two months or so! When I think of the weather in Western Europe! I'm aching all over today. I'm not going to do any physical exercise. A real Sunday!

Monday, last day in Egridir. Met a young man who helped me to make myself understood at the post office. Very nice. We got on well and spent part of the afternoon trying to understand each other. He with his fifteen words of French, I with my ten words of Turkish... A lot of gestures, tolerance and patience.
There are no communication barriers between people if there is good will!

Sent to Geneva my tent, my two rolls of film, my first travel book for my mother and sister, tons of photos and my camping gear.

Three good kilos less! I'm getting lighter. The others have backpacks as big and heavy as containers, compared to me!

We took the tickets for Cappadocia for tonight, in a night bus.

9. The Valley of the Smurfs

Night bus, bus of misery! Eight hours on non-reclining seats and
the driver drops us off on the main road fifteen kilometers from
Uchisar, the town we wanted to go to. At four o'clock in the
morning!
So we walk in the dark until we find a light, a village nearby.
Mariza has a good intuition. She goes to a bakery that agrees to
keep us inside. At least it's warm! They shape their dough and
offer us tea and hot bread. It's smoking everywhere. A great
moment of sharing!
There is snow here...

We take the bus for Uchisar. And there, the shock!
An absolutely surreal, unimaginable scenery!
Millions of years ago, the valley was covered with ashes and lava
from the two volcanoes of the area. With the wind and the water,
the work of erosion is amazing, the landscape is hallucinating!
Fairy chimneys of 40 meters high surmounted by a stone block,
columns, towers, cones. And troglodyte dwellings! It's crazy...
Tuff peaks pierced by a thousand caverns like hoods with dozens
of eyes. Neither lunar nor terrestrial, it's the valley of the Smurfs!
In the past, in case of an attack, the inhabitants took refuge inside
these rocky peaks. And the village of Göreme, big tourist center,

81

is incredible! Bars, restaurants, houses, they are only caves, eroded inhabited mountains, we have the impression to be high permanently so much the brain has difficulty in believing the images which send him the retinas!

We find a cheap guesthouse; the prices here, even out of season, are unaffordable, up to $50 for a room in a fairy chimney. We'll pay ten times less for all the comforts possible outside the cave dwellings, 200 meters away.

Everyone is shattered after this terrible night spent in the bus and the morning waiting, then looking for a pension in this lunar decor. We sleep until 7pm, then it's time to eat.

Comfort, what we were missing at that very moment...
That's a sacred word that no one talks about outside.
His comfort, his precious comfort of life...

This is what creates the sheep, the cold and unresponsive people in front of a cataclysm, a madness on Earth, an eternal famine seen daily on TV, starving children and eyes attacked by flies, a tsunami or a bomb that blows people up.
The comfort sacred, or sacred comfort!
As long as it's there, anything goes.
It's not that we don't care about the misfortune of others, we just don't care when we pretend not to know that others are suffering. As long as comfort is such an important goal in life and in the hearts of men as a life goal, they can be deprived of their freedom, subjugated, even stripped of their dignity; humans are such that they can live with a smile on their face thinking about the nightly show, the Netflix series, or the latest black leather reclining couch to buy next month. The rest of us can die just fine...
And it also creates the "fatties", the soft people, the "spineless"...

And all the sheep we saw out there almost proudly wearing their masks during this fake covid pandemic, when it's useless.
The shee-triches. Half sheep, half ostriches, addicted to comfort. It makes them feel like perfect elements of the consumer-comfort society, spending their days putting up with that stupid mask, only to find themselves in front of the entertainment TV at night, and their damn comfort so reassuring...
What a load of crap!

Comfort should be consumed in small doses, otherwise there is a great risk of losing something vital in us, to the point of becoming stupid, cowardly, sissy... asshole. To be nothing more than a mere bodily envelope empty of dignity.

Great traditional dinner, starting with soup, followed by rice and meat, peppers, tomatoes, accompanied by a very good local wine and the famous Turkish bread, which is a wonder. In the morning, breakfast "Turkish style" consists of a plate containing a sliced tomato, a slice of feta cheese, black or green olives, and a cooked egg. Then, toast, butter and jam, usually homemade, and Turkish coffee or Nespresso.
A great way to start the day with sunshine in your belly...

Today, the first day of rain. Winter has entered Cappadocia. It's cold, ugly, wet. One day to stay inside.
Visit of the castle of the city which is none other than the mountain pierced with a thousand cavities and windows. All in forms that recall the sensuality of the desert and the dunes. All that is worked by the wind during these thousands of years creates sensual forms, without angles or salient edges.
A visit to the local bazaar where everyone shops, including me. Colored hat, scarf... and I flash on a wool sweater, but I have to haggle over the price. It's very technical. You have to try on the

sweater, give the seller a price, usually half of the set price. He usually never agrees, of course, so you take the sweater off with puppy-dog eyes and say that maybe you'll come back before you die. The salesman then makes a last proposal, which starts to become interesting. We can play like this for a long time. Talking about your poor family, saying that you're a student, that your grandmother has just died, etc. without ever losing your smile, is very important. I had a little trouble because the prices are already so low compared to Europe, that it bothers me to go too low. So I haggle for form, and for the following tourists, so as not to get the seller used to them buying at any price. The sweater I want costs $22. And it looks great. But I've set myself $16 and won't buy it above that.
I think tomorrow I'll get it at that price.

We ate a Turkish specialty based on meat, tomato, peppers and spices, served in a sort of large pan where everyone helps themselves with a fork, on Turkish pizza bread. A treat. 2 per person.

Today is a day of spending. This morning, at the barber's, a little pleasure. It's a 12 year old kid who shaves me. And how! Twice the shave with the blade, rinsing, after-shave balm, talcum powder, brushing the hair, all with dexterity and application! He just didn't scrub the inside of my nostrils, otherwise, impeccable service. Tipped.
Then we go to Nevçehir, a local town, to find a bank. I come across a shoe shop. I go in. I come out ten minutes later with a pair of shoes and new sneakers, my old ones had almost no soles. I also need a second pair of jeans. Total: a lot of money...
Afterwards, visit of an underground city on four floors. Everything is perfectly preserved. Corridors so narrow that I have to bend at the maximum and measure 80 centimeters to pass. All this dates from 1600 BC. But we lack a guide to

understand the functions of all these rooms and chambers.

End of the day, back to the pension. I decide to shave my head, I'm ready. Or rather I ask Beto to do it.
30 minutes later, result: I have the head of a G.I Joe. That's what I wanted, or at least I thought so.

At that time only the military had shaved hair. No one else. I don't want to tell you how people looked at me when I came back to France after a few years... Then, year after year, men started to shave their heads. I would have been a precursor on that one.

My head is now cold.
Big surprise, I didn't expect to have such feelings. In the shower, for example. First time the water runs on the skin of my naked skull, it's almost orgasmic, eyes turned upwards, mouth open, little stream of drool...
Another surprise too, the first time a fly landed on my skull. I felt its little fingers on my skin, I could perfectly trace its path on my egg skull. The sensations that it gives me are mind-boggling. So flies are my friends. Now I am amused to think that they come to make me small hugs...

It reminds me of the low season in Ibiza when I was one of the guards at Amnesia, one of the biggest clubs on the island, and during the few months of the winter season there were three of us guys guarding the disco full time. We slept and lived in it. I didn't have a dime and those few months were hard to live with. We spent hours eating nuts with the local dog because there was a walnut tree in the disco. The days were sometimes very long, with nothing to do... So, from time to time, I wrote shirtless in the languor and heat

*of the idle afternoons, and sometimes flies came to land on my back
or my shoulders, my only companions of the day. I thanked them for
their visit, they brought me a little moral comfort...
There too, I considered them as friends who came to visit me.
Since then, I can't stand the stupid killing of flies with a fly killer.
At least they are useful.
They are the prey of a good number of birds, lizards, and larger
insects, the raw material of choice in terms of protein for other
animals.
On the contrary to a good majority of humans who are useless and
spend their lives damaging the planet or killing animals, like those
who still eat dead animals.
So there you go, I like flies.* ☺

This morning, big surprise! Great weather, since the little weather
is not here, and everything is white! It's as cold as a frozen duck,
but if the sun holds out, it's going to be a wonderful day. I slept
badly, too cold. My body was not warm enough to warm the bed.
We walk down into the enchanted valley, up and down the hills
of trolls and goblins for two hours. Two hours of wonder. I
bombard with photos. We meet two Frenchmen from Egridir
and book a pension with heating for the next day.

Saturday 13 November: already two weeks in Turkey. How time
flies! And how quickly man can adapt. The days go by, the dates
go by, and life follows its course.
Thank you to the Gods for allowing me to make this trip and to
see this magnificent country.

We get in touch with the tourism world in Göreme because there
are some travelers, many young people, Japanese among others,
and all the pensions have a wood oven in the rooms. I negotiate
skillfully and diplomatically the price of our new pension. It is

always a subtle and technical chess game. I am good...

I have new sensations with my shaved head.
Feeling the wind on the bare scalp. I wear a woolen cap half the
time because it's cold and I have to get used to my new head.
Psychologically, I'll need another two or three days before I can
show myself to the world, I'm not ready yet. My Argentinian
friends have the impression of having a new companion, a
sergeant major in the legion...

The image!
Ahhh... the image we project to others, the image of ourselves, our
image.
How annoying it can be to always pay attention to this devotional
self-image.
Some people devote their lives to it. Or are captive to it, possessed
by it.
There were times in my life when my appearance was really
important, and then I realized how superficial and lacking it all was,
only serving to fill my inner void with the energy of people looking
at me. A kind of energetic vampirism to feed the empty beings,
nothing else.

After my first marriage, I became single again and went to live in
the south of France. The freedom, the beautiful women, the beautiful
places, the good restaurants, the good life...
I had a nice car and I wanted everyone to know how successful I
was, how good, handsome and strong I was, and for people to turn
around when I passed by and say: "Wow, he's successful...", "Look
at this guy, how good he is! I needed it. An unconscious need,
belonging to my secret part of the shadow, which pushed me to the
extreme to receive these streams and subtle gulps of invisible
energies from all these faces crossed and wrapped up by my
silhouette. I then bought myself a big watch, the biggest possible, it

was already fashionable - and isn't fashion made to be noticed, to be admired? Because my success had to be seen right away.
For me, who had hardly ever worn a watch in my life, it was the last straw. So I had a huge thing on my wrist that annoyed me more than it told me the time. Then, I had big rings, huge metal and stone rings that encumbered my fingers and that I had to take off and put back on several times a day depending on my activities, sports, swimming, sleeping...
So much clutter in my mind!
All this while thinking that I was going to get better and better and that it would carry me higher and higher, that I would grow, that I would rise to the pantheon of my own glory!
Laughs...
What a mistake.

In fact, I was more drained than nourished by this obsessive pattern that assailed me.
It lasted about two years before I threw everything away, watch and rings, and realized the uselessness of these sophistications and the vanity of burdening my life with trivialities of social consideration that were supposed to - I thought - nourish me more than my mother had done when I was a kid.

Because that's where we are, of course! It's all a search for self-esteem in the eyes of the mother who congratulates her little one for his first steps, for all that he will succeed in his first years and that, personally, I was unable to experience.
Mom was not there.
A trace of the wound of abandonment? Probably.
Still, I am convinced that it comes from there, and that a child who has been loved, fulfilled and nourished by the love of his parents (especially the mother for a little guy) will care much more about the opinion of others and his social validation later.
This was not the case for me during those years and I must have been pretty funny to watch.
Or downright pathetic...

I'm sometimes a little ashamed of it now, when I think about it...

It's so cold in our unheated room in Uchisar that it fogs up when we breathe. Yesterday it took me at least two hours to warm up my feet when I went to bed. Tonight, the last cold night, I sleep in my sleeping bag and under three blankets. But that's not enough.

We visit one of the most beautiful valleys in Cappadocia. We walk for about three hours along the local vineyards and vines, and we follow the dry course of a thousand-year-old river, passing under stone arches, in tunnels that the river has dug, but unfortunately, in trying to play the daredevil hero, I sprain my ankle again. As a result, the rest of the walk is spoiled by the pain at each step.

And yes, I must still be or have my head in the stars, and not anchored enough in the matter! A great classic...
When the body speaks, its language is clear. "You can't stand on your feet, you always want to escape your body and go up there. So this is what happens, and now you're going to have to concentrate on every step...". Sprained ankle.
An interesting thing about pain is that the body speaks a language. Its own language. But you have to be able to read or decipher it.

A few dead cells that accumulate in the body can impede the circulation of blood in a micro-vein. If this continues to accumulate and is not drained by osmosis outside the body, one can well imagine that complications will arise.
And I like to think and see this at the cellular level.

For when a sperm unites its destiny with an egg to create us, a very first cell is born. It contains all of our future splendor, our original perfection and light as intended by the Universe in its grandeur and magnificence. I like to think that this cell is always there, somewhere deep in my heart, in its initial perfection. Therefore, if I have a boo-boo, a malfunction, if I am bruised, if I am bleeding, or if I am in pain somewhere, then I can mentally contact this cell that contains my initial perfect DNA and ask it to quickly send pure cells to replace those that are dead or damaged in a part of my body.
Isn't this an absolutely healthy and easy way to heal yourself?

Simple, personal, just project this intention with your heart.

I'm waiting for my first cancer (which I will never get) to test this, because my first wife died of it, and I for one will absolutely never go to the hospital to be injected with their poisons created by dehumanized, money-hungry labs.
I'll just have to talk to my body with love and it will fix everything. Or I'll stop eating for twenty days or so, and then everything should be fine...

I hope - and here I always come back with humor and love to the Gods who play with me - that I will end my life in fifteen minutes with a good old heart attack, and if possible by making love with a chick who will drive me crazy and make my heart explode!
The best ending ever, right?

Let's go, let's schedule it! ☺

Returned to the troglodyte pension WITH heating please! Put a bandage on my ankle and set up my room, i.e. arranged my toiletries in the bathroom, according to my habit of putting toothbrush, toothpaste and hairbrush on the sink... but now the brush is unnecessary! It made me laugh! Here is another thing less that will lighten my bag...

We have dinner in the living room of the pension which is also a café-restaurant-reception, in short, a room for everything, in the company of two couples, Australian and Californian, and our two French from Egridir. We had a very nice dinner and ended with a game of cards. Our room is dug in the rock, with all the comfort and the cleanliness wanted. Painted in white. On the ceiling, we can see the traces of each blow with a pick and hammer that it took to dig this room. Above our heads, forty meters of mountain and two million tons of earth!

Monday 15: Yesterday, nothing happened. Because of my ankle and I felt like living in slow motion. Bought Paris-Match, read it in about 10 minutes, still uninteresting. Played pool, backgammon, cards. My ankle is better. Swelling gone.

It's snowing a lot now! This morning, a good twenty centimeters. Everything is white! It's beautiful. This time it's really the land of the seven dwarfs!

Yesterday, three young Americans arrived at the guesthouse. They left the same evening. They arrived from the south of the country where it was 24° and where they were swimming. They arrived here, it was -4° and snowing. They couldn't stand the Riccans!

We visit Urgup, nothing to see; then some, including me, go to the hammam to be pampered by a big old masseur who does his job very well. Others spend the afternoon with a very professional carpet salesman, who explains all the differences, textures, manufacturing methods, and prices, and they leave with one or two carpets. Useless and cumbersome, but they were tricked...

Then we hang out in the guesthouse, between the bedrooms and the reception-lounge-dining-room-kitchen-living-room-and-possibly-attic, playing cards and backgammon.

Tuesday: same, I do nothing but a walk and karate in the nature. We learn the local game that everyone plays here in the cafes. Only the men of course. My ankle is 80% recovered. I keep losing at backgammon and it's getting pretty annoying! Anyway, at least I'm still learning.

Today, Wednesday, it's dirty weather, but everyone has decided to go riding. Well, I'm following the herd, grumbling a bit because I'm more of a disjointed puppet on a horse. As much as I've spent the last ten years with my ass on a motorcycle in summer and winter, on a horse I'm just a puppet. I don't have the knack, I've never taken lessons.

 So we go to Aramos, the big town around here. It's raining. Too bad, we go anyway. To the stables, 22 Arabian horses, including thoroughbreds. I ask for a mongrel horse, with the least pure blood possible, the softest given my level of handicap. A disabled, deaf and three-legged horse if possible, thank you! They find me one. He seems much too big, strong and nervous for me. First of all, he has to be brushed so that he can feel me and get used to me. Then they have to saddle him up, an operation I don't take part in, then take him out and mount him. It seems simple but in reality they haven't been out for a long time and this time makes them nervous. As soon as we get on, we are already soaked. A 45 minute walk is fine, but I'd like to gallop a bit, or at least get some feel for it. When we're done, we're all frozen. The hammam is closed, it's a pity, that's what we would have needed.

Back to the city bus.

It's amazing how well organized the bus network is in Turkey. You can find any bus for any destination, all the buses are great, very clean, with free water in bags and you can stop them anywhere on the road, on a wave of the hand. But all the men smoke and it gets unbreathable very quickly. I'm talking about a thick, choking smog all over the bus. A nauseating haze that nobody thinks of stopping because almost everyone pulls on their cigarettes. Crazy...

Tonight the boarding house is full. Six new travelers have arrived. Australians, Germans. We eat almost every night typical dishes. Many of them are based on eggplants, Turkish rice which has nothing to do with our rice - rather a mixture of semolina and rice - and veal or mutton, with tomatoes, onions and peppers. A real delight. Moreover, all the bars have their "shish kebab" machines and you can eat at any time. Today, for example, I eat at 3:30 pm.

10. Istanbul

Thursday: we move, finally! We tear ourselves away from Göreme, after five days in this great pension, these crazy games of backgammon and this room dug in the rock. It is certainly not before a long time that I will see a place like this again, for sure!

Four hours by bus to Ankara, the administrative capital. There are barely ten of us in the bus.

Again, contact with the city. Noise, heavy traffic, running and bustling in all directions. When we arrive at night, around 4 o'clock, Ankara seems huge. Buses everywhere. Traffic jams, the facades are dirty as well as all the streets in fact. It's filthy!

We find a pension thanks to the Guide du Routard. And there, it is the brothel! Nobody is happy, everybody talks at the same time, rooms with shower, without shower, with WC, with three beds, with two, we discuss the prices and it doesn't end anymore. I don't care. We're in the cheapest hotel in town and they're arguing like carpetbaggers about a price that's already been reduced by a third by the boss. After these endless boring discussions, we go to eat deliciously in a local restaurant, then we play a game of pool, and for tomorrow the program is already made: we do not stay and we leave for Istanbul the same evening. Quick visit of the city, and pffffuuiit...

Saturday: here I am in Istanbul. Formerly Constantinople for the Romans, and even further Byzantium for the Greeks. It is the door between the East and the West. The crossroads between many civilizations. The train trip was like when you sleep in a train, that is to say, like Pulco-lemonade quite shaken; I slept rather badly, persuaded that the train would derail any time so much the gaps between the tracks were violent and the shakes important. In short, we disembarked at a station. Then you have to go downtown, which can only be done by boat. And so much the better, it is all the more beautiful. On the boat, first contacts with the inhabitants. Rather warm. There are mosques emerging from everywhere. Built on seven hills, the city is cut in two by the waters of the Bosphorus, on one side the Sea of Marmara, and on the other the Black Sea. The cut between the two worlds is clear. East and West.

There is a cheap and comfortable hotel in the tourist district, next to the Blue Mosque.
Coal delivery for the hotel: a mountain of coal in front, in the street, on both sidewalks, blocks absolutely everything. Pieces like rocks, as if the hotel's facade had collapsed. Amazing!

Sunday: walk, alone. I waited 45 minutes for the others at the entrance of a mosque and then I left. Being alone will only do me good.
Oh dear... so many miles in this city! I walk through a thousand alleys until I reach the university, and there begins an improbable open-air market. In the middle of a compact crowd, street vendors push carts of all kinds of trinkets, adding to the indescribable chaos another mess. Almost impossible to move around. This leads me to the mosque of Suleyman the

Magnificent, the largest in Istanbul, with its four minarets. Six kids play with me like fish that eat a piece without ever touching the hook, and make me go crazy. Then I get lost in the maze of streets leading to the sea. Beer stop. My feet are on fire. Back to the hotel and shower.

Everywhere in the streets, between the cars that honk their horns, merchants or deliverymen push carts, hand trucks or carry boxes. It looks like chaos, but everything is moving.

Post Day. To begin with, find the central post office where you can pick up "leftover items". Inquire if anything has happened for me. The guy can't find anything. Yet I know there's something waiting for me. Well, my package is filed under my first name and not under my last. And on top of that, I have to go to the other end of town, past the last subway stop, taxi, on foot, to finally find the right building. And there, the administrative horror. Going from one point to another, from one office to another, from one unfriendly guy to another weary and bitter robot. From one floor to another. A marathon! What a mess.

As I leave the post office with my parcel under my arm, a nice guy takes me back to the metro through a kind of highway. Impossible traffic, no rules of conduct, anarchy. And between the dusty old trucks, the overcrowded buses, the cars zigzagging at full speed, the horse-drawn carts that apparently were not afraid of the cars' fury, we move forward.
It is also a picture of Istanbul, civilizations rubbing shoulders. As well as the bazaars of the 1001 nights stuck between two banks!

For the metro, you don't have to worry about it. One fixed price for the whole line, whether you make one stop or twenty.

Tonight we go to a special place where everyone smokes hoohah.

A kind of big pipe connected to a water container by a rubber tube topped by a small tray containing tobacco, on which an employee comes to put an ember. The result is that you have to pull a lot to smoke, the smoke gets cold in the throat because it is cooled by the water, and after 10 minutes, I get bored... But it's local and the local men come to kill time by smoking their hookah and watching TV. It's a place where you come to be bored.

Like yesterday, tonight I'm eating grilled fish, delicious! No tricks, the fish is opened, put on the grill and served on the plate. I don't know what kind of fish it is, but it's big, good and cheap. That's enough for me.

I twisted my ankle again yesterday, the same one, and it really pisses me off! I'm sick of it. I have really weak tendons and my ankles are taking a beating. Fragile part of the colossus. It reminds me of the legend of the Achilles tendon.

I buy my ticket to Bangkok, $375, which is half of what I had planned. Great news!

The group will soon split up. Laura and Jorge have to stay here in Istanbul to wait for the answer of their apartment in Buenos Aires, Beto will stay with them for a while. Maybe we'll meet again in Thailand. I'm going to go with Rod and Joe, the two Australians who are really nice people.
So, it's moving, I like it!

Visit of the Topkapi Palace, palace of the sultans, more than 400 rooms of which only some can be visited, inhabited since 1409 and until 1800 by these Muslim monarchs. Open to tourists, the exhibition rooms offer to the view and to the Japanese cameras the thousand and one Ottoman splendors, exceptional jewels, solid gold thrones, the seventh largest diamond in the world *(80 carats)*, Chinese porcelain, jewels, various ornaments, weapons adorned with emeralds, rubies, diamonds, etc... These are four hours of marvels, presidential gifts offered to the sultans by ambassadors of the whole world.

Visit also the harem where 300 to 400 women were kept by black eunuchs, raised in a great discipline.

It's full of Chinese, Japanese, Indonesians and some other tourists.
It is very cold today.
In the late afternoon, the weekly hammam. One of the oldest in the city, all in marble. I become a baby again in the arms of a fat eunuch who treats and mistreats me deliciously.

Today Thai consulate, on the other side of town, on the modern side of Istanbul. No problem, two months validity and it costs about $10. Then I walk back with the intention of finding a gym. I need to get in shape as I feel like a limp potato...

The tourist office sends me to a large, very modern center. Not bad. Negotiations at the entrance, student prices. It's still expensive. Anyway...

Two hours later, after sweating on all the equipment and spending 20 minutes in the sauna, I am as fresh as a daisy! Considering that my body is the temple of my soul and that it is my only vehicle for this life, I like to keep it in good working order. And I like to know that my body is a perfectly tuned racing machine. That is, when I don't fall into my excesses...

I return on foot, while passing by the pedestrian shopping streets. Arrived at the hotel towards 5 p.m., power failure. All the hotel is plunged in the complete dark. Interesting.

Friday 26: I'm getting bored. Every day it's cold, it's raining, while there are so many things to do outside under the sun. Every morning I look up to the sky and think about Thailand, soon, where it's 25° in Bangkok because it's the cool season. Four more days to wait!

In one of my former lives, which was revealed to me by an Essene therapist - a life lived in Tibet (I don't know how far back, if back there is...) - I had a sister - who was my first wife in this present life - and we had suffered a lot from the cold, among other things, in this rough life of mountain dwellers, there.
So it seems quite normal to me that in this life I am looking for warmth above all.
It is always difficult for me to face the cold when I am poorly equipped. Emotional scoriae strongly anchored in my consciousness make me run away from the cold! And as if by chance, I am currently living in the tropics... well...

A walk under the Istanbul drizzle, various purchases, gasoline for the zippo, Drum tobacco, finally real rolling tobacco, and two cassettes of music.
Strolling through the spice market, among thousands of strangers, with a good old blues in my ears wrapped up in a hat with the walkman, is a great moment!

Back to the hotel in the middle of the afternoon and meditation, after doing some laundry. I don't feel like doing anything else.

The next day, I didn't even want to go out. Too cold. I'm going to buy some earplugs anyway, so I can meditate in peace or sleep well. Because we've already changed rooms three times! Next to the hotel is a printing house and the noise of the machines can be heard from 8 am to 7 pm, just on the other side of the wall.

Upstairs we had the noise and no heating, now we only have the noise, in a room with six beds. This hotel is a madhouse! The boss is a natural overachiever, a sort of 100,000 volt flesh magma, his son a degenerate who pisses us off every morning at breakfast with his tea. All he can say is "Problem! For him, life is a problem and I think being born was his biggest problem.

Tomorrow, we're off to Bursa, a ski resort 20 km away, because some people want to ski. Not for me, because I don't have any gloves and I don't think they rent them. But I'm a bit fed up with Istanbul and a change of scenery won't do me any harm!

Here is your favorite speaker talking to you live from Bursa, the former Ottoman capital, on this Monday 29th, at 11 o'clock in the morning, in the four by two meters room, with two beds, of a low category hotel. We arrived yesterday afternoon, Beto and I - because all the others are either sick or don't want to come - after two hours by boat and one hour by bus. First day of full moon. Frantic search in all directions to find a cheap hotel. Exhausted, we finally find one. It's not cool to arrive in a city you don't know, on a Sunday, when the tourist office is closed. No plan, few people outside who speak English, in short, it's a matter of survival and instinct.

In the evening, not much to do, except the... casino. So we go there. Search, passport control, it's serious business. I try a bit of electronic poker, and after an hour, I filled my pockets, three times my starting bet. But, because there is a but, I'm still too young and stupid, I should have known that the opportunity to win some money easily must be seized and that after that, you have to leave quickly, otherwise, by pulling on the rope, it can break. Which it did. I lost everything, plus $150 on blackjack afterwards. What a jerk. I should have stopped. I'll know better next time. Always leave the casino when you win a little. Keep the luck going. And don't leave with the shits.

This morning, we go to the tourist office to get information. First of all, the cable car doesn't work today, and secondly, even if we take a taxi to the top (at 2 500 meters), the hotels are astronomically expensive. And three, there is too much snow to simply walk around in our mountain boots in the national park. Which means that apart from seeing museums containing all the dusty old things in the area, there is nothing to do. So we go back to Istanbul.
A fantastic weekend in Bursa, friends!
Bus, bus in boat, re-bus, boat and tramway, to finish at the hotel where we met our friends.
Tomorrow, last day in Istanbul!

Yeah, I didn't do anything today except buy plastic playing cards, dollars, and sit in the den and wait for time to pass, drinking vodka and getting my ass kicked at pool by Rod.

Spanish evening in a restaurant, sitting or lying on cushions around a round pewter table, with an Argentine woman I met at the hotel who spoke to me at length about the kibbutz in Israel. Very pretty but unfortunately sick with glands, 40 kilos too much... Too bad !

Last day : phoned Switzerland + pool table while waiting for 4.30 pm, time when the bus for the airport comes to pick us up.

That's it. Separating with Marissa, Maryse, and Judith with whom we were playing cards, we leave this hotel populated by crazy people and much too noisy for the airport. Intense traffic, nervous driver, us too. After fifteen minutes on the road, no one speaks a word, everyone is lost in their thoughts, it's departure. And it's as if all the tension accumulated over the last few days was falling on everyone's shoulders. Shitty hotel, rotten weather, fed up with Istanbul, fed up with kebabs, fed up with mustached people, desire to leave, need for warmth.

That's it!

11. Destination Orient, Bangkok...

Istanbul Airport. Three hours late, the plane. No big deal. We kill time with the maps.
Magic atmosphere of airports, I love it...
Between the travelers who pass by, the workers who are at their place of work, the policemen, the taxis, all this little world that is agitated, these lives that cross each other and that are all going to different destinations, these people who will never see each other again, the calls over the loudspeakers that crackle and are difficult to understand, the people who sleep on the floor or as best they can on seats that are too small, those who have a backpack, those who pull their suitcase on wheels, those who are elegantly dressed, the backpackers, the young people who don't give a damn about anything and especially about their looks. I like these atmospheres...
We're almost not in Istanbul anymore, we're between two worlds.

Perfect service from Pakistan Airlines who invites us to eat to make up for the delay. Delicious.
22:30, a call and it's for us.
We get on the plane. I'm already gone. Airbus I-don't-know-what, it's fucking beautiful! What luxury, it's modern, electronics everywhere! Movies on a plasma screen, headphones in my ears,

twelve channels with the situation of the aircraft in flight in real time on the TV, oriented on the world map, speed, temperature, altitude, it's great! I love it. 900 km/h, five hours to get to Karachi.

Karachi airport. We take three hours of jet lag in the pear. Plus three more hours in Bangkok, promising!
We start to be disfigured. Tiredness...
And amazement!
Here it is a real show! I can not count the number of different costumes that I see. There is everything. Muslims, of course, but also Hindus and it's a shock when you see them the first time. The religious ones especially. They have only a big white sheet and sandals. I don't know where they put their papers... in their underpants? Intriguing... They seem to have woken up in a hurry, grabbed the first sheet at hand and headed to the airport to leave for another country. The women wear a colorful silk piece fitted, with skillful technique, around their bodies. Other men have very loose silk or cotton street clothes, which must be comfortable to wear. Vision of the first Asians too. Incredible chromatic range. Businessmen in suits. The complexions are very dark. Hindu women wear a bead or diamond on the nostril and colored silk scarves. I like.

In the airport, the loudspeakers distill verses of the Koran chanted by a man. Atmosphere...
There are still women completely hidden behind black veils on black dresses. Impressive and sad at the same time. Like in prison.

It's a bit of a mess. They all jostle to get through the metal detector, and they are brought out. The figures are all slim and lanky for the men and curvaceous for the women with bulges at the waist protruding from their saris. And because they are small,

they fit everywhere in the queues. From the top of my six foot, I observe all this with a smile.
On the heads, many caps or headdresses, as well as shawls. A lot of babies in the arms too.
Hair and beards are hennaed for the men. Is it a mark of distinction or religion? I don't know yet.

We embark for Bangkok.
Unpleasant trip because of lack of sleep.

Arrival in Bangkok.
The breath of heat! 80% humidity! My body receives this like a punch. My legs have to make an effort to carry me.
Everyone starts sweating quickly. We went from -5° in Turkey, the air conditioning in airports and planes, to a good 30° now. Ouchhh... But it's still good.

Taxi to the district I spotted thanks to the Lonely Planet guide and, once there, a crowd of travelers in a multitude of small shops, with music, animated and colorful life, tuktuks *(three-wheeled taxi)*, everywhere food offered on the sidewalks, and people in cotton or silk clothes that I will buy tomorrow. Small evening because I am invisible, disoriented, exhausted.

It is precisely when one is so tired, when the mind and the ego are at their lowest ebb, that the conditions are optimal... and that it can happen...
Out of body experience.

That night I was very tired, exhausted, and quickly went to bed in a huff. I start the night restless, tossing and turning. My bed is wide, I can. Soon I can't feel my body, I know I'm leaving. I wait for that

moment, half-conscious...
The next moment, I find myself beside my bed, standing up, not
knowing how it happened, so fast.
Except that my body is next to me, lying on the bed.
I've heard those peculiar creaks that precede a decorporation, I've
often come close to them in previous voluntary
attempts, but I didn't expect it to happen tonight, I didn't prepare
myself for it...
Usually, when I want to try this experiment, I lie down in the
afternoon in the darkness of my room, ready to experiment.
I relax, I breathe for a good moment, I relax my whole body, from
head to toe. My thoughts go to each muscle or group of muscles, to
relax them, to release them, starting with the feet. And I go up little
by little, with the only objective of the maximum relaxation of my
muscles, of my segments. Then I arrive at the head. Not feeling my
physical body anymore, I visualize perfectly my etheric body which
floats above me, and it remains only the head so that it is perfectly
cleared. It is at the place of the neck, that in my case, it is
complicated. We have already spoken about it before, I have
blockages at this level, and in general, at this moment of the process
I am forced to swallow and, by doing so, this prevents me from
going further and brings me back slowly in my physical body. I then
have to make efforts to free myself from all thoughts, to go back into
the letting go, to visualize myself going further, to see myself going
out of my body, even to project myself outside with will. I have to say
that I have been interested in this for quite some time, I have seen
videos and read quite a few books on the subject, and I am anxious
to get there.

So, in general, it gets stuck at the neck.
On the rare occasions when the mental process stops and I feel that
I can go further, I have the perception that my etheric body is only

connected to the physical body by the tip of my nose. It is imminent and there are sounds and cracking sounds... a little terrifying I must say.

As if something is breaking badly inside my head. A real sound of dislocated flesh, of bones being broken. I had experienced it two or three times in the past, it had frightened me, and my astral body had immediately returned to my physical body. This frustrated me, because I had to do it all over again, and in general it is impossible, you have to stop the experiment there...

That night, I found myself outside my physical body, without having passed these stages. I am surprised, astonished, everything happened so quickly. And especially without me being the voluntary instigator of this experience.

Everything around me sparkles. I am light, I know that I am no longer my body, I am floating in wisps of tiny stars, in a world of fireflies. It is dark but I see everything, everywhere, without turning my head. A feeling of being part of a Whole that I don't know yet. Conscious, I know I'm out of my body. I don't need to turn my head to observe my new world, I see everything at 360 degrees, and I feel like I know everything too. Besides, it seems to me that I have no body, no eyes to see...

I have to remain neutral and calm, because I know that if I give in to my emotions without controlling them, I will immediately return to my body.

Everything happens very quickly after that.

I had read that all I had to do was want to go somewhere and I would be there instantly. But I don't have time to think about it when I find myself in a mountainous landscape, in a green and sunny valley, a pleasant place. I fly over a mountain village at a hundred meters high, with in front of me a kind of church unknown on Earth, a mixture of Christian building and another planet, I could not say, it is an unknown temple with a very pointed roof, a kind of pyramid-church. It's a beautiful day, I'm flying, wondering what I'm doing here... I could be flying over the small village of a beautiful Swiss mountain valley.

I barely have time to ask myself these questions... when I immediately return to my body.

It is already over, I did not have time to see more. It all got away from me, without any control.

I come to my senses, lying on my side on my bed, in total darkness, stunned and thrilled by what I have just experienced. I try to engrave in my memory the previous seconds, not knowing how long it will have lasted. I must be able to tell it tomorrow, I must remember everything...

First wake up in Bangkok. Three o'clock in the morning, eyes wide open in owl mode, impossible to sleep. Jet lag, yeah!
I go to the terrace to do an hour of tai chi, shower, then sleep again until eleven.
Today shopping. I need clothes appropriate to the climate. I buy a pair of silk trousers, two pairs of American silk briefs, a cotton shirt, a t-shirt, all for $20. I feel totally comfortable!

Tourist office, take various information.
Dive into the crazy traffic. At the red light, fifty motorcycles, twenty tuktuks and cars blocking the horizon. The light turns green. In a hellish noise, all start. A toxic cloud that would make all European anti-pollution barometers explode now covers the flow of cars. The policemen at the crossroads wear air filter masks to breathe. The population is, or at least appears, incredibly young. And very friendly. According to some books about Thailand, rice is the reason, because it provides the

nutrients for development until the age of 18-20 and after that these nutrients would not be enough, which is why they would be all small with childish faces.

Personally, I prefer the explanation of the Buddhist religion, which leaves people free, does not deprive them of anything and makes them responsible for their actions. One feels that people are fundamentally happy here.

Bank, change money. We speak in "baths" here. There are televisions in the banks, it's incredible; there's a television up on a wall, oriented so that everyone can watch it and it broadcasts a local program. I'm dreaming, coming from Geneva, the bank that's so boring...

I end up with a centimeter-thick wad of 100-bath notes, the equivalent of $300. In the afternoon, I want to go to the Stadium to see the Thai boxing matches. I have to go two kilometers away. I will never find the place. However, I end up in a place, near a railway line, which must be a slum. Wooden shacks, corrugated iron sheets, small landscapes of earth between the houses. Creepy, almost unhealthy. People look at me with wide eyes, most of them surprised in a friendly way to see this big guy here. What the hell is a foreigner doing here? They must be thinking... lots of kids. I still feel uncomfortable. They're sizing me up by looking at my shoes, just sneakers. As if a man's status is measured by his shoes...

Back on the way to the tourist district, Banglampoo.
I stop along a canal, where, as at a bus stop, very thin, long boats are parked, at the back of which a huge truck engine is placed right at the stern of the boat, the end of which is extended by a steel tube of three or four meters long which plunges into the water, containing the axle of the propeller, then the propeller. Am

I clear? It's very, very impressive to see these pilots maneuvering the throttle without mercy and arriving at the boarding pontoons in threes or fours with extreme dexterity. Dozens of people wait to get on board and jump when the big boat docks. The boat stays for a few seconds, staggering in the confused waves, and leaves again with a deafening noise where the hundreds of horsepower of the engine are let go. It is a pure happiness for me who has always been a lover of big and beautiful machines and frustrated by the European anti-noise regulations. Moreover, surprisingly, nobody is afraid to jump on these moving boats without any protection or safety barriers or anything else you could see in Europe to protect people. Old, young, women, men, all jumping with a smile, as if they were getting on the subway. Except that here they are waves, boats, that everything moves and stirs strongly. Nobody is worried, no real fear. Cool these people!

In the evening, last supper with my Argentinian friends who have moved to the other side of town to a friend of theirs. I don't know if we'll meet again, maybe in Chiang Mai, further north.

This morning, it's so good to be woken up by a ray of sunshine! It's been a long time. Slept badly all the same. The noise of the fan, the street noise, the heat. Tai chi at six in the morning, then back to bed until ten.

I have to be aware that I should not expect better than that as long as I am looking for such cheap pensions. The partitions are like paper, you can hear everything, farts as well as the most diverse and varied moans... Sometimes it goes pretty well, we laugh, and sometimes it's really bad!

Breakfast, and search for a hotel for the next day. I find a travel agency which proposes, among other things, an excursion to the crocodile farm. 250 baths (about $10) for the whole day. I take. We'll see how this organized trip goes, I don't like it at first.

Bus, arrival. Various bland shows, cafeteria, then the inevitable souvenir stop where everyone follows while bleating. A bit pathetic...

Back to Bangkok, and destination the central post office. I must take the Express Boat which goes down the river which crosses the city. Impeccable. The boat does not dock, it directs its trajectory towards the end of the pontoon and leaves as quickly as possible, people have just the time to jump on board by holding each other, and the manoeuvres are regulated by a young person, with a whistle. All this is done quickly and brilliantly. It's good to see people helping each other and not being afraid to do something simple like jumping off a moving boat. But you can't do that in Paris, for example, because the French mentality is much more cautious than that...

I play cards with kids and even do a few magic tricks to see their big eyes of wonder... but nothing, they were neither hot nor cold. Damn kids! Or maybe my tricks are lousy...

Right now, it's the king's birthday. Indeed, Thai people have a king and they worship him and his family. As much as Buddha. Like Lady Di in England. So in the streets, there are bulbs in all the trees, giant posters recalling the events of the life of their king. Tonight, it's the neighborhood party, and in the street, the inhabitants have set up tables, loudspeakers and let's go for the party!

In front of us, Joe, Rod and I, were five very colorful plates. Pork, duck, a fragrant noodle soup, dumplings and sweet and sour shrimp. Worth a fortune in European restaurants, here it's

almost free. Just divine!
All of this is served with sauces containing unknown ingredients
and flavored to perfection. End of the meal with a whole
pineapple cut in ten seconds with a machete. The others take a
coconut opened in front of us, and served with a straw.

I am next to the street of the tourists, or rather of the travelers.
Because it is here that the houses are the cheapest. There are only
foreigners walking on the sidewalks, and of course, in hundreds
of different shops, clothes, tapes, souvenirs, fake Rolex and
Cartier watches for $5, travel agencies, hotels, guesthouses, etc.

My two friends are leaving me. Our roads separate. For a few
months because I have to meet them in Sydney, Australia.

I think I'm going to buy a Rolex watch because it's nice and it
doesn't cost anything, and I'm dumb enough to wear it.
It'll remind me of my youth in Switzerland and I'll show off a bit.

Note : Hum... it only lasted two weeks !

I buy sandals for walking, it's more practical, my feet sweat a lot.
I now have everything I need.

I eat a freshly opened coconut. I drink its milk. Delicious! I'm
going to share my room with a girl travelling alone for the sake of
saving money. Apparently in this street all the travelers from all
over the world meet. They arrive in batches. It's fresh. On the
other hand, there is really an upsurge of "piercing", many wear
rings in the nose, the ears crumble under the weight of the metal
and I was told that a girl had the end of the tongue pierced by a
ring! This morning, to top it all off, I even saw a guy with a
pierced eyebrow! Damn, what you don't have to do to make
yourself interesting! Maybe they all want to show that they have

travelled all over the world and for a long time, thinking that the more tattoos, various piercings, more or less dishevelled or dreadlocked hair they have, the more they are great travelers! I think it's ridiculous. Fortunately, there are still a few brilliant humans left... thanks for the flowers...

Note: twenty years later my body is more or less covered with tattoos.
Only fools don't change their minds!

I'm going to board for the crocodile farm.
Four hours later: well, we are very far from the convenience of Turkish buses! It is in fact a minibus with a faulty air conditioning that drops us, a dozen tourists and me, in a large amusement park made in Thailand: a zoo, huge gardens-bac-enclosure containing hundreds of crocodiles slumped asleep with their mouths wide open to refresh themselves, distributed according to their age in pools more or less large. The one for 3-6 years old, 10-15 years old until 40-60 years old for the biggest specimens.

A show is also proposed with elephants playing football, in a kind of earthy football stadium, and us in the stands. Demonstration of what elephants can do, antics learned by heart. A good child show, followed by the crocodiles that come out of the water and take the guy's head in their mouth. A little twinge of sadness at the idea that one of them might get a cramp or feel a sneeze coming on...

My fake Rolex is weighing me down a bit and I realize that's not me. I'm not the kind of guy to show off with a nice watch on my wrist. For five bucks. I leave it on the bed for the cleaning lady, and I hope she doesn't get outraged.

It's a pain in the ass #2: My belt is gone! With the dollars and baths inside. Oh, not much, maybe $100 but this is the second time this has happened to me and it's pretty inexplicable! In the morning I left it on the bed when I put on the silk pants, then Beto packed up and in the evening I found a note on my bed telling me he had moved in with his boyfriend. I don't suspect him because I trust him and he knew what was in that belt. Unfortunately I can't reach him on the phone he left me. And if it wasn't him, could it be a local guy while I was taking a shower? I can't stand that! It gave me the blues for the evening. I really hate being fucked.

Evening spent sipping freshly squeezed watermelon juice. Pure delight!

Something absolutely inconceivable that I forgot to mention until now is that there is no bread in Thailand! It doesn't exist! Can you imagine that? The first time I asked for it in the restaurant with my omelette, the waiter seemed as surprised as I was, I was surprised, and everyone else was surprised. They finally brought me some imported sandwich bread. So no sandwiches, no toast in the morning either. A wall of my culture that falls down...

This morning I put my backpack in a locker for about two weeks, to be cool and light for the North. With lots of little padlocks everywhere to be safe. I send my sleeping bag to Switzerland by mail because with my last clothes purchases, my bag starts to be quite full. And I don't use it anymore. It will take between two and three months to arrive by boat and anyway I don't give a damn, it's the cheapest.

Bangkok Station. The brothel, but a great brothel! Huge, full of people. Bonzes and young monks wearing ochre and orange cloths, a lot of young people, well young... I don't know. You can't give an age to the people here. They have such childish faces! They look young until... I don't know, fifty or sixty, and only then do they start to age. But before that, it's impossible to know their age.

Half of them are sitting on the floor, cool, relaxed from the knee up. The air fills the atmosphere with a monotonous roar. A few travelers stand out from the Thai with their spectacular harnessing. I'm fine, my little ten-litre backpack is full. Another plastic bag with bananas and water. I'm fine, light, mobile. I left my credit card in my travel bag at the locker because the North is notorious for card theft when guys go trekking. They leave their card in the hotel safe and while they're at it, the boss steals it to go shopping with his cronies and buys expensive hi-fi equipment, then puts the cards back before the tourist comes back. The traveler is unpleasantly surprised to find his account overdrawn by tens of thousands of francs, but it's too late.

I just have a $50 bill that I'm going to sew into a pocket of my silk pants as a spare tire.

One cannot say that the Thai are lazy, they are rather indolent. The synthesis of their Buddhist religion, their character and the climate makes that one sees many of them sleeping during the day and that they move with their legendary shuffling gait. On the pavement, the newspaper seller collapsed on his pile of paper. Everywhere, behind cars, men and women sleep in deckchairs, a few meters from the traffic. Unimaginable in Europe.

Night train Bangkok - Chiang Mai. It is 6pm. I go up in the train. The size of the city is unbelievable! 30 minutes to go out, plus 10 minutes of commuting, in train going 80 km/h. Perfect meal. Green asparagus, grilled shrimp, rice.

But I sleep badly. Light, fan, shaking and noise of the train, cabin too cold. Anyway, I sleep for a while and I wake up thinking we're coming... it's midnight! We will arrive at 7:30.

Arrival in Chiang Mai. I find a nice pension thanks to the Guide du Routard. A wooden house. I don't really know yet if it's the Thai style but it's very nice inside, made of woven bamboo, very serene, and cheap.

This city appears to me as a good big town, with a hundred times less traffic than in Bangkok where, according to what I read, there would be 70% of the national car fleet!
The air is different. Less busy, fresher. I am really a tourist! I am very poorly equipped for this region. I didn't take a sweater or pants, nor big shoes. So trekking is impossible. But I'm not going to shed a tear because there are so many trekking agencies here that the circuits must be jammed with tourists. You can do treks from 2 to 7 days, with elephant rides, rafting or bamboo rafting, but only for a few hours, everything else is hiking.
Moreover, the goal is to arrive in villages where the inhabitants are taken for monkeys to whom we throw peanuts or that we look at with big eyes before taking some pictures and leaving... I don't like it. The elephant, yes, the rafting, ok, the jungle exploration, yes, but not the tribes who see groups of tourists passing by every thirty minutes and who beg for their coins because they have already been poisoned by tourism.

According to the books, the guides you take are not always reliable and of good character, and the trek can turn into a super scam or a nightmare if it rains or if the route planned in advance is not respected, or even into fairy days; it is a lottery.

I'm talking about the treks here because it's really the center of all the trekking expeditions for Northern Thailand.
There is only one idiot who will not have done it, it's me!

This morning my tongue is a real horror show. It's grey, brown, and itches like a big flu. In fact, I'm quite well, it's strange, I don't feel any symptom coming from the depths of myself and there are many causes: pollution in Bangkok, cold during the night, the water I drink little by little, either with ice cubes, or with fruits washed in the tap, or while brushing my teeth. I think that these practices gradually accustom my intestines to the local bacteria so that I am not disturbed afterwards. A bit like with the sun, expose myself gradually, for several days; afterwards, no need for protection.

For breakfast, I go by bowl and instinct. I arrive at a place where they put in front of my nose a kind of very liquid rice pudding, in which the owner has broken an egg, added fine juliennes of ginger, as well as other products unknown to my palate.
It looks more like camel vomit than a continental breakfast, but it's very good. And digestible. At noon, spring rolls to take away with its little bag of sauce, strawberries to finish and I find in the fridges of fresh drinks that are everywhere in the shops, some kind of vitaminized and perfumed
elixirs to recover a tonic youth. I had seen a lot of people drinking them and it's very good.

Evening with a Swiss-Italian guy on holiday here for three months, and two French guys, also nice, on a trip for a year.

We are accompanied by a very playful Thai girl who lives in the pension. We eat very expensive Italian food. Before that, I went to a bar open on the street where I made friends with the two cute waitresses. I'm a little bit turned on by beer, it's been a long time since I drank some, and after two drinks I feel in a very happy mood. I drink some very good Australian wine with my tenderloins, then I have another beer in a "blues" bar, and when everyone goes home to sleep, I go back to see my two cute waitresses. I fancy one of them and I'm super excited. But nothing. Work, so no cuddling. And not the first night, come on Philippe, let's be gentleman! The first hour yes, but not the first day!

I go out two hours later, I walk crookedly which makes me uncomfortable when I pass groups of young people, I try to be confident, put one foot in front of the other and I have the impression that it does not go too badly. In front of the pension the barrier is closed and it's with many acrobatic adventures of a drunk man that I can get in. Belmondo would have been proud... The next day, I will learn that the gate next door was open...

Little hangover this morning but it passes quickly. Hire a cheap and completely twisted bike for two days to visit the city in search of a belt, because my sister is going to send me by mail a "special backpacker" with a zipper inside. I find one for $1 signed Lacoste!

The rest of the day at the pension, under two magnificent mango trees next to the wooden house. Discussions with the Swiss-Italian and Nong, the Thai. Hammock, watermelon, and the hours go by quietly. Time is stopped.

Evening meal in a beautiful outdoor square with dozens of stalls offering food and drink. The choice is huge and all the food, ingredients and tasty dishes are displayed in front of us. Crab rice at one table, noodle soup at another with dozens of weird little things swimming in it, including little fish dumplings, large noodles and other UFOs I don't know about.

We then head to a huge bar made up of a dozen smaller ones, and a boxing ring closed for the evening. Each bar has its own pool table. If you want to play, you write your name on a little blackboard at the entrance and when it's your turn, you put down 20 baths and play against the winner of the previous game.

I was immediately thrown out by a girl who played well, too well for me. Of course, the one who plays well stays. My pool night was rather short. Delightful young girls take care of you by cuddling you, but leave you as soon as a new gogo arrives. It's business as usual, but it hurts your ego all the same!

After a weird night I get woken up by the local barnyard. The first night I came home drunk and heard nothing. This morning I get everything! The house pug dog, a sort of poodle with a granny, chasing a cat under my window, barking so loudly and long that all the other dogs in the neighborhood start to do it too. Hello, the concert. Unbearable! So of course, he keeps on going. And there's a mosquito net on the window, so I can't even throw anything at him. Then it's the mice's turn, or the rats'. I listen to their typical "squiirrkkk" and wonder if they are inside or outside my room, and I hear them moving around. By the time I sink into a gentle torpor, the chickens start reciting their morning hymn in rhythm and echo, for 45 minutes. I am raging in my pillow! One of the hens, or that crowing rooster, is standing five feet away from my window in his pen. I can almost see her vocal cords vibrate with each crow! I'm definitely going to poison them tonight...

So tomorrow night, I'll try the earplugs, and if it's not enough, I'll change guesthouse. But I left the earplugs in Bangkok.

Sports day today, bike to a park, an hour of karate, tai chi and snoring under a fantastic tree. In the evening I feel a bit feverish. Not really feverish but caught a bit in the throat. Without any flu symptoms, cold or anything else. It's really strange. My tongue is still a bit brown.

Dinner at a lovely place by the river with a band.
Early to bed because tomorrow night there are boxing matches at

the beer center.

Grey day today because of lack of sleep and activities.
I start drawing again, except that the result is a failed head of an
old man, with a ballpoint pen. In the evening, visit the night
market, grandiose and huge! It's as if all the shops were open,
with in addition, on the sidewalks of stalls, absolutely everything!
Clothes, trinkets, art, and all the crowd is pressing. It's very
difficult to keep your wallet, there are so many beautiful things! I
fall for a sweater made by the northern tribes, for 7 $, it's not
much and I need it. You can really dress up nicely, even very
nicely, in silk or embroidery, for three times nothing. And I'm
not talking about souvenirs of all kinds, a little more elaborate
than what you can find at Mont Saint-Michel for example.
Dragons made with hair and it's really a whole ponytail that has
been used to make these dragons on legs, whose spine articulates
smoothly. A typically oriental handiwork. Similarly, to eat, a large
open-air public square, hundreds of tables and chairs, you buy
coupons of 5, 10 or 15 baths and pass all the various food stalls
around the square, paying with your coupons. I start with chicken
curry skewers, then pork soup, Chinese ravioli, various vegetables
and finally a very special dish to see and eat: in a plate is spread a
sheet of white dough, and inside are laid loose soy, Thai sausage,
pork, yet another meat, then the sheet is folded on itself and
turned over; everything is closed, you do not see the contents and
the whole is covered with a special sauce. It is eaten cold. And it's
strange.
I end the evening playing like a god at pool, so I stay every time
since I win, and I see a lot of girls and guys who want to measure
themselves. Quiet, beer, cigarette, girls who tease your neurons
and your imagination, it's the miracle recipe.

I'm going to leave the day after tomorrow, there's nothing to do
here except in the evening.

Tonight is the first night of the Chiang Mai Food Festival. A large street closed on both sides, dozens and dozens of food stalls by the river. Beautiful princesses carving vegetables into masterpieces, ice cream too, beautiful, and, most interestingly, what we are going to eat. Fried rice with crab, ravioli of all kinds, with mussels, lots of crayfish, prawns, grilled fish and shellfish, and a thousand other specialties so refined that one cannot imagine what they are made of. On a wooden platform on the other side of the river, there are demonstrations of Thai dance and theatre, incomprehensible to foreigners, which resemble shadow plays whose actors move slowly, full of grace and femininity. All performed and sung by young people.

Speaking of them, you see them working absolutely everywhere, kids directing traffic in cop clothes, kids in boarding houses or restaurants taking orders, bringing food or coming to cash.

Sunday : departure from Chiang Mai, after one week. Bus to Thaton, direction North. Super minibus adapted to the size of the Thai. I'm stuck, badly seated. Three and a half hours of superb road. The vegetation is greener, denser. In some places, it is the jungle on the sides of the road. What a joy to see that! Unfortunately I spend the whole trip between sleep and wakefulness, tossed around by the road, bored by the heat and stared at by an old hen. I'm talking about the animal. I'm half out of it. I still see bits of landscapes that really correspond to the idea of Thailand. Rice fields, ponds where birds and buffalos graze among lotus flowers, jungle with palm trees in the middle of a luxuriant vegetation.

Three travelers and I were unloaded in Thaton *(and not by groping)*, in front of a guesthouse where we were taken care of by a very enterprising landlady. No sooner had we sat down for a refreshing Coke than she started filling our heads with her trekking stories.

I have seen so many pictures of treks that I don't need to see the people of the Akha tribes. Everywhere, any house offers treks. Guaranteed scam. It smells like a money trap. The so called three days excursions where you leave at noon and you come back two days later at noon, it makes three days on paper but it makes only two in reality. These are sweet scams done in a good atmosphere and always with a smile. Same thing for the prices, it's not expensive when you come from Europe but when you know the prices of the country, for ten trekking you can buy a motorcycle here, that's saying something! I think that those who live from trekking must all be rich Thai people.

12. The Golden Triangle

A young man who is on holiday and passing through here has been bitten under the forearm, probably by a spider, which we imagine to be horrible and dangerous. The guy is fed up with it, it hurts him, so he rips off the scab and I squeeze his pus; it will take about ten handkerchiefs to remove all the shit inside the pocket. It's really not a pretty sight!

One thing I really regret every day is that I don't have a telephoto lens on my camera. Every day I see potentially beautiful shots, people, heads, in the artistic sense of the word, and it's impossible to make beautiful pictures of them. I have just seen a tribal woman from the north of the Golden Triangle passing by on the other side of the street, adorned as all tribal women are, with her traditional headdress, with jewels and a ceremonial costume, and her long neck decorated with dozens of necklaces. Beautiful and authentic, because in the street she does not pose. But impossible to photograph with my camera, I would capture the whole street and the woman would disappear among so many bland elements.

In the bedroom, I sleep with a nice sample of insects, big cockroach in entrance, midnight beetle, plus various mosquitoes and big spiders to decorate the place. My favorite animals...

I removed the same amount of pus from Eric the Frenchman's arm as yesterday. I still have pimples on my temples and have had them for three days after arriving in Bangkok. The food or the climate. But nothing to do, it doesn't go away. Boring. The other day, in a beer bar, a girl wanted to pierce my buttons! What a shame. There was nothing to pierce, they're empty, but still...

I buy a ticket to go down by fast boat to Chiang Mai. About four hours of descent. They are dugout boats, very long and very narrow, with always this enormous engine at the back. Departure: the pirogue is full. It starts. It's fine, not too noisy. What a pleasant sensation to feel again the propulsion by an engine, on a liquid element, 10 cm above the water. Everywhere, along the river, reeds, bamboos and luxuriant but not invasive flora. This is not the jungle, but just a very mountainous area and, in the middle of a narrow plain, the Kok River. We stop in a tribal village where a house on the water's edge is marked "Police Office". Everyone has to sign a register, name, surname, nationality, even the passport number for the tourism statistics. Drinks break, sale of bracelets and handmade necklaces by the women of the tribes who are adorned with their most beautiful clothes and smoke huge cigarettes that make their teeth not very elegant.

Back on the river. No hard dwellings. No cement. Only wooden huts, huts and villages. What a strange feeling of harmony and peace. Only green for the jungle, brown for the wood, and blue-green for the sky and water.

Approximately four hours later, we arrived in a small village entirely concreted. We are accosted at the landing stage by a guy who offers us a pension proposed in the Guide du Routard as being the best. It's a good thing. We climb on the back of a pickup and on the road through Chiang-Rai. The pension is beautiful. Typical Thai house, all in wood, sumptuous. Clean rooms, flowery sheets, it's really very good. The owners are nice. They rent motorcycles at reasonable prices. It's exactly what Eric and I wanted.

Eric is a jovial and cheeky 34 year old Frenchman, a funny guy. We decided to visit the far north and the Golden Triangle, the border between Laos, Burma and Thailand. Nowadays we don't risk anything. It's not the opium season and it has become too touristic to meet bad people. We'll see tomorrow. Dinner in town. This city is not really breaking anything, for those who like the night. A few bars with girls pathetically waiting for the gogos outside, nobody in the streets, it's dead. Let's go home.

The perfect kind of evening for writing.

Inside, I'm looking forward to going south to see the ocean, live on the beach, work out every day, which for me is a guarantee of balance and inner strength, and maybe fish. Later, in a week, I'll be there.

Wake up on Monday... no, Tuesday the 14th. I don't know which day we are living. Breakfast in the guesthouse, then we rent the motorbikes, four speed scooter, 100 cc, for two days. We leave for the Golden Triangle. What a good feeling to be again son of the wind, free and independent. We take the main road and after 30 km we turn off onto the main road that leads to Mae Salong, a village of Burmese or Chinese refugees, made of wooden huts. Some tourist shops. Eric buys some fried worms and eats them in front of my disgusted face, but I try anyway, I can't give up. They look like potato chips but with an aftertaste of eyeballs, guts and worm brains...

Village full of authenticity, where Burmese, Chinese, Thai and Akhas (tribes) live mixed. Buddhists and Muslims live together perfectly.

Restaurant superbly inhabited by a large family, kids playing and laughing in such simplicity, and the best noodles and chips I've eaten so far because in addition to the usual vegetables, everything is sprinkled with peanut powder. Excellent!

All along the road, ponds with giant water lilies, rivers, beautiful mountains and hills. And always this feeling of harmony because we are in a pure nature!

On the way back down, we pass two girls sitting on a wall, waiting for a possible bus. "Come on with us!". Two young Israeli girls on holiday for three weeks visiting the North, alone.

There are a lot of young Israelis in Thailand because they all have to do their military service for three years, both boys and girls, and with the money from their three years' pay in their pockets, they go to Asia, where life is not too expensive. So we see plenty of them in Nepal and Thailand in particular, and they have an unfortunate reputation of shame everywhere they go because they are often arrogant, disrespectful, speaking loudly as if they were the masters of the place and I have seen them several times making fun of the locals. So for my part, I tend to avoid them.

But these chicks look nice... And here they are, on our petrol boats. A few kilometers further, police stop us. Some kids. They look like friends. They search everything, our bags, our bananas, our pockets, looking for drugs, of course. Unfortunately for their statistics, we are as healthy as newborns. With smiles on our faces, we take the same road back to the village. A little further on, we fork to go to a place where the Thai people go for a footbath on weekends, a beautiful natural water feature, with huge fish and, most surprisingly, monkeys running free on the roof of the temple, in the trees and on the ground. But beware.... aggressive and thieving monkeys! Signs warn visitors not to leave anything lying around and not to let children feed them. We experience this and get thrown off the clean lawn in order. Dozens of them, with their little ones. That's probably why they are so aggressive.

Another curiosity: a bat cave. About 300 steps to climb to land in a place that, 300 million years ago, was under water. There are rocks and coral and, suspended twenty meters high, dozens of bats that we can see with our lamps. Small, cute ones.

Then there are 20 km to go to reach Mae Sae, the crossroads town at the border between Burma and Thailand. Just before arriving, I get a flat tire. Damn! Fortunately, I'm 100 meters away from a local repairer - that is, three kids on the side of the road - who fixed the tube in less time than it takes to write this!

We then discover the traveler's paradise. A pension all in exotic wood in the Thai style; I have never seen anything so beautiful! Inside each bungalow, everything is made of bamboo and woven straw, it's ma-gni-fi-cent! There are about twenty bungalows. All of them on the edge of the river that separates the two countries. But we arrive at night, so let's wait until tomorrow to admire the show.

Superb hot shower where I can look at my afternoon passenger, a very pretty girl indeed, while peering through the holes of the bamboos. I am enjoying it!
Yes, I know...

I have to ask the girls for a little financial help because Eric is going east and I want to be able to give him back the money he lent me a while ago. I have made some unnecessary expenses and what I have left is too little. The two girls are planning to return to Bangkok at the same time as me. Then it will be fine, I can return their capital there.

I sleep great. Dream night in dream bungalow. In the morning, the place would encourage to stay one or two days more, just to rest without leaving the domain of the pension. Copious breakfast and we leave. Not very far since we stop at the bridge that serves as a border. Lots of traffic on both sides from Burma. Many exceptional trinkets which would be all the rage in our European flea markets because the prices are ridiculous.

We take the road again to stop for lunch in a restaurant. We drive for another two hours to reach Chiang-Rai, the scenery is sweet, fields cultivated in the old way, wooden tools, buffaloes helping with the farming or lounging in the rivers with their young. Unless all this is just Hollywood-style cardboard scenery, set up for us on our picturesque road, dear tourists that we are...

Entering Chiang-Rai. We get lost beautifully. We still end up back at the pension but only for Eric because the two girls and I are leaving tonight by air-conditioned V.I.P bus with thirty seats *(so room for my loooong legs)* for Bangkok. It's a good thing because the pension is full anyway.

Station: bus to Bangkok. 7pm.

Small snack distributed, blankets, aerodynamic seats, TV, it seems not bad!

After nine hours on the road..., we arrived in Bangkok with the two girls, plus a guy we met at the bus exit. Back to Khao San Road, the backpackers' street in the tourist district.

Once again the parade of new trends neo-baba-junkie-fashion punk-you-saw-the-new-loop-that-I-put-in-the-nose-yeah-oh-my-god-you-are-too cool.

I give back the money the girls lent me and we decide to leave for the islands tomorrow.
I'd like to fuck one of them, and it's driving me crazy. I'm

desperate, I need sex...

But I have doubts, a problem of conscience. Because the guy we met did a ten-day Thai massage course in Chiang Mai. And massages were always something I wanted to learn. But afterwards, he's going to spend ten days in a monastery for the experience and the meditations, ten days during which you can't talk and you eat vegetarian; and it's apparently a unique experience for a guy like me who's always wanted to measure himself against that.

So what to do? Why did I miss this opportunity when I was in Chiang Mai? Now I should go back... Should I?

In fact, to be honest, I'm pushed by old fella, the piece of flesh between my legs that sometimes hosts my brain. He worries me and looks sad. He remains pale and not very vigorous. He needs company, he wants to have fun.
How stupid I can be!

I try a Thai massage this afternoon, in a temple in Bangkok. I run into a monk, I don't know if I owed him money in a former life, but he doesn't spare me! Damn, how he hurt me! He's had a field day making me suffer or I must be stuck all over. I've been in the crusher for two hours. On me, above, he presses, I suffer and he continues ... Sometimes when I have enough energy between two ouch-aie-yikes, I open my eyes to see him leaning my face, his elbow in my plexus, and I swear he takes pleasure the bastard ... But no, impassive face of the executioner accustomed to the fragile European tourists. On the other hand, a lot of energy is released because it acts on the nodes and energy centers and releases accumulated tensions in particular in the ligaments and tendons. The energy then returns to the global circuit and starts to energize the body again.

And I'm trying to satisfy the animal inside me, who wants to fuck those two chicks on the islands, to satisfy my bodily senses by living half-naked, surrounded by people who are also naked. What a joker I am, how many decisions I would have made in my life just to follow my instincts of pleasure.

I wonder if I'm missing out on something that would bring me much more than the realization and concretization of these primary instincts. I know it deep down, but it's stronger than me, I love it...

Well, on the one hand, in the islands I will be in a quiet place to meditate morning and evening, doing sports every day for my balance, I tell myself, to calm my inner distractions.
Which makes me think that I can do without the monastery experience. But I'd still like to experience it once, Boudiou! And I would also love to learn the science of massage. It's done with the hands, and hands are my thing. Magnetism, chirology, anatomical studies, I've already started these studies...

I have made my decision. I will still go to the islands with the girls to feed my vices, but I pray to the Gods that my path will once again cross a massage center to learn these techniques.

It must be said that the beast in me needs flesh, it's been a while since the tension accumulates, and the monster demands its due. Otherwise it will growl, and I will suffer!

To add to the discomfort of my indecision, I went to pick up the mail left at the post office, and I read the one from my mother telling me that my sister is going to lose her job; it pisses me off. And the endings of the letters quickly bring tears to my eyes,

feeling a powerful rush of emotion each time. God, this
sensitivity!

There is a lot of noise everywhere. In more than two weeks, I
couldn't find a single moment of calm. Every time I wanted to
meditate or clear my mind, the chickens, people, kids, cars, the
whole city was against it, all making such a racket that it was
impossible. That's also why I want to go to the sea. Those
magical moments of dawn or sunset are good for meditation.
And after a session, I don't feel disturbed like I do now.
Right now I'm drinking beers and smoking like a locomotive
amidst the deafening noise of music in a trendy bar. I still have
this duality between getting high and living a healthy life. Today,
the high, and I'm looking forward to the healthy life...

Last day in Bangkok: still in the street of the permanent
backpacker show. I do some gymnastics on my bed, in my room
of the shitty pension we found. We walk with the two girls along
the counters, in view of the last purchases, a T-shirt for me
because I tore the one I had while getting dressed this morning.
Then we get on the bus that takes us, about thirty tourists, south
to the big island of Koh-Samui *("koh" means island)*. Painful
journey, more than ten hours of discomfort and lack of sleep...

I'm going to have to play it tight because these Israeli girls, who
are rather strong in character, are not easy to make fun of.
They're serious and I want to have fun. So I must have lost the
instructions because I don't really know how to deal with them,
and what I'm testing doesn't really give gratifying results. You
have to wonder if they're laughing in their country...

13. A descent into hell in Koh-Samui, I hit rock bottom.

The search for balance, or the permanent fight between the shadow and the light.
Yin and Yang. We are all the same, we humans.
I think we all have the same emotions, and in our life course, we have more or less the same inclinations, tendencies and flaws, assumed or hidden, and stemming for the most part from our childhood ailments. The more we develop our light, the more our shadow grows too. We cannot be only luminous, it is impossible. Or we must have transcended this part of the shadow that can no longer harm us, like Christ, Buddha and other mystics who will no longer reincarnate on Earth.

This half-baked theory explains why some priests have turned pedophiles. I guess the Church never really paid attention to that, too busy as it must have been to make as much money as possible for the Vatican. But then, no one taught that to monks, abbots and the whole clique of men engaged on the road of piety, carrying their shadow zone which grows as their light increases in them.

Still, it is necessary to be able to manage it, this dark area lurking in us that nobody talks about, and for which there are no teachings. Can you imagine if, during a sexual or violent impulse, we could consult a Great Book of Impulses, in which everything would be

132

described and explained, with the proposed remedies?

Having said that, mine, my shadow zone, is doing well, thank you, and I like to go there from time to time, just to see if all the cogs of my dark and machiavellian being are in place, so that all the machinery is in working order.
Hence my dear excesses...
Who says excess, says imbalances...
Imbalances coming from childhood ? From parents?
Well, well...

My mother, and her sad story.
Get the Kleenex ready...

A woman incarnate with limited means, who has spent her entire life missing out on a path that could have been brilliant if she had the strength to fight her demons and other drug addictions that have clouded her vision and potential all her life.
Soon she was caught up in the karma of her own mother. And she would project it onto her children. The patterns that repeat themselves...
If she had accepted the fact of having been abandoned by her own mother, without continually mourning in abysses of regret for the rest of her life, her destiny would have been quite different.
The holy word is acceptance.
His mother died after the war when she was young and his father took another wife. So there was another woman in the house who did not accept her naturally because she already had other children to take care of. So my mother suffered a lot from the lack of love and looked for a mother's love all her life. She did not find it.
If she had relativized this later, once she was an adult, by crying once and for all, by shouting and by evacuating her anguish and her needs due to this lack, she might have been able to have a life and a normal relationship as a mother with her children.
She never knew or could do it, blocked as she was in her emotions and feelings; her energy attracted confused and negative situations, with men who corresponded to this vibration, or at least who would

be able to prove her feelings right, by confirming that she was really a nobody, that she didn't deserve to be happy, that she wouldn't know love, etc.

Yet she underwent therapy with various psychologists for about fifteen years, filling notebooks with useless notes, because my mother had already tried drugs, and she knew that there was a magical and easy way out of suffering.

This woman who was not cherished by a mother could not love us as an adult, and thus created in turn the family pattern she experienced as a child. She saw us very little, she could not adore us, and she also abandoned her own children, in a way, to other hands.

The extraordinary and frightening magic of repetitive patterns. Isn't it beautiful or magical? There is something amazing about these mechanisms...

As for me, I was lucky because my instinct was to travel far away, as far as possible. And it was much later, around the age of forty, that I realized that all these distant trips had had the sole intimate goal of staying as far away as possible from my mother. I was able to rebuild myself and it took me twenty years. Alongside brilliant women who helped me, because alone, I don't think it would have been possible; I needed help too much.

This was unfortunately not the case with my sister, who, not having the same saving impulse as me, stayed by her side all her life. Naturally, she developed her little cancer after fifty years, as a result of a life of maceration of negative emotions in her body gangrenous by destructive energies which stagnated, and which destroyed part of her organs.
A classic cancer, after all.

It is in the acceptance, after the understanding, that these energies begin to dissolve and disappear to leave room in the body and the heart, so that a new light settles there. So that there is again space for the Universe to flow.

Acceptance - kneeling down with humility - is central to inner transformation. Accepting that there is a higher pattern that dictates our current conditions in our incarnation, which can change if we welcome them knowing that what we are experiencing has a meaning and a reason that may have come from far away.

For my mother, go figure.... perhaps she had to be abandoned because she herself once rejected another life? Why not? And thus understand the sufferings that it generates so that it does not reproduce them any more?

I love you mom, and I'm glad you'll be going into the light soon and that you and I can really talk deeply.
You will have missed out on your life, lost in all those meds.
Your head hasn't worked for so long, you can't understand it all. A life of drugs, Mom, fifty years of drugs that have killed your brain, that's what you will have lived. You have consciously hidden your existence and your feelings to forget this childhood trauma. That's all it is. And it's huge...

Was it worth it to attempt suicide several times? No, but I swear, throwing yourself several times under a vulgar bus... instead of a big German sedan! Mom, sometimes you're really full of shit! You really wanted to be a Breton pancake, huh? You would have gone for the "diplomatic corps in a hurry, driving at full speed in the line of the bus", then we would have been fine, you know, we could have won some serious financial compensation at least...

What about the motorcycle, Mom? Why would you throw yourself in front of one? Because your son has been riding for a long time and you wanted to try? It hurts, it breaks bones two hundred kilos thrown at 60 km / h!

A whole life wasted in the voluntary numbing of your emotions by these chemical molecules prescribed by robot-doctors unable to

suggest anything else, so as not to feel the distress and suffering of abandonment in you.
Was it worth it to have ruined two precious hearts at your side, that of your children?

I still don't know, Mom, whether I blame you or not, fifty years later...

Despite the fact that you have been my greatest teacher, raising in me my most intense questions.

It would have been such a relief to hear sacred words like "I'm sorry", or "I love you"...
But my sister and I have given up on that. Your brain is far too damaged now, at the dawn of your passage into the afterlife.
It's a huge waste, and a great sadness for us.
I can't wait for you to go into the light and for this life of torment to end, especially this lamentable end, which is only pain, suffering and sadness.

Your daughter and I will continue to rebuild quietly, until we all meet up there to discuss it with our glowing hearts.

Happy to have arrived this morning of Saturday, December 18, in Surat Thani, the port of embarkation for the island. Everyone is waiting with feverish eyes for the minibus to take us to the boat. Discussion with the girls about our accommodation on the island. There are many beaches more or less frequented, more or less pleasant from a reception and price point of view. Thanks to the Guide du Routard, on my side it is all decided. Calm, beautiful beaches, a nice village in the north of the island. The girls better follow.
At least I hope so...

Bus for an hour, discovery of the South, a lot of water, floods everywhere, a family goes home with its feet in the water carrying its belongings and the children. The rainy season, the monsoon, is not over. Besides, here, there are only clouds!

We arrive at the port, we take a ferry. Shaken up like Orangina, the two girls puke overboard, a lot of people talking at the beginning, but after an hour, everyone is pulling a face, including me, focused as we are on the horizon and the refusal to vomit. An hour and a half that was downright painful.

Our asses were so sore, we finally arrived on the island of Koh-Samui.
It is the very type of image that we have of paradise.
Beaches lined with coconut palms, very green, and everywhere a luxuriant vegetation. The tropical island, obvious.

Taken in charge by the recruiters who watch for the arrival of new potential tenants, we go by van to the desired beach in the north of the island.
In fact all the beaches are lined with villages of bungalows overlooking the beach, with more or less space between them.
The difference lies in the welcome, the price and the beauty of the shelters.

I'm alive again! How quiet! God, it feels so good!

And the ocean is so beautiful, as always, but here the water is green and all the shades are in green.
I am inwardly delighted to have found my sea again.
I haven't seen water since Turkey!
Big waves come crashing in a noise so pleasant, it's good to hear that again!

I eat deliciously, play cards with the girls, and sleep. I need a week

of fitness with jogging every morning, meditation and karate, or tai chi in the afternoon.
I started this morning. I feel good! But it's a bit hard to get back into it. It's been a month since I've done any regular sports.

As for the girls, I don't know, it's not going anywhere. It's stagnating in the "bof" category. We have a good laugh, we're good friends, but there aren't really any sparks, apart from the youngest's formidable pair of balloons that light up my retinas. We'll see if they're putting in a bit of effort, or just decoys. Because they're not really hot, in the perverse and naughty sense of the word. They feel comfortable with me, and I have company.
For how long?
I wonder what the hell I'm doing with them anyway...

Visit of the beach this afternoon. There are luxurious complexes and villages of bungalows more routine and less well equipped. For example, there is no sink in my bungalow, and after I relieve myself, I have to pour water with the can into the basin so that the excrement goes away. To brush my teeth, it's special. You have to take the water from the can and do everything with it. But for $6 a day, we're not going to complain!

Tomorrow we will go with the girls to "Coco Palm Beach" which has a good reputation. For 20 baths more, there is the sink. Not that I'm being picky, but I'm only spending on food and nights, so a slight increase in rent will fit perfectly in my budget, with less cockroaches.

First head in the ocean. About 26° or 27°. A treat! Playing with the big waves is a great pastime. I fall back in childhood. On the beach, Thai people pass by to sell fabrics or offer massages.

Evening in the more luxurious "Resort" next door. Super

beautiful, but atmosphere a bit boring. On the terrace-cafeteria-resto-bar, lounge music, chic and noisy Americans. In short, I prefer the Thai or backpacker atmosphere.

For the last two days here in Coco Palm Village, it's been ugly and grey, cloudy and windy. Nothing dramatic but we can see that the nice season is not here yet. So the rhythm of the day is a bit slow. Beach, reading, eating. Right now it's a storm; the rain has just arrived and there's a wind that could blow the buffalo around; the palm trees are bending, and on the horizon, the sea is invaded by a layer of fog. We tell ourselves that what is coming from the open sea is not very reassuring. A nightmarish atmosphere...

It lasted an hour and a half with a lot of rain.
Then, wake up from the grey. Well...

I'm bored today. Back to the village where I was two days earlier because I had forgotten my walkman. That gives me at least one walk in the day.

It's nice in the interior of the island. Big coconut forests, the grass is high, buffalos are grazing peacefully.

I don't know if it's morale or a physical decline, but I'm getting royally bored. It's crazy. Before it was cars, noise and pollution, now it's the opposite, but I have nothing to do. And nothing to learn either. I still study my book on palmistry - the study of the hands - but barely an hour a day. And I still have a good dozen to fill.

I just didn't belong.
Going around in circles, getting pissed off like I was, normally I

should have felt that I had to change course, go towards something
else, find another place. There are signs that show if you're in the
right place or not...
But I wanted to fuck too much, my senses and perceptions were not
well tuned.

In fact, I had bought this book in Switzerland to study it and
learn this science because, as my goal was to go and find my life
partner, I wanted to put a maximum of chances on my side when
I would meet girls that I would consider interesting... and what
better than to propose to read the lines of their hand to naive
girls, hey hey hey... predator that I am...

With girls, it's just company, it's been too long for them to turn
me on anymore. But hey, at least I'm not alone. Okay. I have an
insidious, guilt-ridden feeling inside me that I wanted to follow
my dick's instincts and urges instead of learning about massages.
And this is the result!

I'm not really proud of myself, slave of this piece of tail! Maybe
tomorrow I'll move to another village...

I'm introducing the girls to Tai Chi this morning but they don't
seem to be biting. Indifferent.

Last night I visited the night spots of Chaweng Beach in the east
of the island. It's the "sex" beach, sex on every corner, but not
the sex I like. I don't like girls who sell themselves. I've never
been to the whores in the cities, so I'm not going to start here, on
this pretty little fisherman's island. In this street, there are mostly
assholes from all over the world, to talk about ass. Guys, you can
see what their level is, and that they come here to play with chicks
they would never have had at home. It's pathetic. And it makes
me feel bad for those good girls who just want to support their

families by playing with foreigners. But there are some of them, the level is so low, they are testosterone bags, and I feel sorry for the poor chicks who fuck those guys...

It's Walt Disney compared to where I live now. A huge area in the palm forest where bamboo and wooden nightclubs have sprung up. It's the carnival. I find bars with pool tables, I play ping-pong with a beer in one hand, a cigarette in the other. We eat cheaply. We have a good time, especially me, because the two girls don't move their butts while I play ping-pong, billiards, dance and even do a little rodeo on a mechanical bull between two games of shotgun on cans of drink. In short, I'm having a blast. Not them. Are bland...

I drink quite a bit too, I need it, and my beer bill is maybe the equivalent of three nights in a boarding house. It bothers me, because I start drinking again, and the little bubbles helping, at the end of the evening, the bill is heavy! Because of my roots in Haute-Savoie and my childhood, I can really drink a lot...

This morning, I move, I move. I'm going to the party, party-pulses oblige!

I pack up all my things and say goodbye to the girls. I don't know if I'll see them again, may God take them in his Holy Guard, and may he be bored with them... And off to Chaweng Beach "the depraved".

At the side of the road, you have to wait for one of the collective taxis that criss-cross the island, and agree on the price with the driver. It costs nothing. The taxi is full, there are even two people on the roof.
Arrival in Chaweng. I have to find a bungalow and it's very crowded. I find a cheap one, super baba cool atmosphere, the

first thing the owner asks is if I smoke. "Yes, only cigarettes". But it sucks. The bungalow is tiny, the toilets and showers are shabby and it's ugly. Well, we'll have to find something else.

But later. For now, I'll take it, thinking that the beach is full.

I eat, and on my way home, I come across a fantastic garden. All the trees are trimmed like in "Edward Scissorhands", the movie with Johnny Depp. It's idyllic, magnificent! Out of curiosity I ask the price, and it's the same as the other shabby one next door. I book a much cleaner bungalow with a less baba atmosphere...

I have to go back to the first one, pack my bag again, tell the crazy boss that I'm leaving him, three hours after my arrival. Everything goes smoothly, but I still pay 50 baths.

14. Sex, alcohol and rock & roll...

In the early evening, all the bars offer videos. The films of the evening and those of the following day are displayed at the entrance. So there is a choice.
I wander from one bar to another. I started the evening by watching Helen Barkins play, then ate with "Sliver".
Everywhere, until 9pm, people are eating and watching movies.
Afterwards, without a drop of alcohol in my blood, I head for the night party.
This is where things usually go wrong...

Alcohol and addictions:
I, for one, have always been an addiction man.
Phil "over and above"...
My friends, women, gambling, money, alcohol or cigarettes, it has always been "always too much, always too much...". It seems to me that people who have water in their astrological sign are very prone to this, or let's say, more than others. And I have water in my sign. I know the extremes well enough to have been around them at a very early age.

I started drinking a lot when I was about 17 because we went out clubbing with our friends three times a week, on Wednesdays, Fridays and Saturdays. All of them, and every week. We couldn't escape it, we had too much fun, we drank booze, because it was the cheapest way to get drunk. How many mornings did I get up to go to work with my head in the toilet?

It's a good thing that drugs weren't too present in my life because I could have fallen into them and enjoyed them. I've tasted everything, whether it's strong drugs (heroin, coke, acid) or soft drugs (shit, mescaline, weed, ecstasy...). I must say that I spent a year in Ibiza, it helps to get acquainted with all these explosive substances for the head and the party.

As far as alcohol is concerned, I always drank to party and not to drown a sorrow, a depression, or to forget. I leave that to my poor mother. Later, sometimes, because I was bored...

Alcohol makes me happy, makes me want to laugh, turn up the music, dance. Alcohol does not make me bad. I didn't get into many fights in bars when I was drunk. On the other hand, it didn't really belong to me.

Alcoholism was passed on to me.

Let me try to explain something essential that few people think about: the family hierarchy, the ancestral dynasty, which greatly influences our lives, and without our knowledge.

Genetics and the energies of those who passed on our genes have a lot to do with it.

My addiction to alcohol belongs more to my biological father (whom I never knew) than to me personally.

That bastard passed it on to me and I am somewhat addicted to it, unknowingly. Yes, this man, who behaved obnoxiously towards my mother when I was a child (pimp, remember?), drank a lot of pastis - up to 18 or 20 according to my mother - every night. Well, to his credit, his mum ran the local village bar with an iron fist, and used to bottle up all the drunks in the area. For the son, it was rather easy to get drunk every day with his friends.

144

And me, I find myself twenty or thirty years later adoring pastis.
Why pastis rather than rum or vodka? The mysteries of genetics, I
don't know... The fact
remains that I believe in the energies passed on by those who came
before, by the lineage of our ancestors.
This explains why, now that I know it, my "passion" for pastis has
waned, I know that it comes from him, it does not belong to me and
it has no place in my life.
So I consciously decide to cut this invisible thread that links me to
him and to this addiction.

By this action I also prevent the transmission of this energetic
charge to my daughters, who will never be alcoholics, at least not by
the pitiful genetic heritage of this biological father.

At the Reggae Pub, I am accosted by the prettiest Thai girl I have
ever seen, very sexy, too much so perhaps. I can't tell if it's a guy
or a girl because the result is amazing, I'm stunned. I'm amazed,
drooling at the corners of my mouth, fine droplets beading on my
temples... Immediately after the usual "What's your name", he or
she offers me to have sex, because her parents are poor and she
wants to get an ostrich clitoris, something like that. It was too
quick anyway for her not to be a whore who whores. Well, gently,
I tell her to fuck off to the smurfs and get herself another sucker,
but she doesn't know smurfs. I go back to the bar. There, I meet
another Thai girl, pretty, nice, not aggressive like "hello, what's
your name, you want to fuck ?", so more in my idealo-romantic-
obsessed state of mind. We spend the evening dancing, kissing.
God, it's good to touch a woman again!

The show is also on the dance floor, with tourists dressed as neo-punks-babacool-branches or lady-boys having a great time. Have a good night. It's incredible, because every time I go out to flirt or try to party, it's often a failure. And here, I play it cool-abdul-tranquil-émile, clean spirit, no-alcohol-I-will-not-go-late, and I enjoy myself.

Except that, what can I do with my blue flower-everyone-is-good side! How could I think she wouldn't want my money? We get home around three in the morning, we get eaten by mosquitoes that make a real Christmas feast - it's normal for everyone to eat - and we have divine sex, or rather she rapes me like a tigress. Now I know she's a pro. She dances on me in an impressive way! Thai women's skin is different, soft, little hair, beautiful color, silk... I love it!

I put my heart into it, I give it of me, I devour it sensually and slowly. We fall asleep. But we sleep badly, we touch each other, we move, and in the morning we do it again. Normal.

Damn, this flow of romance could have held if she hadn't asked me for money when we left: "Normally 500 baths," she tells me. Shit, fuck, I'm so stupid!

I give her 300, and out of my sight. That'll teach me. How naive! Well, it's nothing and these poor girls have to live and feed their families. Besides, it's Christmas.

I'm far too naive...

Friday 24th December: I can hardly imagine that it's Christmas. It's my first time in the tropics! If it weren't for the signs announcing it and the decorated trees, nothing would tell us that it's Christmas Day. All the criteria that built my end-of-year logic are falling apart. No snow, no mountains, no Switzerland, no parents, no presents, no winter. That's a lot of Christmas elements missing!

December 25: Here it is, Christmas is over. I imagine everyone
sitting around the family table and the poor turkey in front of it,
tongue hanging out and ass full, and especially all those people
from the same family pretending to love each other on that night,
giving each other presents, most of them stupid.

I wake up, destroyed by the bottle of Mekong - the local whisky
also used to unclog toilets - that I sent myself yesterday during
the evening that started with boxing fights, supposedly the most
fantastic of the year, and that turned out to be null. All of them
were young, under 35kg, puny kids, babies fighting, not much of
a show. Then I went to the Reggae Pub. It was packed. I danced
like crazy until I couldn't control my legs or my head.

And that's when everything went wrong...

There was this guy I had met on my way in and who had
immediately struck me as unsympathetic. There's no explaining
the immediate repulsion. The perfect badger, pretentious,
cunning, dressed like I don't like, a jerk's face... Anyway, I start
drinking, the bar is full of festive people. After a few slightly
drunken and hateful looks, I find myself facing him in a corridor.
Everything happened very quickly. Contemptuous looks, lips
slightly curled up like aggressive dogs ready to fight. And we
grabbed each other. Arms outstretched, our bodies too, we knew
it was going to rain... Barman, a cocktail of adrenaline-
testosterone if you will? Then the shots. The first one starts with
a generous impulse from me, my right fist is going to smash his
left cheekbone, and in spite of the music, I can hear perfectly the
sound - very enjoyable - of the bone being violently hit and
cracking. The guy's a good accuser and now he's the one who

sends his fist on my eyebrow. Boom, my brain takes the shock, and especially the noise. But I know it's holding and that it's nothing. By the time I cushion it, my head moves back a little and I shrink. Quick and nervous, he hands me one, and PAF another one, in the same place, above my left eye. Boom and boom again. My skull hears and digests, but I'm not stunned and I stand up. The people around me are shocked, no one really moves, the sound system is on full blast in the box, the scene freezes, freeze frame. The guy runs outside. My face is bleeding, my eyebrow is blown out and blood is gushing out, I'm so happy to finally get a taste of fresh air. I quietly go to the bathroom to wipe my face, make myself beautiful again, and go back out to climb the stairs leading to the exit. The doorman didn't react, because everything happened too fast. The guy just took off. I wish we could have gotten to know each other better, but I'm told he left.

A girl I had seen inside comes up to me, I guess to console me, her maternal instincts telling her to help me, and her certainly wet panties whispering to her to come and sponge my fresh blood, you delicious little vampire. I sit on the sidewalk, we chat, the current passes, she wants to take care of me, cuddle me, she lives not far. I pretend to be a guy who's losing it, and it seems to work, pity takes over, and she wants to comfort me.

Oooh the manipulative villain that I am...

We head for her house because I don't like making women sad, and I want to prove to her that not everything inside me is shocked and traumatized...

Testosterone and adrenaline helping, the night is tender, cuddly... unforgettable.

Some women like violence, it opens them unusual perceptions, and their body vibrates with these bestial stimuli...

Three hours later I look in the mirror. Nice hematoma on the left side, we call it a black eye. On a white face. But there's no need to blush, it's the others who will be scared to death, or who will be green with fear.

The next day, not too hungover, I'm fine, I'm recovering from these emotions.
The weather, like every day, is grey with some sunshine. You can feel the wind from the sea, it's hot and humid, maybe 28° or 30°. What am I going to do today? Nothing. Let myself live, a bit of sport in the late afternoon. It's Christmas, damn it!
I've been moody all day. Walking around in circles. Not knowing what to do with myself, with my body.
In the evening, all the bungalow villages offer free, all-you-can-eat meals, and then the party. The table is beautifully laid, there are about fifteen dishes and at the signal, all the beasts - about twenty people - pounce on them. It's delicious, there's everything, and there's plenty of beer and whiskey. Tonight is the night I should have gone on a cheap bender!
With my face, some people look at me with curiosity, that adds a little to the mystery of the great stranger who is among them.
Everyone is then invited to the next village to continue the party. As I decided not to drink a drop of alcohol, I must seem a bit sad compared to the others who start talking and laughing loudly...
Not far away, the election of miss I-don't-know-what takes place, in a good-natured atmosphere. One of them even shows his ass every time he passes. And he wins, this idiot! Because he/she is elected Mister Biggest-Ass-Hole! I
'm
going to bed early, because even though I'm getting to know

some of them, I'm bored
sober.
Phew, it's over. There's still the "New year's day" to deal with.

This morning, up earlier than usual. It's only sunny in the
morning, until about eleven. So I take a sunbath. It's good!
The voracity of the mosquitoes is incredible. When I took the
bungalow, there was already a double mosquito net. Normal, it's a
big bed. The first night, I slept badly, spending most of it
scratching myself.
Well, I'm going to install my "single mosquito net" because the
big one has holes in it, and I think those smart mosquitoes have
been trying to find the entrance. I put it in place. Second night, I
spend it with the Thai girl. Same scenario. They don't seem to
appreciate the local blood, so they make a feast of mine. I can
hear them lining up at the entrance of the mosquito net, taking a
ticket, their cutlery, putting on their bibs, and diving in to feast on
me. Third night, it's getting better. My bed is like a fortress. I
installed the mosquito net so that it fits perfectly on the bed. No
more free space. The only sensitive moment is when I go out to
pee. A high-risk operation! I still kill four of them in the middle
of the night and I still don't know how they do it. My sheet is
starting to get stained with blood. Every time I crush one - and I
must have crushed thirty in the last three days - there's a fresh
stain of my blood, which the bastard has soaked up, on the sheet
or on the mosquito net. No mercy then! But it's getting a bit
nasty! And I'm not the only one... I see people who arrive in the
morning with whole patches of pimples on their thighs or back.
One girl is even covered in pimples, damn it... A mosquito even
bit me on the lip yesterday! On the lip, shit! It's crazy, these

bloodsuckers don't even have any shame anymore! Fortunately I have an ointment against insect bites of all kinds, it's very soothing.

Another peculiar fact about this island is that there must be a disease among the dogs. Almost all of them have half their coats scratched and they can't stop scratching. It's pitiful, it makes them look like dogs with AIDS. People are afraid of them. I've seen so many times the Thai chase them away, these poor creatures. With their feet, with a book, almost with the sign "vade retro satana", when they hang out on the terraces or at the edge of the beaches. The locals don't really like dogs, even if they respect them as Buddhists.

Thai particularity, people do not show their skin or their body at the beach. They bathe with their shirt or their t-shirt. Especially girls when they are young.

There are several things you should not do here: pointing your finger at someone, touching your head, because it is the most sacred part of the body, and pointing your foot at someone. For example, when we are sitting on a terrace, we like to put our feet on the chair in front of us, as a way to relax. But since the feet are considered to be the ugliest and most ungrateful part of the body, it is an offense to point your foot at someone here.

I meet a lot of interesting people today. I play on the beach with some swedes who are leaving tomorrow, a funny Chinese guy, two French guys from Montpellier. A very nice day.
In the evening, I'm having a great time by measuring my drinking - which is already an improvement for me - and by dancing with

all my guts until 2am. The to-tale fun! Wow!

The next day, not too creepy, I'm hanging out on the beach. I would party every night, but I can't! My body and my head couldn't take it.

The weather is getting better as the days go by. It's nice in the morning, the sun is shining more and more, each day is getting brighter.
The beach is starting to get crowded, a lot of people are coming with suitcases, so holidaymakers for the end of the year, and most of them are coming for one or two weeks. Spend a lot of money, fuck a lot of nice and sweet girls, and leave with empty pockets. All of them. Lots of Germans.

I also see disturbing scenes. Because you shouldn't think that Thailand only welcomes the beautiful people. And yes, the degenerates from Europe and the perverts with unhealthy sexual urges know that they can afford in Thailand little guys who know nothing about life, for almost nothing. And they are there, I see them sometimes and it is frankly disgusting.
I saw a fat bearded German guy sitting in a restaurant with a little Thai guy, who must have been only 14 years old, and I was overwhelmed by contradictory and violent emotions, and I didn't know what to do, because everyone - Buddhist and necessarily tolerant of human deviances - seemed to accept this new couple in the restaurant. I still think about it now and emotions of anger and violence rise up in me. Fucking perverts!

Tuesday 28 December: Full Moon Party day.
 Every month at the full moon, there is a huge party on a beach

of Koh Panghan, the neighboring island. Many people go there. This year, there is talk of 2,000 to 3,000 tourists for this full moon party. I'm not going to go because you pay a lot of money for the boat, you drink like a fish and you wake up the next day on the beach half-conscious. I'm not interested. There are also a lot of drugs on this island, and no police. Hallucinogenic mushrooms, pot cakes... but I'm not interested in drugs. Beer, sex and sports are my new addictions. So goodbye full moon party, I'm out...

This morning they cut down three palm trees, too old, which threatened the safety of the bronze workers. You have to see them climbing up the palm trees and fixing the ropes like monkeys. Beautiful to see. Sad for the palm tree that falls.
Jogging at eight o'clock, shaving, breakfast, a good start to the day.
In fact I fall asleep as soon as the clouds appear, hop! Up at 6pm then. Classic start of the evening. Movie-video on a terrace, direction where-everything-goes, because let's not forget, it was the full-moon party yesterday. My prayer or wish for this evening is to have my own full-moon party with a girl, and to finish with her. It will be largely fulfilled, but that's for later...
Jealous and envious as you must be, so mop up that little trickle of drool that's oozing from your lips...

So, the evening starts in the bar by playing pool. Yesterday I got thrown out immediately, but now I'm beating two Thai girls and an Australian, before being thrown out by an Israeli - but I wasn't feeling it and I played like a potato. Anyway, it's a good omen for the future because I prefer to be unlucky in the game and... you know the rest.

After three beers, I go "on the dance floor". I wiggle on the podiums like you-see-how-well-I-dance, good atmosphere, great house. In this club, there are lots of lady-boys and girls looking for the "falang" *(tourist)* who will pay for a blowjob or a semblance of love. They are there wiggling their asses and baiting the foreigners. You can imagine that I've been there too. And for the past few nights they know I don't want to pay. One of them is really beautiful. I'm not sure if she's a real woman because she's absolutely perfect. She's got beautiful breasts, whereas Thai women have very small ones, a beautiful face, beautiful legs, an ambiguous girl with a strange voice too. Yesterday, she told me that she had her period and that she didn't want to work. So I thought maybe she was a woman. I go for it. And she snaps. She'll wait for me outside. Yeeeesss!

I'm still dancing, still drinking, with the delicious thought that I'm not going to sleep alone. Two hours later, drunk, I collapse outside hoping to see her. She comes in and tells me she just blew a customer for 500 baths. Damn, when I think of all those beach vendors who carry their heavy load of trinkets all day trying to sell them for pennies, these girls must be the richest on the island! Yesterday, five clients she made. Sex pays! Besides, nothing here is dirty. Everything is "sanuk", fun, funny. It is normal for the population that girls have fun with foreigners. Just like gogo-boys and lady-boys are normal. Sex is fun, not taboo! And it keeps the whole family going, so if everything is good in the pig, everything is accepted!

We left on his moped. To eat first. I was quite drunk and disturbed by this otherworldly creature of absolute eroticism. We agreed, no sex, just sleep. We go to her place. I was a little embarrassed when, after kissing her passionately, I asked her to show me her sex. Thai women are modest because they don't show their skin at the beach. So sex, you think... But she showed it to me. It's a girl! Yippee... champagne! I can sleep with her... I leave in the morning having respected my contract, no sex. I know, I'm an idiot, but I like to keep my word.

Beautiful day the next day. Backgammon against an Australian who plays well. My repeated humiliations in Turkey, in Göreme against the guy who played so well, have paid off, I'm playing better now.
Great group of Australians that I hope to see again. They're really cool, these Australians! They're always in a good mood, they're always relaxed, they smile, I feel good with them.

Made an important decision. Besides,
it coincides with what we usually
decide in the New Year.
I'm going to work on my future, perhaps towards a new direction. I'm going back to Chiang Mai to learn massage. Two weeks of classes, six hours a day, and a final diploma.
It could be serious. But we have to look at the dates, there are two courses a month, the next one around January 15. I'm going to take care of this seriously this week with the travel agencies.

I have fun in the water with impressive waves that only terrorize the spectators. I love it! I almost died several times, but I like it! Tonight, a big boxing gala with real fights, not an exhibition. A little blood and bone-breaking should be good.

The next day: indeed, it was worth it. Beautiful fights, the show around the ring too because people bet, they shout vehemently when the boxers are unleashed *(so when their chains are removed)* and it's madness in the stands. Each blow is taken up by the spectators who shout "ole" Thai.

And there were two fighters who left on a stretcher. A bit of blood on the ring too... In short, a very nice evening.

Then, everyone goes to the "Reggae Pub". Bamboo and tropical atmosphere, and a lot of lady-boys. It is quite common in Thailand to see guys transformed, with or without operation, into women. These are the lady-boys. Some are successful because of their small ass and small shoulders. Others are really laughable, like this young guy with a rugbyman's build and dressed with lace everywhere. I laugh a lot...

Last night, no luck. There are two of them, with beautiful curves, who titillated my senses and were very endearing. But, even though I have a well-developed sixth sense to sense true femininity, I wasn't too sure of myself when I asked one of them if it was a man. Other than that, good club, good atmosphere, full house, closing at three in the morning. Then everyone went to the "Doors", a big bar that closes much later.

Then, my head being no longer available, my feet took me back alone on the road to my bungalow...

And on this road was a lady-boy.

He had urges, which I felt very well. Of sex.

And I, being a generous person by nature, well, I gave him what he wanted. Well, not what you think, because my little hole is and will remain hermetic, even to the most intrusive of requests, and his, I didn't want it. But his mouth will have done my business, on the side of the road, at five o'clock in the morning.

Drunk, a mouth remains a mouth

Unfazed by the shame, I dragged myself to my room, soothed and drained.

Shame: One of the worst human emotions.
I have been ashamed several times in my life, and they were real lessons.
I particularly remember coming home from a party at five o'clock in the morning on an island in the Indian Ocean, after having hit the local discotheques; I came home drunk on my motorcycle.
Alternating one eye open and the other closed, I decided to stop in a curve, staggered to try to put the bike on its stand, and let myself fall here, like an idiot, on the ground, so much I could not take it anymore... I fell asleep.
I was awakened in the morning by a car that stopped in front of me. A father got out with his three sons, teenagers I suppose, to help me, not knowing if I had a problem or not. When they saw my crooked face and my unopenable eyes, they understood, and the father said something to his sons, like, "You see what alcohol can do...". As I stood up, staggering, I was frankly ashamed. Ashamed to the point of tears. There I was, a big drunk guy on a street corner, still drunk at six o'clock in the morning, unable to start his motorcycle, with a dead battery (of course I had stopped with my headlights on), I felt pathetic, pitiful, pathetic. And here they are, kindly helping me and pushing my bike, which agrees to start again.
I left with my tail between my legs, not really proud, I just wanted to be an ant and disappear...
I don't want to go through that again.

First long day on the beach. Lots of vendors. The nicest ones are the ones carrying a scale on their shoulders with a basket woven at each end of this long flexible bamboo rod. On some of them is a charcoal stove with corn grilling. Sitting there, without moving, you can eat, get dressed, get a massage. This beach is better than the previous one because there are more people, more life. Swimming, nap, staring, a good afternoon that ends with a long jog on the beach, with U2 in the ears. Great !

Once upon a time...

At the time of the Pharaohs, in ancient Egypt, a beautiful young woman dressed in white, an apprentice vestal, is about to take a test. It is the ultimate test. She has been working and preparing for it for many years.
There are about ten of them who have so far succeeded in their elimination course, which is littered with various challenges. Years of work and learning to get here.
The temple is looking for a new diviner.
If she succeeds, she will be appointed priestess.
If she fails, she will die.
The purpose of the ordeal is to remain locked in a sarcophagus for four days.
With nothing. No air, no food, no help.
She gets out alive, she'll be a priestess.
She doesn't come out, she'll have failed, dead.

The young woman slips into her icy marble coffin. Several assistants then close the heavy granite lid over the reclining body, sealing the sarcophagus.

Four days pass...
The sarcophagi are reopened.
Bodies are found lifeless, without breath.
Most of them are dead, the aspiring priestesses.
Amelie was one of them.

Amelie, who we find in 2005, married and with two children. My beloved ex-wife.
She has had several lives since those ancient times, lives that she has forgotten.
In this present life, she joined a circle of light therapists a few years ago. They are called Essenes. She follows a guide, she learns and she loves it powerfully. She shines from year to year, and becomes a

beacon. She gradually climbs the steps of light within the group, and soon finds herself assistant to the priestess.

It is then that her conscience gives her a powerful, irresistible, wildly attractive suggestion.

At her ascension stage, she will have reconnected with considerable emotional reminiscences, recreating the same density of emotions and vibrations as those experienced in a distant other life. But she doesn't know it yet.

Life is a great game, will she dare to play?

All the factors are there, the triggers are present, thought-forms, consciousness, soul, everything pushes her to play again this once lost game.

And her body recreates the sarcophagus of old.

Acute leukemia.

Boom!

At least that was the term used by the robot doctors who examined her body.

She who didn't drink or smoke, she who meditated and practiced love through light, she who cared for others, who practiced yoga daily, here she was with cancer?

Can you believe it? It is impossible! How could it be?

Except that her destiny is so much more noble than the sum of all our earthly beliefs.

In truth, she will have recreated her once-failed ultimate test. To play.

Having once again reached a high level of spiritual studies and vibrations in the light, she offers herself in an unconscious personal challenge the possibility to finally reach her Holy Grail, to reach the final goal that she has secretly nurtured deep inside her for lifetimes and lifetimes... to finally become a high priestess

So here she is, bedridden and weak, prey to her worst fears, including the fear of dying. Dying again. With her family, nowhere near imagining why, pouring waves and waves of fears into her, all from the Matrix. And this Medical System and these life-saving robots pouring into her the infamous sticky liquid, supposed to change her blood, as if the cause lay there...

She struggles.

For a long time.

Alone with her conscience, trying to know why this is happening to her.

Wondering why the Gods are sending her this ordeal.

She only understands this towards the end, during her multiple exits from this body that never stops deteriorating, when she becomes aware that her body envelope will soon no longer be able to support the vital space of her soul trying to reintegrate it, and that she will soon have to leave it forever.

She left, taking her secret with her.

She had failed again.

Leaving the humans to their pains, and she sailing towards a next karma, a next life in which, no doubt, she will start again to create the conditions to win this ultimate personal fight which pursues her.

She has gone high, very high up in the upper layers in the hierarchy of light, to help break up some of the negatively charged egregores that are weighing the Earth down.

See you soon, my dearest Amelie, we'll see you soon.

15. End of the holidays

Horrible vision this morning of a young dog huddled behind the toilet, dying, his flesh raw from scratching. Unbearable! I would like to kill him to help him. I don't know how to do it.
Those who went to the full-moon party come back broken, crazy, corpses. They say it's the craziest thing there is, 5,000 people dancing on the beach until nine in the morning. Lots of drugs, even hard ones. Holy shit!

Now it's almost totally beautiful in the morning, it's crazy. Blue, blue and blue again, green water, yellow sand. And my coffee is black.
The sea is less rough. It's almost impossible to have fun in the waves.
I'm having a wonderful day with the Australians, who are really offbeat. I have never known a normal Australian before...
Ping-pong, backgammon, I'm an animal. Usual evening, food with them, pool, and afterwards, we go and wipe ourselves somewhere. The music's no good, can't get enough of it. I can't wait for the year to be over because I'm spending too much and

there's a kind of tension in the air that fills everyone's bodies and hearts. We are tension bombs. The accumulation of a whole year, 365 days of emotions, is soon too much for the senses. It demands to explode. It will dissipate on January 1st...

Yesterday, one of the dogs on the beach came to me because he was being mistreated by another dog. On his chest, a huge hole. Deep. I could have put my thumb through it. The ribcage was completely perforated. It's hard to believe he was breathing through it. The disease is getting deeper. God, I wish I had some needles to stick them in and make them feel better.

Personally, I see our relationship with animals as similar to that of angels. There is a hierarchy in the light. And we'll all get there, at every level, higher and higher...
I think we have to take care of them, as we take care of the beings of light in the invisible. Our angels... I see it as a duty received at our incarnation. Like parents who naturally take care of a child.
This would explain why all children without exception have an infinite love for animals.
Whether we believe it or not, entities in the ether are there for us, close to us, always ready to help us. Some call them our guardian angels. They watch over us. They vibrate higher than us, and by duty or by a force of unconditional
Love from the Light, they take care of us.
We therefore have a duty to help our animal friends who, on the scale of vibratory planes, are placed below us. We all feel it in our hearts, it is inexplicable.
But once we are adults, and our good feelings are buried by our lives in concrete cities, always running after money, we are hardly

interested in the pigeons on our sidewalks, and in our pets who are more there to mop up our ailments than in a relationship of equal to equal.

Normally we should all respect them, and communicate with them. There are trainings for that, it's exciting and easy, my daughters and I have followed one.

Last day of the year: everyone is quiet and getting ready for tonight. On the beach, all the bungalow villages decorate their terraces and announce their menu and the evening's program. Around 11pm, the tension is palpable. Everywhere people go out, they have celebrated in their bungalow with bottles bought at the supermarket. And everyone is heading towards the Reggae Pub which is already full to bursting. It is almost impossible to dance because of the crowd.
Midnight. It's crazy! Everyone is wild, for almost three hours people are dancing everywhere, on tables, chairs, madness! I love it... I try to entice a few girls with a frenetic dance leaving no doubt about my intentions, but I come across some uptight English girls and a lot of young girls. Around three in the morning, I move to the "Doors". I'm pissed, I'm a bit blue, I'd like to celebrate this night with a girl, and finally, after hanging out and eating, I go to see the first dawn of the year. Great! Sleep at six in the morning.

The day after, day in slow motion, of course. You can feel that something has passed, the air is lighter. Some are already packing their bags, who had come just for the party. On the beach, a lot of dead bodies.

I walk quietly to a village of bungalows, I had spotted a girl. I show up, there she is.

I realize that during these last three days, I have really lost my balance. Drinking every night, the mental state is taking a hit. I feel fragile, like I need my sunglasses. I don't dare approach her. On the other hand, more than once when I wanted to approach a girl and I waited for the right moment, soon after the boyfriend or her husband arrived. So I don't rush...

I don't talk to her, I act shy. And as the good Lord does well, an hour later I see her walking alone on the beach. I go there. We get to know each other for two hours. Yum, I see her again tomorrow.

Hearty dinner, sautéed rice with shrimp, two plates, and sleep. Tomorrow, I get back into shape.

Yes, and it starts with a tai chi session at six o'clock facing the rising sun. Then a walk to the bungalows where my new girlfriend is. Things are looking up...

Stormy day today. And when it rains here, it rains! The sea is covered with mist, we can't see anything at 300 meters, the sky is black, it's impressive. There's nothing to do. And I didn't do anything. Slug. Running in the evening and good food. Too tired to join Jennifer, my beautiful American girl.

Monday, January 3: tai chi when the sky is still red, set ablaze by the stretching sun. I begin to master my embarrassment to practice my tai chi on the beach. A part of shyness, a part of modesty always holds me back at the time of launching me. Especially when there are people around. Oh, not many in the morning at six o'clock, but still a few drunks and dawn lovers.

Actually, it's stupid and if I do it it's for my own good, and
everyone does it in China. So I'm starting not to care.
I'm in a bad way right now. For the first time in three months, I
have diarrhea. Not really powerful, but since last night I've been
taking the appropriate medication, so we'll see tomorrow if it gets
better. I also have a lot of pimples on my knees. And some
unknown pain, it hurts when I run or climb stairs. Why the
knees? I don't know, it itches like an allergy. I've got my insect
bite ointment, it helps a little. And I have a cough, like many
people here, a small cough from time to time.

The knee, or the "I-we"
(in French "ge-nou" means knee, when you say 'ge' it means 'I'
and 'nou' means 'we' which brings us to the I-we)

I will explain…
So many people suffer from it, every day.

In the series "our body speaks to us", there are a lot of men who
have pain in their knees, or in one knee, it is a great classic.
This need to control everything all the time, which leads to
frustration when it doesn't work, makes us forget that there is
something bigger than us…
Like "God", or the Creative Forces of the Universe, just that. So, by
forgetting that, and not kneeling down sometimes to humbly bow to
something bigger than us, the energies can get stuck in the ligaments
and tendons especially, and the body tries to talk to us, screams at
us that it's not right. We start to limp, a pain grows, which scares us.
And the evil-saying. The disease.

This happened to me a few years ago, and I went to see a specialist
because I assumed I had gone too far in sports, thinking my

cartilage must be affected. It was also a time when I wanted to control external events, even if it meant getting my foot in the door to make sure everything went my way. I was in hyper-control. Of course I was.
But the Gods didn't see it that way and played on that attitude...
After I had an MRI and my file was consulted by a professional, it turned out that my cartilage and synovial fluid were damaged, and that... "Oh dear, my poor man, you won't be able to run like before, it's over. Ohh la la, my poor man, you won't be able to run like you used to, it's over...".
Ouahhh... Paf, bim, ouch...
Uppercut taken, I got up with difficulty.
It's clear that when physical and medicinal medicine doesn't take anything else into account, it's scary. If they would just understand that there is not only the flesh, but also the other energetic bodies of man, as well as his fears and apprehensions, we would be better advised. Our western medicine is so limiting. Of course, the drug industries do not have energy to sell, but chemical drugs. They prescribe us only that.
And we don't have the time to go and see all the alternative doctors to look at our complex being, and see the problem as a whole.
Fortunately I believe in other energies, and especially in myself!

So I quickly forgot the pessimistic verdict of the other one in the white coat, and went into positive mode. "It came like that, it will go like that too! And that's what happened.
Not only because of this simplistic conception of self-healing, but also because I became aware that higher than my little person, there are other energies that I will never master, other elements of colossal power that I will never be able to control, that they have a role, and that therefore it is good sometimes to kneel down to bow respectfully, like a knight before his king - before something greater than myself, and to accept my powerlessness to want to dominate, to control everything, to welcome the letting go of what presents itself to me. To accept.
The acceptance of not being able to control everything is the

beginning.
Accepting what is, as it is, is sometimes difficult for committed
people, or fighters, or programmed to always move forward.
But...
Acceptance = possible transformation, because the struggle is over.

My pain went away, and six months later - anything involving
ligaments and tendons takes a long time to repair - I started running
again, with the joy of a child who had been told he could never do it
again.
To think that I should have had an operation, according to Mister
White Coat, if I didn't have this celestial belief in me...

Medicine on Earth is at the service of pharmaceutical laboratories,
and must therefore sell, and we, consume. The responsibility of
doctors is immense, and many will find themselves with much
torment once back in the light, for the hour of their own judgment.
This will have been seen a lot during this fake pandemic of covid,
how many doctors will have cowardly sold out to the labs.

The "I-we" also concerns the couple, and the tensions that can
accumulate within it. We will see it later...

There must be a lot of microbes and bacteria in the sand.
Between the dogs and the people, that's a lot of infectious
sources.

Last night was a blast! I had a great time. And so much the better
because today there is nothing to do. It's blowing and it rained a
lot this morning. It's a day to write.
Good news, it's going to happen for Phil's! I was able to get the
number of the massage school in Chiang Mai. Next Monday, I'm
there!

It costs half as much as I thought it would, and the Chiang Mai school is the most famous. So, Tuesday it is. That leaves me a day or two here, then back up to Bangkok by train, and Chiang Mai after that. If I can do it all in one go that's even better. But I need to know if the trains are full first.

Tuesday: ok, I take the boat on Friday, then the bus to the train station once I get to the coast. Train to Bangkok and another one to Chiang Mai, that's two days of travel, I'll arrive exhausted, but happy and on time.

I'm enjoying the last few days at the seaside, because after that, it's a big deal for two or three weeks...
I've lost my city shorts. Where? I don't know! How can you lose Bermuda shorts? And the famous Lacoste 1 dollar belt! I bought another one, expensive, but nice.

Epilogue: well, I'm sick of it. Two weeks here is fine.
The girls are scared or intimidated, it doesn't go down well. The two I talked to again this morning were as cold as icebergs.
I've seen and drank what there is to see and drink here, enjoyed the nightlife to the max, got wasted, had fun, danced, hung out on the beach, swam, got a tan, and got laid. Not as much as I would have liked, but still, I have a lot of naughty memories, enough to make me a little old man with laughing eyes later...

Now it's time for something different. At least for a short time. Going back to school. I hope I'm right in wanting to go, that it will serve me well in the future. Anyway, my next wife should be happy!

After that, I'll fly back to the south.
A little pleasure after the intellectual and manual effort.
Phuket, Koh Pee Pee, the most beautiful waters in the world, and Krabi.
I think that Thailand is good, I will have done the tour.
But this is another story...

Expenses :
Turkey : about 800 dollars.
Thailand so far, about 800 dollars.

16. Back to school : Thai massages

Friday morning, 5.15 am, the time when the big mosquitoes gorged with my blood snore, their stomachs hanging, and it is under an eye tenderized by the idea of seeing their flesh burst that I crush them with a sharp snap of both hands, a grin of satisfaction on my lips. Gargl, how good it is! How I hate them! I've had a bad night because of these mosquitoes. Again, before I turn off the light, I take a good look at the screen and usually kill one or two of them with a fatal Mawashi geri. And it is with joy and killer fever in my eyes that I turn off the light, knowing that there is not a single one left.

Two hours later I wake up scratching, turn on the light, and there are two or three of them taunting me with their guts swollen with my blood. I put on the ointment that soothes, take the winchester and shoot up the room. I don't know how the bastards do it, but they ruin my nights.

Further north, in the cooler weather, I hope there are fewer of them.

After having packed my things, I wait for the first taxi to Nathon, the town of Koh Samui, at the side of the road, at 5:30 am, time at which the mosquitoes return home gorged with my blood - well, we won't come back to that - but also the whole panoply of insects that have finished their night of shopping and victuals, and return to their homes to shake their wives before going to sleep, except for the scolopendra which, as everyone knows, is a hermaphrodite and can be self... ahem.

In the taxi, or the covered van, everyone is pulling a face. It is too early for the first smiles, which come later. On the way to the port.

Port, boat, half-consciousness. Watch, sleep, battle of the eyelids that fight the activity of the brain that tells them to stay up, since it's daytime, but they don't give a damn and want to make up for the hours they couldn't get off and rest. It's a tough fight.

I tried to close one eye after the other but nothing helped, they were united and wanted to rest together. The journey lasted a few minutes of wakefulness and attention, a few blinks of the eyes. In reality, two and a half hours.

Arrival in Surat Thani, on the mainland, bus to the station. Train.

Every time I took the train, that is to say once so far, it was at night. So I saw nothing of the landscape. Here I see flooded rice fields, it's a beautiful day because little day is not here, the countryside is very green and there is water everywhere, so the land is just covered with what Uncle Ben's needs to be satisfied. The harvest will be good. Thousands of unknown trees, palms and rubber trees and as many buffaloes grazing without a pester.

In the train, the air conditioning system is leaking, drops are falling from the ceiling and several passengers are wet. We laugh... It reminds me of this traditional Thai end of year festival that people celebrate with big buckets of water on the faces of their neighbors, or passers-by. In the streets, everyone is spraying each other laughing and it must be really liberating to be able to throw water on people, without distinction, just for fun, in a festive atmosphere, like children would do.
But for the moment I've had enough, I'm disconnecting all the circuits, I'm putting them on pause.

Eight hours later. Bangkok. Phew, here we go! First leg passed. Half of the boring journey done. Creepy and a bit out of touch, I'm in Bangkok station. I know it since I have to take the same train I took last time to Chiang Mai. Same train, same platform, same atmosphere, same "same".
Moist atmosphere, messy atmosphere, no doubt, we are in Bangkok!
The first time I had slept really badly. I hope it will get better. This time, I will dress warmer to sleep.

Ten hours later, on the train: I slept well because, knowing the trick, I took the bottom bed, as the light upstairs is disturbing, and I was well dressed, so I didn't feel cold. Anyway, I thought I'd be completely dismantled, but I'll arrive fresh instead.

I had coffee in bed this morning, or rather a spilled one, but not like at home; here they spill it on me, a coffee shower! Let's not get upset... She's a young girl and when she asks me for 50 baths for a sandwich and the coffee I have to drink in the blanket, that's too much. I refuse, and the bitch gets away with 20 baths and my sandwich. Well, I think I've been fooled!

I find the vegetation of the North, luxuriant, an inextricable jumble between the jungle and the palm trees, full of unknown trees and plants. It's a bit colder. That's good.

Chiang Mai, here I am. Here I am again! "You again, Philou?", "Yes, old chap!".
Nothing has changed.
I rent a bike for two weeks. Find a nice guesthouse for one night. Phoned and went to see the Institute of Massages. I speak with the owner who seems very competent because he has studied and taught in America.
Two colored pencils, two photos + copy of passport, that's what I need to start. And, of course, my indispensable hands.

Tonight, I have to go shopping, buy a new pair of city shorts, expedition-safari-style-who-wants-to-look-like-Rambo-but- more-classy. I have to have a talk with my wallet, sometimes it closes too fast...
Night bazaar, you can really find everything. How I wish all the people I love were here! It's Ali Baba's cave. In one area, all the shops are open, it's 9pm and on the sidewalks, it's a huge display of various goods, crafts, everything is beautiful and cheap, and if

I listened to myself, I would come out with my arms full of packages. I find my new safari shorts for $5.

Sunday: eight in the morning, the alarm clock rings. Damn, how good I felt. It's a day to sleep today.
 Last night, after playing pool like a champ against several opponents, I rode my bike home and got completely lost. In the end, I had to ride 10 km, and I was pretty tired. I have to say that the bike is an old lady's bike, with only one gear, so I have to deal with it, whether it's going up or down...
So today, I have the pod! But I have to move because I don't like this boarding house. There's no one
there and it's gloomy. Check-in is at 9 o'clock, so I have to leave before.

Ok, I have a new room in another pension. It's crowded, even old tourists, which I hadn't seen before. Sleep, sleep and sleep again. In several stages, because I pee every two hours like a metronome. Late afternoon, while walking around I witness the second most popular sport in the country, a kind of volleyball played with the feet, head, knees or elbows but not the hands. These kids were playing spectacularly well, it's very acrobatic to see. In the middle of the city.

Monday 10: Here we go, first day of class. I'm already getting ready to go. The morning starts with a sprint, um... that gets me in shape. Well, I arrive on time. Introduction of everyone, it's quite heterogeneous, we are eight new and some who are doing their second or third week.

Protocol. First a prayer to thank the founder of this style of massage. It is a mixture of yoga and a little Chinese for acupressure. The purpose of these massages is to relax and stimulate the internal energy flow. A session can last two to three hours!

This morning we study the feet and the beginning of a massage session, which means washing our hands, praying for the good practice we are going to do and the good care we are going to give to the person. Then we warm the hands by rubbing them together. Then the massage can begin. We all have a booklet with drawings to write our comments in.

In the afternoon, after a break of an hour and a half, we started the legs. For the legs alone, it takes about 45 minutes!

After the explanations, two by two, we work on our new knowledge. And it goes fast. No time to daydream. At 5pm, I'm a bit tired. I need to rest a bit and study to get this knowledge into my brain. In the lower limbs, all the work is done on the meridians and energy lines along the outside of the legs. Inside and outside. In one day, we learn for about 1 hour 45 minutes of massage.

Tuesday: second day of school. Prayer that the master recites and that everyone repeats aloud. It is about thanking the founder and wishing to receive the knowledge of the medicine of the Universe so that through our body, bring happiness and health to the patient. An hour of yoga afterwards. My thigh muscles hurt because these are stretching exercises that they are not used to. Theory then, and practice in the afternoon. All about the legs. The figures become artistic! The positions look like yoga ones. I memorize quite quickly and well, and when I see the others, I think I'm quite good. There is a Canadian couple, 50 and 58 years

old, who, once their four children became adults, left their
country to discover the world while developing their knowledge.
Among other things, Thai cooking and massages. Bowler hat and
Canadian boots!

Like yesterday, I'm exhausted. I'm going to make myself very
small tonight. Alas, no more pool and beer. Early night.
But I'm glad I came here and started these classes. I've been
looking for a long time for a way to connect with people to help
them or heal them, and I've found it. What I can't do with words,
as a stutterer until I was 21, I can do with my hands and my body.
Express myself.

*Didn't I tell you that I was born unable to express myself? I grew up
stuttering.*
*As soon as I opened my mouth, people would usually look at me and
their eyes would start to crinkle, and then a little hurtful mockery
would follow. For the more respectful of course.*
Sometimes I got a good bite, I must say. It stung!
*It's complicated, the life of a stutterer. We have to look non-
stuttering as soon as the first sounds come out, we have to
concentrate on reciting the sentence we have to say in one go, but
there's always a fucking word that we know very well when we see it
coming mentally that we're going to get stuck on it because it
contains the two or three letters that get stuck. And we, in our
stuttering brains, know exactly which ones. The "M", for example,
and the "L" are terrible. And since they're in almost every sentence,
we always have a hard time finishing them. Sometimes we find a
way out at the last moment, another word that doesn't contain an
"M" or that damned "L", and it can go... But in the song and the
melody of the sentence, people realize that the guy wants to finish*

his sentence way too fast, and it feels weird, it's suspicious. When it's impossible for us to counteract the famous word, well, usually we stumble, and that's when it gets stuck. And that's when people start laughing. And that's when it hurts.
And when it comes to relationships with women, I can't tell you how much it hurts your manhood, your masculinity... and your confidence takes a hit. And what about when I'm tired? It's huge. Sometimes I can't get through a sentence without stuttering. Strangely enough, it's mostly in French. Less in English or other languages. Probably because I have to think more.

Having said that, as a child, my mother took me several times to see a speech therapist, or logopedist. I found these consultations amusing because we played with words, and I always liked that. I liked learning sentences by heart and reciting them as fast as possible. But it didn't really work in the long run. Always this stammering, degrading my pride.
I was able to speak almost normally again around 21-22 years old. Don't ask me why, I have no idea. At that time, I started my first trips alone, and something must have come loose; I could feel it when I could finish a sentence without having hesitated and/or stuck on a word. An explosive and enjoyable revelation for me, normality for the other person in front of me, who must not have understood those exalted
eyes looking at him...
It still happens to me sometimes when I'm tired, and now I say it without any complex: "Be careful, I may start stuttering...".

I often thought, during these past decades, imbued with this philosophy of reincarnation, that it could also be a matter of a previous death by hanging, having perhaps even been a victim of an injustice. Wouldn't I have been a bad guy in the 19th^{ème} century in *the American Far West, having ended my life with a rope around my neck, hanging sadly on a gallows? Go figure... why not. I was always a big fan of westerns as a child, I kind of grew up with these movies...*

The slow death of a hanged man must create such a powerful emotion that it must be engraved in the universal and immortal consciousness of the being, to, back in a new body, in a next life - to see with the hierarchy of angels the why of the how - impact the human and limit him in his language. Why not?

I believe it, it makes sense.

But back to my hands.

I remember the psychic I saw in Paris. According to him, I had to do something with my hands to give energy, and free myself from it to be more balanced. I feel that I can achieve this goal through this practice. I want to know it more. I asked the two Canadians to buy me a book in French about Thai massage.

Wednesday: great day. I start it with vitamins, little bottles that you can find everywhere, it's fragrant, fresh, you drink it in ten seconds. And it's great for the body!

I'm working a lot today. The positions are becoming acrobatic and I hope I'm going to memorize them. I didn't get lost this morning on the way to the institute. I did to get back. That's crazy!

Tonight, I'm going to meet a Brazilian girl who's taking the classes, for dinner at the Thai Cultural Center.

Thursday: stiff! But completely exhausted! I didn't sleep. I didn't sleep I tell you!

The Thai Cultural Center is a real tourist factory: you pay for a bowl, you are directed to a large room where there are already 300 people and, barely time to look around, the food arrives. On a tray are eight cups containing specialties. It's really good. Salads, pork, chicken, fried rind, vegetables, fried noodles and, for dessert, fried bananas with rice cake. Some of them didn't touch their tray like this old British couple behind us, Sophie and I devoured their part.

On the stage, dances. Nice dances. But after one or two, we've had enough. All in all, it will have lasted an hour and a half, and everyone is driven back to the guesthouses by minibus. Good organization.

So, after... well, Sophie and I... tac tac boum boum!

Or rather, it went smoothly. "Can I sleep here?", "Uh, yes, of course...". And at night, all pussies are grey... I knew very well that it would be impossible to sleep. But neither she nor I had a condom, so no ticking! But with imagination, you can find some very naughty
hand-games...

So, today, I'm dead. No sleep.

I go to the bank to fill up my pockets. I feel better afterwards.

Tonight, with Sophie, we eat Italian.

She's going away this weekend, so we enjoy being together.

We dine like gods in a pizzeria. Ravioli that had been lucky enough to be stuffed with spinach and cheese, lasagna, baked bread and a glass of French red wine. Divine! The dream...

Sophie goes to the bazaar to buy a few last things and joins me in my bed later. I love...

Friday: how good it is to be woken up by a fresh body and to make the bed squeak afterwards! As the English say: the queen squeaks!

Last day of level I for massages. Tests and practices. Full massage. Good, I remember it well, and all those who have passed through my hands tell me that I have just discovered a new profession! Many will not continue next week, including Sophie who is taking the train tonight.
I'll see her again, normally in a week's time, in Malaysia, on the island of Penang, in George town. We have agreed on a guesthouse to meet again, as my visa expires on January 28. This means that after the second advanced course next week, I have to fly to Malaysia and apply for an additional two-month visa for Thailand.
In Turkey, they had given me a non-extendable visa. So I have to go out of the country, to go back in with a new visa. It will cost extra, but I want to visit the South and live in the islands there for a while. Phuket and Koh Pee Pee among others, where the waters and corals are said to be among the most beautiful in the world.

Last night I renewed with my old friends, Mr Beer, Mr Pool and Miss Cigarette. Good evening. We get along well, all together. I'm really playing better and better. Miss Masturbate didn't come to see me afterwards.

17. End of Thai massages

Saturday: got up late, it feels good. Gargantuan lunch in a restaurant that makes special cakes, like banana or lychee cakes, then a walk in the afternoon, and in the evening we go again to the pool table, Thai boxing and sound system for deaf people. I have to spend less from now on. I eat a bit too much European food, and it's costing me a lot of money. I buy sunglasses, rolling tobacco and another pair of silk pants. The glasses were 280 baths, I got them for 100, the trousers were 350 baths and I paid 200. They still have quite a margin!

Sunday: Everything is going well. I dreamt that I was giving massages to all the staff of my former employer. Every morning when I wake up, I do some visualization exercises. I perform a full body massage to one person, accelerated of course, to memorize the order and logic of the figures and limbs to be massaged. For the upper body alone, arms, legs, stomach, head, there are more than 63 figures and sequences of massage. So the hardest part is to remember everything. But with this technique, morning and night, I can remember everything and anchor it in my brain.

As usual, the weather is fine! I learned that there were terrible floods in Paris, I read an English newspaper to see the temperatures, I felt cold just by opening the page for Europe. That was enough for me. Here, it's the end of winter; outside, it's a little warmer every day, maybe 28° to 30° during the day, and 18° to 20° at night. European summer.

Wake up around 11 am, I have lunch next door, at the "Lamchang Guesthouse" where I stayed ten days the first time. There is a small garden, trees, a hammock, and the lunch is more successful than at my current residence. I am waiting for a German girl who is taking classes with me, to go to the zoo by bike, a little outside the city.

One thing I like about Thai people is their nonchalance, their casualness, wherever they are. I like this way of not giving importance to their behavior and attitudes in society. They are in flip-flops, in sandals, anywhere and anytime, and in the evening in the bars you see the tourists in jeans, Lacoste polo shirt tucked into their trousers and shoes when the others are in sandals and simple t-shirts! The difference is striking between those who complicate their lives by a whole network of obstructions and restraints towards others, of long and complex protocols, and those who don't give a damn about all that.
It makes you think. For me it's easy, I feel so good in my cotton or silk pants, I just put on a t-shirt, one of those pants, and my sandals. Lightweight, perfect.

We went to visit the Chiang Mai Zoo, which is actually a

mountain next to the city with enclosures for the animals. It's sad, we walked ten kilometers, and biked ten kilometers to get there, for not much. In short, we come back exhausted!

Monday: back to work. Second week of learning. New faces, those who start. I feel like sleeping today, soft, gelatinous, sluggish, brain swollen... That's
all. Pool table in the evening.

The next day: progress in the art of massage. In the evening, I am massaged by a teacher, and it is effective! I feel new, fresh and perfectly calm and awake.

Second time I've had the shits. I don't know if it's because of the massage that caused an acceleration of the photon-intestinal particles by having reactivated all the energies down there... Maybe. Anyway, it's growing strong...

Wednesday: I buy the plane ticket Bangkok-Penang, for Malaysia. 5 050 baths. Oops! I allow myself to fly only because I have worked hard during the last two weeks.
I'm a bit tired of this city. I can't wait to finish this course and get moving. On the other hand, I'm in great shape!

Important decision today: the chance of this incredible force called Life and its synchronicities made me, for the second time, meet people who tell me about this Buddhist monastery which proposes courses for foreigners, eleven days of meditation and harmonization with nature.
I think this is a sign that persists, I must go there.
I don't mind, because when I went down to Bangkok to go to Koh Samui, I had already met a guy who had told me about it,

and I was excited about it.

You bet, an experience like that is for me! Eleven days without a word? In total silence. Silence made of smiles and looks. Learning to meditate, to put myself on the same level as nature, to listen to the rain or to watch an ant live? Of course it's for me!

Buddhists are different in that they include in their values humans, animals, plants and non-living things or minerals. And all are their friends, all are connected. This is exactly the relationship that I understand of the union of all that lives in our Universe and the interconnection of all that vibrates.

I read a little booklet explaining this course, and it's the kind of thing I like to do to explore or push my own boundaries, forget my ego, push myself a little.

So yes, I'll do it.

Early February: in the meantime, we finished learning about Thai massage. We have seen the top of the body, the legs, the two sides with the arms, the back and the head, and the sitting position to finish. Now I have to ingest, digest, sort and spit out the unnecessary, to give birth to my beautiful personal massage scheme, which I will apply.

Last evenings when I have fun playing pool against high level people. It's great when you start to get good! I'm also starting to smoke less, I'm sick of smoking just to keep myself busy in the evening. The same goes for beer, I haven't drunk much of it in the evening for two weeks now. In fact, apart from the places where there are constant parties like in Koh Samui, I don't feel like drinking. I naturally adapt to my environment.

In short, it is not good for me to stay too long in party places, that's all.

Friday, last day of classes: phew! That's it.

It's hard today because I work and massage all day a guy, an American, who is certainly great at milking a cow with his hands, but as far as vibrations are concerned, I don't like his energy, too fast and he doesn't have the sensual and animal touch. Sweaty hands, no feeling...

I wash myself well afterwards because, by touching people, they leave me their vibrations, their negative or positive energetic imprints, especially in their hands and arms. We all received our diploma, 60 hours of practice for me. Hugs, photos, and goodbye!

Time to move on.

I am looking forward to the next part of my program: Malaysia for a week, hopefully with Sophie, and the next two weeks in this monastery.

Not bad! I love my life.

Tonight I'm having dinner with this Canadian couple. They are coming back from the North and have done my itinerary. They are very nice and I have a good feeling with them. Normal, they have three sons of my age. We eat Italian food, mamma mia... Great evening. They are really people full of sensitivity and finesse. I'll see them again in Toronto, if I'm ever there.

Chiang Mai airport: the primitive behavior of some Europeans is really starting to get on my nerves. Like this idiot Englishman in a hurry, who is passed by an old Thai man he had pushed a little earlier, and to whom he makes a scene. What a jerk! I hate holidaymakers, credit card in their pocket, who go to another country with their habits thinking that it's up to the others to adapt to them. A good life lesson on the right brain of Europeans and the left brain of Asians. I love it. Everything is reversed. And witnessing this kind of scene makes me think that it's good to change brains. For example, to lose your temper and start yelling is to be strong for a Westerner, but it is the opposite for an Asian because, in his eyes, the angry person will have lost his control and will be considered weak. This is also observed in Thai boxing, where the person who gets angry in the ring will make the audience laugh.

Bangkok airport, two hours later: pleasant flight, full plane, beautiful weather.
This airport is a bit complicated. You have to change building for international flights, go up to the third one for check-in, pass a lot of metal barriers. Moreover, I do not know why, everything is expensive in the cafeterias, to make my shaved hair stand up. My coffees and orange juice this morning are the equivalent of a night in a pension. I'm paying six times as much for my share of watermelon! Why is that?
 Funny, on the electronic bulletin board, no European city. Ho-Chin-Minh, Saigon, Peking, Phnom-Penh, Penang, Singapore... What exoticism under these names! All these cities I don't know yet...

The government will take drastic measures to curb the traffic problem in Bangkok. In the newspapers, they talk about private car and bicycle days. This is really a worldwide problem...

18. Discomfort in Malaysia

An hour and a half by plane later. Seen from above, it is much greener and denser in vegetation.
Airport, first contact with the Malays.
Here come the veiled women without smiling. Shit, I didn't miss that! Yes, Malaysia is Muslim.
Taxi to the hotel where I have an appointment with Sophie.
Shit! She's not there.
I take a room anyway. Expensive...

It is much more modern than Thailand, the buildings, the streets are better organized, no noisy tuktuks. The most striking thing is the Chinese. They are everywhere. I read that they own the streets and the businesses, the politics being left to the Malays. The culture is Hindu or Chinese. Everywhere the inscriptions are in Chinese, the food is Indian, the transporters on their rickshaws *(three-wheeled bicycles)* are Indian, in the street the people are black and the Chinese are white. Or yellow. And I'm a little tanned. I'm in the tourist district, it's convenient for information, travel agencies and food. The houses are old, haven't changed for at least 100 years. My room must be at least eight meters high, with an old yellowed fan on the ceiling. Colonial style, except it's not made of wood.

No smiles on the street. We are bathed in Islam, with the return of the mosques and the muezzin five times a day. The Chinese are too busy trading to smile.

Ahhhh... Thailand, where are you?

I weighed myself, I lost four kilos.

I ate twice tonight, to compensate. Indian, curry rice with vegetables and mutton, and Chinese soup with fish presented, horror, the head cut in two! The dogs of the neighborhood came to feast in my place...

Everywhere old Chinese, in the halls of hotels or in the streets, in white camisole or bare-chested. Not the same notion of embarrassment or restraint towards others, they don't bother with these typically European considerations...

I hope Sophie will come tomorrow!

I think back to Thailand, where if you have a mole with hair on it, it's a sign of good luck... so they let it grow. In Europe, we rush to the surgeon to have it removed, too much shame! Sometimes, I feel weird talking to someone who has a big mole with ten centimeters of thick hair on it, I can't help but look at him, praying not to laugh...

And all over the place too, these lizards, on all the walls. One even fell into a simmering pot when I was eating Indian food, and it startled the cook, who quickly backed away, wondering what could have fallen from the ceiling. He came out alive. Scalded, but alive...

In my room tonight, a surprise guest. A cockroach of at least six centimeters long, a monster! I can't squash it, because first I start following the Buddhist precepts of not killing anything alive, and then if I squash it I'll splatter the room and my flip-flops with its horrible putrid juice. I don't want to clean up afterwards. But of "it" I could never make a friend!

Quickly find a pan or a colander, then take a sheet of paper or a newspaper. Find the insect and hope it hasn't run away, slam the bowl down on it with a sure hand, then respectfully slide the sheet under the colander without breaking its fragile legs, and turn it over and hope it holds up, that the hand is large enough to cover the width of the container, and run to the window to throw it out with a loud cry of relief, hoping the thing doesn't stay at the bottom of the pan. The same respectful approach to insects applies to the dreadful spiders that sometimes haunt my nightmares. Well, I have to, I can't kill them...

Sophie arrived. I was meditating. Great.

"Hi, how are you? What were you doing?" Food night, we are both tired.

The next day, we rented a scooter and went to Penang Mountain, a tourist attraction. Cable car up to 700 meters. Impressive view. But once up there, not much to do. It's cooler, that's something. We go back down to see the temple of snakes, the second biggest attraction in Penang. Talk about a joke! Not a single snake, but lots of tourists, there were! Fortunately the entrance was not paying.

After two days here, something bothers me, not to say "pisses me off". It is the inhospitality of the people. Especially the Chinese! They are rough. In the restaurant, it's "sit down", without even a "please". Everywhere we are spoken to like dogs. At first, my sensitivity made me react violently, now I slip "assholes" or "dickheads" into my sentences with a smile to all those who are not friendly. It helps me cope with my first contact with Chinese communism/Confucianism. Anyway, they don't get it and don't care about us. We are just dollars on wheels. So, for me it's "Hey, what do you want asshole? We're not going to let this happen, are we?

When I think of Thailand, I realize that Buddhism is really a philosophy of total freedom for everyone, reconciling the harmony of the being with Nature and the Universe. Perhaps that is why everyone is happy to live there and smiles with kindness and friendliness.
What a difference with the Muslims who may have the sun in their hearts but keep it to themselves. In the streets, they are serious and concentrated, the vertical line between the eyebrows on all the faces shows a concentration without any possible bullshit, and the welcome is felt. Like a world without sensitivity, and little gentleness.
For the Chinese, communism does not allow fantasy and personality development since everyone is modelled on the same model. Perhaps that is why they seem sad and distant. As far as business is concerned, they will be the masters of the world because of their seriousness and their business sense. But let them leave tourism to others!
Well, I'm going to go and eat outside, to see the assholes with Sophie.

Tuesday: in the end it turns out that only the Chinese are not nice. The Malays are pretty cool.

We go to the north of the island by motorbike. Discover the beaches and the place where I can stay until Saturday. The beaches are not as beautiful as in Thailand, not as clean and especially here, it is lined with luxury hotels. Big chains have settled there and, in the lush vegetation, huge modern hotels stand out.

Anyway, until Saturday I'm going to the beach, it's cheaper and I like it.

Sophie left by bus, towards Kuala Lumpur. She's a good girl, strong, romantic, a bit stuck up with her London manners. She irritated me a bit, but I like her. I have her address in Brazil but I don't know how long it will take to see her again.

Here I am, alone again, my head full of projects, I have my passport with two new months for Thailand, my train ticket to Surat Thani for Saturday, I just have to enjoy my stay here, preparing my mind for this renewal, this experience of the next week.

Another subject since I'm in a hurry to write: traffic.

Here, I think it's worse than in Thailand. People overtake on the left, on the right, they forget the intersections, they go in all directions and like in Thailand, it's full of mopeds. The people ride two wheels. Models that we don't have in Europe. And what a pity, because they are great! Four automatic gears, it's small, it doesn't consume anything. Some of them make a hell of a noise. I have to take some street pictures because it's amazing to see all these houses on two floors, with these Chinese signs. I'm in the old Chinatown.

Full moon tomorrow. Everything here is about 20% more expensive than in Thailand. Where it hurts is for the rooms in

guesthouses or hotels, because I can't do without them.
Food, I can always eat cheap. But sleeping on the beach, that's not done here, and secondly, for the last two or three months I've gotten used to sleeping indoors for cheap, so I'm still going.

I move to Batu Ferringhi, the big and beautiful beach west of Penang.
In fact, between all the hotels that have rooms for the equivalent of $ 50 minimum, there are a few pensions in which I got a room after hard negotiations, certainly the cheapest on the island. Okay, it's not called a room but a cubbyhole. One window, no light, but alone, I don't need more. I pay $5 a day. Well, for the eight hours I sleep there.
The beach during the day is completely different from what you see at dusk, when the natives go for a dip, sometimes dressed from head to toe. There are kids playing, it's very colorful, the light is soft. This time of day is truly divine.
This is the moment I choose to go jogging. It's been a long time. It feels good to have my body running like a Formula 1 car when I'm pushing it hard. I've always loved running on beaches around the world, it's a blessing, I feel so free and happy. Moreover, while running, the horse - I mean, the stallion! - that is in me, shudders with its nostrils and runs to lose its breath.
In the evening, visit of the main street and the luxury hotels and restaurants.
At the entrance of a restaurant specializing in seafood are dozens of transparent aquariums, not very large, each containing dozens of crustaceans and fish fighting for their survival by swimming in their excrement. Sad to see. In front of the lobsters, shrimps, sea snakes, small and big fishes, people walk around and ask the guy

in charge of the collection to bring them the one they have chosen, pointing at the unfortunate one who is living his last seconds. After spending several days in its glass coffin, it will end up being scalded for the pleasure of an ogre who will have taken its life for a paper bill.

I suffer in front of these fish and crustaceans, I can hear their cries and moans.

I wonder if I will end up a vegetarian...

I didn't know it yet, little worm that I was at that time, that I would become one later on.

Unfortunately, I had this revelation about food and what I was feeding my body late in life. But more than that, was the food I was feeding my body in harmony with my philosophy, my love of animals and my conscience? No, it was not, because I have always been a friend of animals, and I kept eating them, dead. Eating their corpses once they were dead. Something we would never do in the wild, we are not scavengers after all! Well, yes.

The System doesn't want to show us this way, but the meat, dairy or other lobbies, such as hunting, have always given us beautiful images so that we don't see animals suffering, so that we see happy cows dancing while producing their milk, pink pigs full of joy, and the same goes for rabbits and chickens, so happy to be in such a bright and welcoming henhouse! Of course, afterwards we don't really see the animals objectively, nor their living conditions and especially their end of life. I, who grew up on a farm with every animal imaginable, know the almost perfect conditions for them...

The Matrix-System wants us to consume meat to feed its chains, to drink milk to fatten the bosses and shareholders of the factories that produce it, it consciously misleads us so that we imagine that drinking milk in large quantities would give us strong teeth and that we would be strong forever, thanks to the calcium it contains. What a mistake!

The Matrix also wants us to be sick, because on the other side is a greedy, money-hungry financial world of ours. The hospital world, the doctors, the pharmacists and, of course, the Big-Pharma monster which is an ogre with ferocious and merciless appetites.

So no, nothing will come from the Matrix, I am well aware of that, it is up to us to wake up and change our prejudices!
Just turn off the TV, and everything is fine, everything goes back to normal.
Personally, I haven't watched TV for more than 10 years now.
So, it took me 40 years to finally open my eyes, remove my blinders and see things a little more clearly, and be more in line with my philosophy of life.

I no longer want to eat the meat of dead bodies, especially when it comes to lambs, pigs, quails, pigeons, chickens and roosters, pretty ducks or turkeys, and what can I say about the little calf that is quickly taken away from its mother and that cries real tears...
No, fortunately my daughters pushed the envelope far enough for me to follow them and to become a convinced vegetarian in my turn.
And happier than before, because not only do I have no more inflammations in my body, but I feel much better spiritually because I am more in tune with my conscience.

And I hope that the consciences will wake up on Earth and that we will put an end to these monstrous egregores of sufferings which stagnate above us. Because, whether we know it or not, it is a fact. The energies of the animal sufferings join together forming a kind of terrible dark clouds around the Earth, and this influences the

healthy radiation which should normally circulate there and influence us.
This has no business being in the Aquarian age.
It keeps us from evolving and keeps us in low vibrations.

This morning tai chi on the beach with the sailors who leave at dawn for their fishing day. What calm, beautiful feeling of renewal. The birth of a new day... It is night and I see this red globe slowly rising and the light embracing the sky.
The evening air is soft and caressing. All the children are there, playing with a pebble here, splashing with water there, laughing, shouting, running. The fishermen prepare their nets under the tenderized eye of the cats, the left eye, because the right one watches on the other side the hens and the roosters which go everywhere in freedom, even on the beaches. We also see beautiful horses, ridden by riders for the evening ride. Everybody is walking around, Muslims in djellaba, tourists, Malays, horses, hens, watched over by cats, who must still miss their tails that they must have lost when they were young because none of them has one! No swing to jump, strange... what are the mummies doing with their cubs?

At noon, I share my meal with one of these cats to whom I give pieces of beef, and with a hen to whom I give rice. It's the first time I've ever fed a chicken in a restaurant!
Suddenly, she attacks the cat who is thrown off the terrace. "Oh but, it is that one does not make it to me!", she cackles with contempt for the feline.

What a day! It's terribly hot, it's a furnace. It's not possible to stay more than thirty minutes in the sun. It is cruel. So everyone mingles in the shade of the few trees around.

The atmosphere in the guesthouse, which is in fact a fairly well made arrangement of corrugated iron sheets and cheap partitions, is not like the other guesthouses. Here, a lot of tired old backpackers, some broken faces, some good-looking tourists, some young people, it's quite mixed. The partitions between the rooms and the toilets are so thin that guess what? Not only can you hear all the grunts, farts, hummm, oohhh and ahhh, and in the toilets, I won't even explain the holes there are, because man being what he is, whether he is Muslim or Buddhist, when there is a beautiful girl next to him in the showers and there are holes in the partition... It is better that this partition is clean, otherwise the voyeur will come out of the shower with a grey circle around his eye, and that can be embarrassing...

I eat beef sautéed with bamboo and black mushrooms, excellent, while waiting for the storm that is coming.
With all this, to add to the omnipresent exoticism, the singing of the muezzin from the minaret. It's really great. The Muslims wash themselves with buckets of water that they pour over their heads. Always this religious purification.

An important fact here, and one that reminds me that I crossed the border, people are fat. Not obese like some Americans, but fat, even more so. The women especially. Coming out of Thailand, it's shocking. Over there the national sport is boxing, so everyone keeps themselves trim more or less, and they are thin by nature. Here, they are rather square. Not all of them, the old

Chinese are like 150 year old scrolls, almost fossils and still full of life as they ride their bikes.

Saturday: it's time to leave. I've met some nice people here in the guesthouse, including a very charming girl, but our destinies are separating. That's life, our lives.

I got stung or burned by a fish yesterday. There are signs on the beach saying "beware of *jelly* fish", but up until now I'd only seen tiny ones on the surface and they'd brush past me, so I'd be startled as they'd swim past me, anxious or scared depending on my imagination, and then I'd laugh. But this time it must have been a big one that swam underneath and must have grazed me. They have poison on their filaments.
I think I'm going to have to have my leg cut off...
unless I just put a plaster on it.

Sunday 30 January: As I go to press, I've had two really emotional days. Yesterday morning, I'm still in Malaysia. After a few hours on the train because of the infernal noise of the rails and a change of train at the Thai border, I meet two interesting girls that I hope to see again. The train deposits us in Surat Thanit around 11 o'clock in the evening. All the hotels are either full or closed, or the guys don't want to work. So we find ourselves like two idiots, an Italian and me, on the street. Tired from the train, irritated by carrying our heavy backpacks, we pass by a temple and decide to sleep there, outside, rightly thinking that anyone can enter and sleep in a Buddhist temple. It's dark and we don't really know where we are. It's just a temple compound. There's a dimly lit plaza, we settle down, and sleep.
Two minutes later, there are too many mosquitoes. I have to put

up the mosquito net. Okay. I try to sleep again. A racket! A racket! The hell. Of course we were behind a wall that led to an expressway, where motorcycles and trucks were running at full speed. On top of that, some guy must have had problems with his engine and was running it for tests, like full throttle. Bad luck, right under our noses, at midnight.

Ok, we move again. A little further, on a bench, the noise reduced, we try to sleep again. Mosquitoes are definitely merciless. And I can't stand to hear the high-pitched "zzzziiiiuzziiiuzz" of these creatures near my ear. It drives me crazy. As a result, around three in the morning, after having turned my bag inside out to get my raincoat - while fighting against these bugs that were attacking me - I find myself in socks, training pants and a raincoat, with my hood turned upside down and tightened all the way over my face, so that there's only a hole in the middle for my mouth and nose. After being bitten on my lower lip, I decide to sleep with the mosquito net rolled up in a ball on my face, and I can finally sleep for two hours, suffocating, but protected from mosquitoes. I can't stand them anymore!

I wake up with my lumbar vertebrae screaming for mercy, separate from my companion of misfortune for the night, apply ointment to my pimples and leave for the bus station.

Imagine the state: creepy, bloated, tired, oozing, irritated, weak...

Bus to the meditation temple, about 30 km into the jungle.

19. Monastery Retreat

I arrive at the temple. In fact, a private property, a natural reserve, a huge forest. Divided in two, a part for Thai, and the other for foreigners.
Reception. I am shown the men's dormitories where I will stay until tomorrow, and then go to the second part, the one for foreigners. Immediately, I fall asleep, to wake up at noon and go eat.
In another corner stands a house, with a group of tables and chairs, and already a column of people helping themselves to the pots. About fifteen men and twenty women. The food is wonderful. Vegetarian, of course.

Vegetarianism: When you think that the animals that contain the most meat and muscle only eat grass! And we eat these animals thinking that, to gain muscle, we must eat another muscle, meat... Poor us, what blindness, what limitations, what children! How could we lose our common sense in front of our televisions, blinded as we are by those beautiful commercials that have brainwashed us!

I always think of the other civilizations that are watching us from space.

To them, we must really be reckless children, because we are doing something very wrong. No birth control on the planet, as if it could feed billions of people indefinitely, we treat other forms of life with disdain and disrespect, we enslave the fauna and flora according to our needs, as if the Gods were us...
How childish and unevolved we are!

I hate our crooked, and mostly corrupt, leaders!

For my part, it is clear that we don't need to kill animals to live, they are here on their land too and participate more than we think in its balance.
It's about time people took off their blinders and looked at food in a different, more reasonable and sensible way.
We have omnivorous teeth, we should mainly eat fruits and vegetables, our canines are relics of our prehistoric past when we were only great apes without brains. Now that we have evolved, it's time to move on to something else in respect of all animal and plant life. Besides, some great sportsmen testify of their only vegetal food and they would be much more listened as models if there were not continuously the lobbies which push to the consumption, so that we swallow always more their denatured industrial food which we do not need and which harms our bodies, making us become obese.

But why don't we still have a council of true sages to rule the planet, like we see in science fiction movies? When? How much longer to wait for this global wisdom?
When everything is ready to be lost? Or when there is no more money on Earth?

Will I live my next incarnation on an empty, burnt, dry land, without
any animal except a few scorpions?
Well, not much of a program...

Introduction with a little prayer, said by a monk, I did not
understand anything, and everybody eats in silence. Then, the
people disperse, free quarters, because the course does not start
until tomorrow. We visit the place quietly and go for a walk in the
forest. There are specimens of spiders, ouaahhh... as big as the
palm of my hand! Widows, I'll know later.
And I also see a snake, I do not know what else, which hides
when I pass by. Yep, that's promising!
Super cool afternoon, writing, reading, with the eternal chickens
in the distance, the birds, the rustling of the leaves in the wind,
the flies, and some nonchalant cats and dogs in the background.
How nice, how quiet. Finally!
Another nap until 6pm, then a small snack of soy milk and
bananas. Still in this strange atmosphere, people don't know if
they can talk or not. We look at each other funny, with questions
in our eyes. Average age, I would say 30 years old. There's
everything. I don't know if there are any couples, because the
women keep away from the men. There's a sense of maturity in
the group, no one is there to break the rules, which will certainly
be unusual.

There are insects on the trees that sound like crickets, but ten
times as loud. When I was sleeping this afternoon, I could hear
the sound of a sawmill, or a metal cutter. In addition, across the
street from the dormitory is a hut in which some monks were

doing work this morning. And in my half-sleep I was thinking, "Boy, some worker forgot to turn off his machine! Can somebody go and turn it off," because the noise was so loud. I had to go out to the foot of the trees to realize that the noise was coming from their tops. It was a hell of a noise. There are thousands of them! I hope these insects sleep at night!

On my way back from the snack, I pass by a small park where there are always many chickens and dogs. I stop to watch them, sit down, and after a while I see three puppies, big playful puppies, running after a hen. As the hen weakens, they grab her and start playing with her limp body, nibbling her wing, grabbing her by the neck, throwing her in the air... I think it's funny. For a moment. But those stupid dogs won't stop, they'll kill her...
So what
?
Hey hey... Philippe arrived ! ...just in time to save what's left of the half-conscious, half-bewildered, half-shattered hen and put her on a tree three feet high, so that she can get healthy and beautiful again!
They were going to kill her playing those dogs!

First lesson this evening: around 7pm, everyone goes to the big "hall of meditation". It's night, we hear some bird and insect noises, it's hot and humid, many shadows are quietly converging towards the place. A large room, completely open, with candles in the background and people sitting in the middle, with corridors on each side. A feeling of serenity and peace. We listen to a tape. It is a monk who speaks in a little negro English, very easy to understand. "*You have to be able to stop running, to say to yourself I have arrived, no need to run anymore. Just feel yourself in the present, here and now*. Repeat this to yourself with each breath.

Walk too. Each step must be a communion with the earth. Feel it under your feet. To feel like a foot massage when we walk, especially barefoot. Walk with love for our earth. Evening lesson. Back to the hut and sleep.

The next day: now the serious things will begin. We move to the second monastery, three kilometers from the first. It is a huge estate, populated with coconut trees and strange buildings. In fact, it's a sort of convent for men, and another for women. Convent, because it is the impression I get so austere, with the shape of the building, rooms around water basins and a huge lawn in the middle, as big as a football field. A kind of closed hotel where each room is identical, three meters by three, no bed, a blanket, a mosquito net and a kind of concrete surmounting for sleeping, with a 3 cm thick straw mattress. A simple wooden door, and small openings at the top of the room with no windows giving onto the outside of the compound. In the middle, this large lawn.

Two other important buildings. The meditation hall, where everyone has taken a fixed place and put cushions on it that they will keep throughout the seminar, to settle into the lotus position - well... if the flexibility of the members allows it - and the kitchen, which is an open house where people sit on the floor to eat, women on one side and men on the other, face to face.

The instructions were given, the registration fee paid, 600 baths (about $35) for the eleven days of food. It is good, by the way, I am pleasantly surprised. Rice, two vegetables, one of which is made with Indian sauce, and a fruit. Drinks: tea or soy milk. Coffee with soy milk too.

The meal schedule: 8 am, 12:30 pm, and nothing more until 6 pm when bananas and soy milk are served. That's it. I can take as much as I want, so that's fine. I can put my initial apprehensions about food to rest.

This evening, introduction by the monk in charge, and initiation to meditation.

I put here in this book the concept of past lives.
For the Buddhists it is the basis of their philosophy. For the Hindus too. So are some other dogmas that would lead one to believe that the souls of the ancients have returned in trees, flowers, animals or spirits.
The Christians could have believed in it if the church - the very dear Holy Church - had not, around 800 AD, voluntarily erased this concept from the Great Book, the better to keep all its lost sheep under its insidious control...
For my part I strongly believe in it and I created the basis of my new life on this concept. The immortality of my soul, which, from life to life, can experience and collect emotions in the form of energies, and learn at best what our beautiful planet can allow us to record, because of its dense matter.
Sometimes I was a man, sometimes a woman. And very often I found myself in the same group of souls in order to settle past karmas, or to create new ones.
Here is a little briefing.

Therefore, the scenes of "but, I've seen this somewhere before...", or "I've been here before...", make sense, if we've already lived in a place, or hung out with a person who seems familiar at first sight. Because that's how it is, at least in my opinion.

I think I have already lived dozens of lives on Earth, in different times, among the Atlanteans, the Egyptians, the Romans, various barbarians in crusade, I have already died on many battlefields following Genghis Khan, Alexander the Great, Caesar or Napoleon. Like many of us, moreover...
We are all more or less dead on various battlefields, with arrows or spears still stuck in our etheric bodies.
The Essenes are good at removing this from us.

I know this because I have been in contact for a long time with the great family of light that are the Essenes, these therapists/healers who heal by sounds and chakra rebalancing. They are used to reading auras and the thought-forms that are sometimes attached to them.
If, for example, we have a powerful experience in this life, the same emotion experienced in another life under the same circumstances, can revive the memories experienced at that time, reminding us of the sensory environment and elements of that past life.

So there was a time in my life as a father when I was very adamant with my daughters, telling them over and over again that "this is the way it is, and nothing else". And of course, I felt guilty afterwards, calling myself names, because I loved my little fleas deeply and didn't understand why I was treating them that way. In fact, I had recreated a sensory set with targeted and recurring emotions, which thus triggered emotional reminiscences of the same experience in another life. I knew this because I went to see an Essene therapist, whom I was in contact with, with my wife at the time, to talk to her about this feeling of guilt that I felt every time I yelled at my daughters, and I felt that it was not mine. So I went to see her, and as I entered her office she said at once, "It wasn't you I saw come in, it was a Manchu notable, with a long heavy colored silk robe, and this notable was in a state of confusion because he was known to make irreversible decisions and to be intransigent. They had already tried to kill him, he was into politics, etc...". Wow...

As she tells me the story, I feel the particular haircut of the Manchurian men, I also feel the weight of this ceremonial dress, and everything she tells me at the time speaks to me... Placebo effect or not, so I would have created in this present life a series of emotions that strongly coincide with the same emotional sequences experienced in this life in Manchuria, hundreds of years ago.

 From then on, the fact of becoming aware of it allowed me day after day to get rid of this thought-form clinging to my aura, and which influenced my life without my knowledge. It left me quickly.

Thus I learned during ten years of follow-ups and internships among the Essenes, and thanks to my wife who was also a light therapist, that she and I had lived together several times, in various family and karmic relationships, in various places on Earth.

We had been lovers in a life in Madrid, brother and sister in a life in Tibet, suffering a lot from cold and lack (which makes, among other things, that in this life I am irresistibly attracted by heat and tropical countries, and that I like very much to have fun with my senses and to please myself...), we also rubbed shoulders during the French Revolution at the end of the 18ème century, during which time I was a writer (and as luck would have it, in this life, I was always the only one in the family with an innate sense of writing).

In all those lives together - and I'm sure there were more - this woman and I were never married, and we never procreated together.

So that's what we did in this lifetime: with two beautiful children in the process.

The groups of souls almost always reincarnate together to find each other, to repair, to free themselves from the karmas created together, and to lighten themselves etherically so that they do not have to reincarnate on a dense planet like the Earth, in order to continue to ascend higher and higher in the radiant spheres of the kingdom of Light.

Then, I imagine that we will be reincarnated on another less dense planet to continue to dance from life to life, learning and improving ourselves more and more, until we don't need it anymore...
These are my beliefs, shared by Buddhists.
Our experiences charged with strong emotions are engraved in our consciousness, and we can find them or feel them in another life, since they are forever in us.

Another obvious example of the energetic charge of past lives on our present life: In this life I have often been to Spain, and every time - don't ask me why - I feel at home. This has been the case since I was 20 years old, when I went there for the first time; I have never felt like a stranger there, I have loved these people from the very first day, and they have returned it to me well.
Another example: since my early childhood, I have always been fascinated by stories of shipwrecks, books about shipwrecked men fighting for their lives, Moby Dick and so on, the kind of books I liked to take from the local library and devour afterwards.
Knowing this, one day I read an advertisement from an English professor passing through my town, who was offering past life regression through Ericksonian hypnosis. I called him and made an appointment. I arrive at his house, he makes me lie down on the carpet of the living room, puts me gradually in hypnosis and it starts...
I have to go down the steps of a staircase, which I create in my imagination and visualize it perfectly, as well as the walls which

surround me. I must then progress in the darkness and go down the steps. After a while, he asks me to stop in front of a door, to observe its hinges, the texture of the wood, its handle, and when I am ready... to open it. I'm ready, and I open it.

BAM... I'm suspended high on ropes between masts, standing about 50 feet above the deck of a large wooden ship, facing out to sea. I feel the sun on me, the wind from the sea, all the hairs on my arms stand up, I am in joy, I know it is me, I am young and Spanish. He asks me what year it is. I say, "1618.

It turns out that it is the period of the conquistadors, a lot of ships were launched during the years by Spain to go and conquer new lands, and I am convinced that I was one of them, the same skilled discoverer that I am in this life, it is obvious to me. Like all those books I read about shipwrecks, my inexplicable love for Spain and its people. For the sea too. This plus that, it is so clear to me that I have lived those lives and that they have enriched me and left powerful emotional reminiscences.

In fact, I tie boat knots without worrying about them, and without ever having studied them. Weird, isn't it?

Come on, one last example for the road: I was once told that I had been a gladiator trainer in Roman times. Ok, it can make you laugh, why not?

Except that before that, I must have seen Ridley Scott's movie "Gladiator"

at least twenty times, always with passion, and that I spent at least fifteen years of my life learning to fight, at the highest level since I finished black belt 2ème Dan in karate, then later started Thai boxing and finished my career at the French national level.

So I say to myself that .... why not... there are too many coherences with my current life for me to ignore these ideas, this concept.

For those who are curious, I advise you to do an Essene treatment once in your life, with a therapist, which you can easily find on the Internet. There is bound to be one in your city.
I am sure that it could already bring you a great well-being to have your chakras balanced again, and perhaps also rare answers to your intimate questionings about your deepest identity.

Wednesday: already the second day of the course, the third in the monastery.

Life, for everyone, takes its rhythm. We get up at 4 a.m., are awakened by a gong that rings for ten minutes, less and less loud, very pleasant to hear, and we all go in silence to the meditation hall. First, a reading. A girl, appointed on the first day, reads to us for thirty minutes. It's hard not to fall back asleep, but that's not why I'm here. It's about various aspects of "how we should live to live better". Outside, it's tropical night, there's a moon, it's 5am. Then meditation for 45 minutes. Here it gets more complicated. Concentration on the breathing, always have the same flow, and as soon as an idea or a thought comes, we have to chase it away to come back to our breathing. That's ok. But the posture starts to hurt after twenty minutes in the knees and back. The first day, the neck and shoulders hurt. Then it's okay. We all have various cushions that we can put under our legs, where it hurts. For my part, I adopted the "Japanese sitting" posture, used as I am to the practice of karate. It's starting to work. Above all, when a discomfort arises, you have to let go. The pain is temporary, it is not in us, it does not belong to us. With patience, it goes away. So, relax... You have to learn and stick to it.

After the first 45 minutes of meditation - the last ones are really painful - we do an hour and a half of sport. Yoga is offered, the girls in one building, the men in another. I tried it the first day but I don't like this style of yoga. Those who want to practice freely can. Between the yoga I learned in massage classes, tai chi and karate katas, I have a choice. So I sweat a bit independently on my side.

Then, showering, which is done with the big water tanks, six in all, arranged in the inner enclosure of the men's dormitories, and which collect the rainwater. We dipped a canister and sprayed ourselves.

Every time we have to go and do an exercise or eat, or start again in the early afternoon, the gong calls us to order. So it's simple. As soon as you hear the gong, you have to go.

After the shower at 7am, gong. We meet in the hall. It is one of the senior monks who speaks on the microphone. He teaches us how to breathe, to meditate, to reject the ideas which interfere in our mind, this during thirty minutes. Then, "walking meditation", or active meditation while walking. Everyone spreads out in the palm grove, and walks, cool, relaxed, even a bit in zombie mode. If you watch the group from far, it can be scary... It's to relax from the sitting position, and meditate on what has just been said, by concentrating on the breathing.

Gong: 8 o'clock. Breakfast time. Everyone goes to the refectory. We serve ourselves, in line, women on one side and men on the other. When everyone is served, a guy says a prayer to thank the Earth. The guy is from the room next to me, and is a confirmed farting maniac, damn the farts he releases! Well ok, I'm not going to shout it out loud...

An hour and a half then to eat and go about our business. Gong. 9:30 am. Back to the meditation hall. Everybody in his place and here we go again for the speech of one of the monks on the "dharma" or the law of all nature. Then, sitting meditation, then walking and that leads us to 12:30 where the saving gong comes to deliver us for 90 minutes.

Lunch.

2pm: gong for ten minutes.

This is necessary because everyone is deeply asleep.

It's very hot and it's hard to get out of the mosquito net. How good I felt!

Back to the meditation hall.

The afternoon, until 6pm, is structured with sitting and walking meditations, and a speech to gradually take us forward.

At 6pm, after the famous gong, it is time for chanting.

Songs in Sanskrit, the ancient Indian script, that we all recite together under the direction of an old monk, as wrinkled as what he holds in his hands, and who has a fantastically melodious and pure voice. Then comes the English translation which everyone recites together.

Gong at 6:30.

I can do whatever I want. Break bread with bananas and soy milk, or tea. I can also go to the thermal baths. In the monastery compound, there are two natural hot springs, the water must be at least 50°! It's very difficult to get in. I go there if I want, otherwise, I have free time until 7.30 pm. I can do my laundry, write, whatever I want.

Gong for five minutes.

After each big break, the gong lasts a long time.

From 8 to 9 pm, sitting meditation in the hall.

9 pm, sleep. Everyone is a mess.

In fact, we sit in one position without moving, with our spine as straight as possible, keeping our concentration, for eight hours a day. Plus another eight hours of meditation while moving.
I can't wait a few days, when my muscles, bones and tendons will be used to this treatment.
 For us Westerners, this is not easy. We are used to sitting on chairs.

20. Buddhist teachings

Dogmas on Earth, and how to break free from them.

I grew up in a Catholic family... well, Catholic was just a vague term because no one was really practicing. My mother forced herself to go to church on Sunday, more to see and be seen.
My mother's confused and distorted perceptions.
So I stupidly participated in more or less idiotic protocols, in which I was dressed like a beggar, wearing this silly burlap outfit and a string around my waist - like Christ's son going shopping - for the big, beautiful first confirmation parade. Most of the family was there idolizing me, unless it was more for the fact that they could once again get drunk after the ceremony and eat their hearts out.
So I concur. What? I don't know, but it's called "confirmation".
Vows of fidelity to the Church I suppose, and especially a call for generosity during the collection in the ranks.
To this day, there are still beautiful photos of me holding a candle, looking sheepish and distraught, smiling stupidly at the delirious family. I also received a bracelet that was supposed to make me a man (!?), the gold necklace that I lost very quickly afterwards, in short... the paraphernalia of the child-puppet who has to follow the

adults in their religious protocol delusions.

As you can see, I grew up with a Christian doctrine according to which, among other things, we didn't eat on Sundays because "the Lord's day" was compulsory... and that allowed my mother to save money on food, and also on clothes because, as a result, I didn't put on weight very quickly...

Brotherhood, hospitality, self-sacrifice, generosity towards others and compassion, on the other hand, were not often seen at home. My mother was too focused on her next suicide and the number of drugs that would allow her to get through the day without throwing herself under a bus, and my stepfather was too absorbed in his role as supreme master at home, doing nothing when he came home in the evening, and above all, not maintaining any intimate relationship with the children under his roof.

You talk about good Christians, damn good morons, yes!

Above all, I could not conceive how a fat bearded man with a good head could look at me between the clouds, and how - if I behaved badly - I could fall into the abyss of incandescent lava of hell, and burn there. It didn't go down well.

I was even forced to take catechism classes after school and, fortunately for me, I never had to suck on anything but candy during those after-school studies.

It must be said that Geneva-la-Prude, in Switzerland, is not known to be a nest of abbots and perverted priests, or of debauchery. They are rather quiet there, thank God!

My spiritual quest was embellished with new sensations and colors when, for the first time in my life, I went to Asia. I immediately felt that things were moving in my head and heart, that empty spaces were being filled with new information that suited me very well, that I understood... The basics of Buddhism.

The concept of reincarnation - voluntarily erased by the Church in 806 - foundation of everything for Buddhists, will have allowed me to apprehend a good number of misunderstandings and I found myself rather quickly with the flat forehead by dint of slamming it, shouting: "Damn, but it is of course! The highlight was my time at the monastery in southern Thailand, and there I really took it hard, but in a good way. Everything was almost full in my head, everything became reasonable, my life took on meaning and I had the impression of understanding a thousand times better what I was doing there, and who I was...

But it is still a dogma with its rigors and protocols, we agree. People like to follow old writings. They venerate old precepts taught thousands of years ago, as if our human sensibilities had not developed and improved, as if we were still living as we did 2,000 years ago for Christians, or 5,000 years ago for Buddhists.

With time, I tell myself that the basis is good, but that it is addressed to people who have little character, or who have not yet found their true Self, their essence, probably not having yet reconnected to their soul, or perhaps not even knowing that they have one...

Because now it's obvious to me: on Earth, people follow paths written by others because their family conforms to them, because their social environment follows them and because, as a child, they were told to do so. Indoctrination of children so malleable. Once they are adults, with this program in their skulls, it is difficult for them to think differently, and they have to hit a wall at 120 km/h to succeed in breaking the patterns, breaking these false beliefs and finding themselves naked. Not an easy task.

I was saved and liberated because I was able to travel and meet spiritual women sometimes. Some I married.
Thanks to my first wife in particular, the mother of my children, I was able to grow in my own way; she allowed me to do so.
She will have opened doors in me which allowed me to dive in my entrails, in my unconsciousness and subconsciousness. We meditated together, we cried a lot, we followed personal and couple development courses, and all this allowed me to realize that I did

216

*not need to follow old protocols invented by others and perpetuated
by men who want to maintain a power over others.*

*Yes, because it's all about power, all these dogmas that play elbows
and try to capture as many people as possible on the human market.
Look at the Vatican - shame on them - sheltering a colossal fortune,
even downright indecent, and having no desire to distribute it. Yet it
would be the Church's place and duty to redistribute it to the poorest
of the poor? For the past 40 years, I have seen French churches
almost empty, sad and grey, filled with depressing music, played by
those old organs that make you want to die rather than be happy.
What is the Vatican doing? It is getting richer and richer. Unless I'm
mistaken, it must be one of the richest countries in the world today.
What a scandal!
Where was and what was the Vatican doing for Christians during
the covid, the wars and the famines in the world in recent years?
Why isn't it playing its part? Unless Christians are idolizing bankers
and real estate investors?*

*But they are not the only ones. Let's look at Daesh: they are waging
war on an oil-rich land between Iraq and Turkey. Why is that?
Because the nerve of propaganda is money! Rich as Croesus now,
they can make great proselytizing videos to attract young people
from all over the world, arm themselves and plan to conquer more
and more new lands belonging to infidels.
Bunch of assholes.
Religions are all about money, power, and unthinking or weak
people.*

*That said, I think we're currently reliving the period of the
Templars, the Cathars, the war between Christians and Muslims.
Not good. Boring.
Back to the medieval era...*

*Personally, and to close this chapter, I had the chance to go out of
my body twice recently, astral trips, as they are called. Not for long,*

as I am still a youngster who is starting out in this field, so I have not really been able to take advantage of them, but I have seen and felt enough to know that the other life, the one after, in the light and divine energy, is waiting for me again, as well as all those I love and have always loved; they will be there to welcome me at the exit of the tunnel of light, when my turn comes, and I am looking forward to it!

We don't need to be told where to go, what to believe and who to follow, where to bend over and pray while showing our ass. We don't need to be told if we should eat this or that. I don't want to be told that on a certain day, for example, I'm not allowed to touch animal hide. So stupid, huh, Jews? We should be able to dress however we want. Marry whoever we want. Think and say what we want. And also to learn as we want... and it is not the young Afghan women who will tell me otherwise...

Let's meditate, let's take time to do things, let's cherish ourselves, let's find our personal essence, we will inevitably reconnect little by little with ourselves, and this will give us the strength and energy to face Life and its trials with a smile and an unshakeable faith in ourselves and in the creative forces of the Universe, or the God you want.

PS: In the series "the truth is elsewhere", take a look at some very enriching Youtube videos which teach us that Jesus would have been touched and taught by the Buddhist principles, during some of his wanderings in the north, and that he would have taught his way of seeing things, based on these precepts...
Of course, it was already 3,000 years ago that some tribes followed these teachings, it seems consistent.

After three days I feel fantastic. I have absolutely no desire to smoke, which is already a good point, I feel good about myself, I eat enough, I can do my daily dose of sport and, above all, I have peace. I don't have to talk to say stupid things, and the same goes for other people, I don't have to listen to bullshit. Royal peace. A feeling of harmony when everyone moves in silence. We all float, like Jedis...

We are now about 35 men and as many women. The older ones must be in their forties and the younger ones twenty.

Some of them have gone. After the second or third day, they wondered what they were doing there, and left. And the monks gathered everyone together, so that they knew what they were doing. I simply watched them, increasing my confidence in myself. The most pure or motivated ones stayed, the bravest ones too.

Gong, we got to go.

I'm sure you've never eaten bananas with seeds in them. I have! And every day. Little bananas with three or four seeds, black, big and hard. The first time I ate them, I thought I was biting a bug.

Rich teaching today. And self-analysis of myself, of what is wrong with me.

Quite a few things, actually. I have to be: "the captain of a boat, whose broad keel sinks deep into the water, which ensures perfect stability to take the favorable winds that will inflate the sails of my destiny." *(that deserves a little swooning there...)*

And I think regular meditation will make the keel grow in me. Without an inner refuge, a reservoir of strength, I am like a rudderless boat. It gets swept away by the slightest current.

Another thing: all my life, I have let myself be dominated by my desires and my sensations. Slave to my senses that I am. When I smoke, when I seek sensuality, or am subjected to too much agitation, all this creates instability.

And everything that is mental or material is **impermanent**, therefore not lasting.

Emotions: someone says, "How happy I am...", it will last for an hour, a day. The person has bought a new car, and in a few times, it will deteriorate, until it breaks. The person has a new lover or friend, and in a while, the feelings will not be the same.

The law of nature, of all nature, is simple: NOTHING IS PERMANENT.

Only this law is permanent, and it will always be so.

Everything evolves, everything is destroyed. Just like our body. This is why Buddhists advocate non-attachment, because attachment is synonymous with suffering, and suffering prevents us from being happy.

Thursday, third official day. It is raining. I haven't seen rain for a month and a half. It's really a day to meditate. Well, that's a good idea, that's what I'll do today!

Every morning, for an hour, someone comes to talk to us about life. There, with the message of a seventy year old woman monk, as kind as anything and with eyes that streamed with love, I got a slap in the face. It was so strong and right. Among his message, I can extract this:

"We must not think of the past, because it is past. We must not think about the future, because it is not here yet. Just think about the present moment, and enjoy it. But the security of the future, how can you not think about it? You see, the second law of all nature, and there are only two that are eternal and will never change, is THE LAW OF CAUSE TO EFFECT, and vice versa. Every effect or thing in a state has undergone a cause. And every cause will cause an effect. If the apple is on the ground (effect), it is because it fell from the tree (cause). So as far as the future is concerned, if one thinks or acts in a sound, pure, clear and correct way (cause), the effects will be the same later. One will reap the same effects!

As simple as that.

The second terrible thing that is thrown in our faces is our selfishness.

When we do a service or something for the community, we expect something in return. Why do we do this? To stroke our ego. When we go to a place and dress up to be noticed, it is to flatter our ego. Our whole life as westerners is based on "I", "me". But this "me" is empty, it is nothing, since it is temporary... Besides, can we really control ourselves? Can we control our emotions? No! Our moods? No! Then we cannot call "my soul", "my consciousness", something we do not control, it is insane.

Even altruists think of themselves first, thinking of others.

The primary cause of misfortunes, wars and problems on our earth? Selfishness.

And it takes courage to accept that we are selfish. It takes courage to admit: "Yes, I am selfish". Many people know this and do not want to face it.

The monk who makes us sing in the evening tells us:
"I have to visit a friend in the hospital who is 86 years old. He wants to see me before he dies, so I can tell him something. So I'm going to tell him that I might die before he does. Why? Because nothing is permanent. Because nothing is permanent." And he bursts out laughing!

Thailand, the land of smiles. That makes sense.

I believe that all Buddhist countries, India *(in part),* Tibet, Nepal, Bhutan and Laos, among others, have this mentality that makes them joyful, and they want to enjoy the happiness of existing, because nothing is certain about tomorrow!

In bulk, some translations of the songs in Sanskrit, and some beautiful sentences read:

The 5 commandments of the Buddhist order:

- Avoid killing any living thing.
- Avoid taking what is not given.
- Abstain from bad sexual behavior.
- Refrain from speaking "wrong".
- Refrain from taking intoxicants and from negligent conduct.

Song of the Excellent Refuge:

When danger threatens, people rush to sacred mountains and forests, temples and shrines. These are not good refuges, they are not really safe. Depending on that, there is no escape from suffering. Those who go to Buddha's refuge, through right wisdom, they realize the four noble truths. They see the suffering in them, it rises, it expands, they see the way out and the noble path to perfect Peace. This refuge is really excellent and safe. Its realization, the fact of realizing it, frees us from all suffering

Reflections on the body-mind (Sanskrit chant):

All material and mental things are impermanent. Once they are there, they cease. Possessed, they are lost. These are difficult sufferings to endure. For once they are born, they grow old, fall ill and die. All material and mental things are not "self", have no soul, should not be taken as "I", "my", "my", or "myself", "my soul".

To check if we are on the path of wisdom, we can ask ourselves this question: are we always prone to anger, envy, anxiety? To be often prone to anger, or to have thoughts of hatred or malice for others, as I do towards morons, is not helpful, for we do harm to ourselves by clouding our minds and bringing confusion to them. We must keep our hearts pure and, instead, in such cases, think of them with compassion, for because of the law of cause and effect, if they do something wrong, they will have to pay for it later.

Friday: A new energy is coming from everyone. A lot more energy in between the downtime. My forehead is also flatter, from hitting it with the palm of my hand so much I realize how stupid I was, and how I lived like a child until now.
The first few days, it was difficult for me to get up, and after meals to go back. Now I have a lot of energy, I feel much less tired.

An hour later, I don't say the same thing. Last night, I had the heebie-jeebies, I was like in withdrawal. I was dreaming of a juicy cheeseburger, filet mignon with morels, pizza, a coke, a cigarette, sex, in short, all the old demons were coming back to the surface. I was sick of sitting still, sick of doing nothing, and above all, sick of not being able to concentrate while thinking about it! Sick of being sick of it all.
I tell myself that this is the transit stage after four days, deprived of all distractions. It's hard...
As you can see, you can't really control your moods.

People are still leaving. The natural sorting out happens in the mass. It's getting hard for everyone.
What the hell are we doing here?
I can't leave. Morally.
Rigor and discipline, please, Phil...

Internal reflection: in fact, for us Europeans who have to think and plan our careers, our happiness, confronting others with our worries, this path and meditation are a help to solve our problems, and live in peace of mind.

The following is the pure Buddhist teaching, or the way of the Dharma (Dharma is that which is, that which endures, that which is always there, that which is not born and does not die)

Some doctrines that can help us live more quietly:

- "No expectations, no attachments", not expecting anything from anyone.
- "Every day, I do nothing," to detach from the ego we put into everything we do. Let's just do them, and that's it.
- As long as we have problems ourselves, we cannot deal with the problems of others
- "This is just that. Why taking it so seriously?".
- Do not get attached to our feelings, good or bad. They are impermanent and unsatisfactory.
- K.I.S.S. (Keep It Simple, Stupid!), or don't get mad, we don't need much!
- And the last one, which I really like because of its simplicity: "Buy what you need, not what you want".

List of emotions that can hinder progress:

- Sense desire (when we want to receive something).
- Bad temper, or unwillingness.
- Lassitude, or torpor.
- Anguish, distractions, remorse, anxiety.
- Doubt, lack of confidence.

Harder now, and which can be dangerous:
- Greed, avidity.
- Anger, hatred.
- Illusions.

Like big waves crashing against the rocks, these latter emotions can sweep away and kill people. When we become aware of these disturbances, we must see at once what the cause is, then stop our brain on that cause, and breathe, IN and OUT, until calm is restored. If this is not possible, we must direct our attention to something else, the rain, walking, doing something with our hands...

Some tips to get rid of certain moods:
Lassitude: breathe deeply, take a shower, don't sleep too much, get up quickly, don't eat too much.
Restlessness: walk, look at a tree or something quiet, listen to the rain.
Doubt: think clearly, know what you know and what you don't know, stick to facts and not ideas, know what you want.

Vipassana method: meditation through attention on the breath.
 Duration: 2 or 3 hours

- Long, even noisy, forced breathing to start with, get into the swing of things. 20 minutes.
- Long and gentle breathing, nose-heart-stomach concentration and reverse. 30 minutes.
- Short breaths (for hyperventilation). 3 minutes.
- Feel your body, the wind, the sounds. 1 hour.
- Put your attention on the tip of your nose and feel the changes in temperature for example.

The mind must be clear, pure, stable.
If this is not the case, do not go any further.

Next:

- Contemplate the constancy, the impermanence of everything, and concentrate on an image, with the breath.
- Concentrate on the joy, feel it to the point of ecstasy. With each breath, seek ecstasy.

21. Dancing with the cobras

I found an occupation during the "walking mediation". When everyone disperses in the huge palm grove, I climb the palm trees. Like a monkey. It requires physical strength and good feet, control of my emotions *(if I fall...)* and concentration. It's good, and I like it. When will the "palm tree climbing" take place at the next Olympic Games?
For the moment I'm climbing at about four meters. The descent is technical, with a steep climb...

Another very exciting thing in this cloistered world of evolving ascetics: snakes!
I remind you that we are in the middle of the jungle...

The other night, I enter my concrete hut, and what do I see upstairs, curled up in one of the openings overlooking the back jungle? A baby cobra. Oh the pretty creature of death!
Thin, about a meter long, it sleeps there.
So I take it gently to put it on the ground, so that it goes away. No fear, I want to play with him.
Always this damn attraction to danger. But he's a baby, with a small head and mouth, so where on earth could he bite me, except at the tips or between the fingers?

Yesterday, I saw another one of about 1m80, much bigger, black, shiny, a good head of killer, a beautiful beast, crossing the lawn to throw itself in a gully of brush bordering the coconut grove. Superb contrast between the light green of the lawn and this shiny black undulating.

Today, I see one again. Maybe the same one, I don't know. A black cobra. I gently grab it by the tail before it hides in the brush again, just to tease it, and release it. I can't help it, stronger than me. Intense exhilaration, adrenaline shot, or sudden death wish. Then I start again. It's an extraordinary feeling to be in friendly contact with one of nature's most terrible assassins, a born killer. I discover in myself a phenomenal attraction for snakes, close to love, to veneration. A real jubilant attraction. I want to play with them too much.

He hides, wondering who has the affront to disturb him, who has the most powerful venom in his kingdom. I force him to move so that he comes out into the grass, towards me.

And we run together! Well, if I may say "run". He undulates calmly, I suppose to get away quietly, and I run alongside him. What a splendid creature! What a crazy feeling! This is life, this is the wild truth! Impossible to cheat in this world!

So exciting!

Well, I realized it much later, anyway..., running with death next to me, I didn't realize it at all, so full of my own energy, kept inside me during all those days of meditation, ultra-healthy food and inner calm.

All this power that is not distilled outside the body provides a rare inner state, you have to experience it to realize it. And so... no fear. Not even the thought that it could be dangerous. Like walking quietly on the edge of the roof, 12 meters high, during my active meditations.

In short, I became an Avenger.

Hollywood, 10 million dollar contract signed.
Snaky-Phil.

Sunday: lazy day.
I got up late, I don't care. It's Sunday.

Nice teaching this morning by the old lady.
In the afternoon, I give a two-hour massage to a German with
back problems. He really enjoys it. And so do I. That he enjoys it.
It's a nice reward. I had told the seminar coordinator that I
wanted to do the massage, and he sent me this first client, who
broke my back a bit.

This morning's teaching is about sense pleasures and the
impermanence of things, according to which we should not be
attached to our desires, because nothing lasts. Example: We want
to eat a delicious pizza. We dream about it. We buy it, it is
appetizing. We cut a piece, put it in our mouth, is it still the pizza
we wanted so much? No, it's not the same one anymore! It has
changed and is not so appetizing anymore. This
shows that there is no point in following all our desires and
desires to the letter, because in fact, it's just a pizza, and we risk
suffering if we don't eat it...
First, there is the contact with the eyes, therefore a sense, the
sight *(the pizza is beautiful)*. Then the smell, another sense *(it smells
good)*. So there are sensations. Good or bad. If the sensation is
bad, ok no problem, our mind detaches itself from it and moves
on. If the sensation is good, there is desire. And there, if we let it
go, it can lead us to attachment to the thing, thus making us
prisoner of creating a "self", "mine", "my", and suffering one day
or the other.

That's why the old lady advises us to tell ourselves, for anything and everything: "that's just that". That's just that, and nothing else. That frees us from attachment.

For everything, the most important thing is to have the right vision and then the right intention. Then everything will come in the right way so that our mind can live without suffering. How and to what extent can I apply the Dharma in my daily life? First cultivate and strengthen my determination. To be adamant about smoking, for example. Then through the practice of meditation. Then, to stop being a slave, to free myself from my desires. And each time there is desire, there is desire to possess, therefore creation of a "me", and sufferings.
Also develop my concentration. Always stay in the present, think about my breathing, the thoughts that come to mind, and get rid of those that haunt me. To regain a good moral character.
But that doesn't mean that I won't allow myself any more pleasures. I will only control them, I will not be a slave to them anymore *(like beer in the evening for example)*. And above all, I won't be attached to them.

That's why I really liked the basics of Buddhism. They leave me free, I can do whatever I want, knowing that if I fall into excess I will suffer. But I will have decided it. Only me, no one else. This makes me equally responsible for everything that happens to me in my life. It's nobody's fault but mine. I like that.

Active meditation on the roof of the dormitory building this afternoon. Or more precisely on the edge of the 30 cm wide wall. Twelve meters high. No fear, absolute calm in my head, just walking around the building. I could be singing or dancing.
Is this due to my now regular practice of meditation, or is it due to the fact that I don't talk, so I concentrate my energy as much

as possible inside rather than scattering it? It changes you as a man, that's for sure! A very intimate communion is established with things and nature. A new dimension is created. And fear is no longer present. It no longer exists. Whether it is with snakes, or with the vertigo of the void, the calm is absolute in my head. No more fear, just an incredible and powerful force within me. Isn't fear just an emotion?

Tuesday: 8th day. I realize how right my intention and action to shave my head was. Unconsciously I felt the need to get rid of a too cumbersome ego, to clean up my appearance, my little ways, all those ticks with the hair, just to look good and satisfy this ego. I felt the need to make this change in myself. Now that I am here to understand many truths, I am on the right path.
Where will it lead me? I do not know. But I will apply the moral reforms and my new precepts.
The future will be all the better for it.
Cause and effect.

It's amazing how conditioned we all are by food. I haven't eaten in the evening for almost two weeks now, or a banana and a glass of soy milk, and I haven't lost an ounce. On the contrary, I've gained muscle with the gym every morning. And in the evening, I am light, I am not hungry, I sleep well and wake up well. Can you imagine that in Europe? In the evening, we don't eat anymore!
No more eating at each other's houses, no more eating out in the evening...
Why has this never been possible? And I specify "in my head".
Because I was bored!
So I looked for every way to satisfy my senses, my sensual desires, and good food is the dominant one.

Because we lack spirituality in our cities. So we let ourselves go to the pleasures of the senses. And we usually eat only to do something pleasant, to forget our dull days. We are slaves to our desires.

How many times have I eaten in the evening, either to fill my stomach or because it was the only pleasant thing planned for the evening. How many times have I felt empty inside? So I had to fill myself up. But I wasn't hungry.

So we eat to fill our inner voids, we give our bodies work, we pollute the earth more with our excrement and farts, all because we are not awake, we are slaves and dependent on our desires. We are small...

Fasting, stopping eating for X days.
When I was a kid, living on a farm, we didn't eat anything on Sunday. It was a fasting day for Cretins-Christians, and it suited everyone because... we were poor. So, a day without food couldn't hurt, and it also relieved the family purse.
A good point for Christians and those who fast to Lent, because apparently, putting your body at rest one day a week can only do good. When the body is at rest, no longer working to ingest, assimilate, metabolize and transport nutrients throughout the body, that's a lot less work, and a lot of savings in calories and energy. All the organs are at a standstill, and can rest for a while.

Around my 40th birthday, I did the test of stopping eating for a few days, just to get back the drive and the serious desire to eat, to be hungry.
Like the hunger of the little boy who has played ball for several hours and comes back with a hunger in his stomach when he yells to his mother: "Mommy, I'm hungry!
I wanted to find that feeling again.

Here is a transcript of this week of fasting:

1st day, Sunday: easy, nothing to say, no special discomfort. I have to say that, as a kid, we always did the diet on Sunday, so no worries about not eating anything that day.

Day 2: coffee this morning, followed by another, with soy milk and water. I get fear signals twice during the day, furtive thoughts of withdrawal, am I going to die if I miss another meal? Things like that... Once or twice my stomach asks for something, it gurgles... I drink a big glass of water and it passes. No worries, I feel fit to continue. I appreciate having time in my day, the time I usually spend going out shopping, preparing food, digesting. That time is now available. I worked this afternoon and found myself very focused. I also feel quite light.

Day 3: slept well. My tongue is getting mushy and white, a few little dull pains in my kidneys, nothing bad, I guess the body is starting to eliminate blocked toxins. No sign of hunger. I drink a lot of water, and go and buy a litre and a half of fresh fruit juice. Between the litre I drank at night and what I take in during the day, I'm up to about 2.5 litres a day.

Day 4: Everything is fine. I have energy again when I do sports. I'm amazed at how my muscles behave, they don't seem to get tired! I like that... I'm still not hungry. On the other hand, in the early evening, I get cravings for tastes on my tongue, my palate starts to demand flavors and textures. It irritates my calm mind. From time to time, I speak loudly to recondition myself: "Strength and honor, Phil, rigor and discipline!" because I know I could break down; there's no one to see me...
I'm starting to get into the game. Four days is not nothing, the game is on...

Day 5: no need to say it, I'm at my best! I feel super light, I've lost 2 kg so far and I'm quite happy about it, I feel fresh, I sleep well, I wake up light...
People really need to know this, it's important, it seems to me, because it goes against popular beliefs and urban legends such as "not eating means dying", or "I miss a meal, I get weak"...
As far as sport is concerned, it's crazy. I feel that my muscles can give more and more, it seems to me that I have found a new energy that I didn't have for a long time, I feel more enduring, my muscles don't hurt anymore after 15 minutes of activity like before. I'm still not hungry, but I'm getting more and more bored in my days because I'm missing moments of pleasure! My palate is demanding its due! It moans every night at dusk like a vampire... 2 more days to go.

Day 6: still at the top, waking up impeccable, my mouth is no longer pasty, but rather fresh. I don't really have this pain in my kidneys anymore, my urine is clear, and... still not hungry! I do twenty minutes of sport in the swimming pool, nothing to say, I feel good. I drink two coffees in the morning, lots of water, fresh fruit juice, and I have plenty of time during the day, because between noon and 2pm I have nothing to do. Same thing in the evening. That must be 3 hours a day more for activities. As for concentration, it's crazy, I love it. I can concentrate a lot more than before, I can work a lot better.
I dream of eating again, because I need these moments of pleasure in my day. I'm not made for an austere life... At least now I know that. Only tomorrow to go...

Last day, Saturday: not hungry. Still not!
What is wrong with me? How is it possible?
I'm being strangled by my desire to taste... That's what's getting hard.
My energy is fresh, I want to do lots of things. I can feel the electric currents running through my body, faster than usual. My thoughts are racing. I feel like people might be confused if I talk to them as

fast as I think. My intellect is more powerful than before. I try to meditate but so many ideas and thoughts come up, I can't. I don't want to sleep either, so I'm not able to. I don't want to sleep either, even though I usually take a nap every afternoon. So much for digestion, eh?

Another important fact is that I haven't done the heavy lifting for at least three days now. I'm a bit apprehensive, because what's still left in my intestines should still come out, right? But if there's nothing left up there to grow, what can I do? The last time I did a 14-day fast, I did a purge with 3 and a half litres of warm salt water, and that irrigated everything downwards, perfect cleansing.
Well, that should hold until tomorrow.
I'm off to the gym, to see how my body reacts. My energy is there, fresh and available. I have less strength because I have few carbs in my body (sugar, energy), but much more tone. I can see it when I lift 30 kg in the biceps as before, it becomes difficult after a dozen or so, however the exercises like "gaining or pilates" are easier than a week ago. So I'm clearly getting more toned, both physically and mentally.

End of the fast.

Conclusion: after seven days without eating, everything is positive! Lost 3 kg, first fats.
Much more tonus and intellectual energy, a crazy focus and still not hungry ... while I am a sacred gourmet!
The first time I went on a fast, I started eating again after four and a half days, because I had a Meetic date that evening, and I couldn't see myself standing in front of my girlfriend without eating when she would order... I forced myself to eat again in the evening, for my date. But I still wasn't hungry.

I then tried fasting again about two years later, this time with the goal of seven days without food. Only liquid. Drinking various drinks like coffee in the morning, fruit juices, lots of water, but also

after 4 or 5 days, a glass of wine or a beer, even a little rum - naughty that I am - because, well... anyway, I always do things my way.
Everything went smoothly, just like the first time. It was quite simple despite the first two or three days of usual tensions, and the stomach commands that were sometimes insistent. In this case, a big glass of water, and everything calms down...

I have never committed myself to a strict protocol for a diet or a fast, as one can sometimes read on the Internet, like: start two days before, by changing your food, to prepare yourself, and ditto, at the end, before you start eating again. It's boring. I do it my way, as I feel it, at least I'm sure that my body will manage it well since I don't impose anything on it that doesn't come from me...
This second fast was a great experience because I was relaxed, and after my first attempt, I knew that everything would go well. And it did. By dint of watching for signs of hunger, the days passed, and I arrived at the seventh without having found the hunger of the little boy screaming for his food.
I started to eat naturally again, in small doses.
Result and balance: I lost three and a half kilos, which suited me quite well, I found a crazy energy, totally crazy because, my body not having to work intensely three times a day to metabolize the food I brought, all this energy was there, available, and I sometimes found myself working for eight hours in a row without even noticing it, so concentrated was I. It's crazy, you have to experience it to believe it.
It's also worth noting that I continued to work out every other day, just like before... just to push things to the limit, to not have any qualms at the end and to be able to say: "I continued to live normally".

For my 3ʳᵈ fast, I wanted to push my body a little further, always further, you are starting to know the man...
I set myself 14 days.
Yes you read that right, fourteen days without eating.
And guess what? Everything went well. I only lost 5 kg, hardly more than the 7-day fast, and... I was still not hungry after those 14 days.

On the other hand, I was entering into an ordeal worthy of Koh Lanta to test my limits, to test my body and the mental strength I can keep on it, to push back the borders of my psyche and to test my intentions, and my fears. The fear of lack, the fear of the end, the fear of dying, the one that is engraved in each of my cells since 30 000 years of survival.
And just this sweet fourteen-day inner battle was a pleasure, a delicious game. On the other hand, not having any more pleasure slots during the day became a torture. The first few days I would challenge myself to do it, I would let myself go with my feelings and sensations, and then I would get used to it, until everything was fine, eating would fade into my memories, I would lose the habit. But for a man like me, an epicurean enjoyer, it became painful at the end of the day not to have my little reward, my sweet pleasure of the palate...
It was he who urged me to eat again. He begged me to put some taste back in his mouth, and several times a day, if possible. His sensors would electrify at the thought of something juicy or tasty in his mouth. It was becoming painful. I dreamed of food. Of pleasures.

For those who would like to go further, at this point, they need to start with a deep cleansing of the very nature of their cells and their programming formatted by 30,000 years of hunting and fear of starvation. Our cells all contain this program, and it can be erased through meditation, through reprogramming techniques so that they no longer contain this pattern.
This, plus other techniques that are well mastered by breatharians (I let you search on Google), will allow them to pass the 21 fateful

days so that a complete reprogramming can be done in them, and that they no longer feed on solids, but exclusively on prana, the cosmic or solar energy.

Yes, it exists, people are currently living on Earth having stopped eating for several years, and even great athletes. We can discover their testimonies on Youtube and it is fascinating.

22. End of the monastic retreat, a new man

It's getting very, very hot. Summer has begun. In the afternoons, you want to do nothing. All life is spent in the shade.
I'm getting tired of it. Fortunately, it's the ninth day. We've acquired a good base of reflection and practice. I'm itching to be free to run my life again, to meditate whenever I want, and to feel the change again, the escape, the discovery, the journey, being free.

Another story of snakes: while returning from meditation, it is 9 p.m., the guy next door also discovers a snake coiled in the ventilation of the wall of his room. Immediately, I take a picture and then have fun with him when he is on the ground. If only I knew more about snakes, I could keep him for a while or play with him again. Crowd. Finally, I take him by the tail and we put him in a bag to release him outside the dormitories. Well, it's still a cobra...

Thursday: tenth and last day!
This morning, excitement on the program. I exchange 3 words with a Hawaiian, who shows me a mountain next to us and tells

me that there are caves to visit. So much for the morning speech, I'm a little tired of it anyway.

We sneak away, like kids doing something stupid. We have to climb a small limestone cliff full of rough spots and holes, it's a real pain in the ass and razor sharp! It's hot and humid, full of vegetal smells. First cave. They follow one another, there are defiles and narrow passages. I think that no one must come here or has come for ages. This adds to the excitement of the discoverers that we are. We do some caving. Sometimes we come across bats. Pictures.

A little further on, in a stupid passage, I twist my ankle. And here it is again. Always the same one! I limp away. After a very impressive passage of descent in climbing, we find ourselves in a place closed of any access, which must have 10 million years. We find a shell! It must be from the time when everything was covered with water. So these caves and tangles of corridors, it's as if we were exploring underwater, thirty meters deep. And there, lost in the jungle, is the largest of the caves. Already, at the top, before climbing down, a very strong smell takes our throat. We know what it is. A mixture of bleach and rot, there is ammonia. And the further down we go, the closer we get to a sound we know. We walk on a green and brown smelly molasses. The droppings of bats! Hundreds of thousands of them, in whole clusters, on the ceiling, others fluttering in all directions. John, who gets too close, is hit on the head by two or three. Just startled. Less than us... We continue, bent over. The whole ground is covered with excrement with that particular smell. These are the ones we see at nightfall, scattering and flying in all directions in search of insects.

After having had our fill of emotion - John saw another snake afterwards - we returned to the monastery. Drink up! We have lost at least two litres of water each! No one will have noticed our escapade.

Today, all morning outside, and in the afternoon I sleep until 4pm; I'm not doing anything. Tonight there's usually something special planned for the last night.

A line is drawn on my monastic life.
Here I am, free again, in Surat Thani, on Friday February 11.
We left the monastery this morning.
Last lunch in silence. We packed our bags and left our prison rooms.
Exit from the monastery, farewell to everyone.
Bus for Surat Thani. I am with a girl, Ute, a German, intelligent and smiling. We go in the same direction. The South. We are also accompanied by a Canadian who wants to teach English here. We find a nice guesthouse on stilts made of wood.

I am nervous. After so much silence, all this noise and this new agitation make me nervous. As proof, when we board the motorized dugout that takes us across the river to the guesthouse, I slip or stumble and my bag, the small one, falls into the water. Damn it! Fortunately, it didn't sink. Almost everything is wet, books, camera... I pester!
Two hours later, settled, my mind a little calmer, back in town, I devour a local candy store full of cakes and, with Ute, we eat a lot of junk food, or good things, depending on which side you look at it...
Goodbye Buddhist precepts! Goodbye to the beautiful doctrines on the slavery of the senses! Goodbye to food and drink!

Tomorrow, we leave for the island of Phang Nga.

I still realize the importance of all that I have just learned and experienced.
I feel more complete, more aligned, almost happier.
More at peace.

Arrival in Phang Nga. The scenery changes. Everywhere in the countryside, rocky peaks, domes of 30 to 50 meters high covered with vegetation, are bristling, as if pushed by the earth.
Everything is incredibly green, of a crazy tropicality.
Arriving at the bus station, we book a cheap half-day tour for tomorrow to discover the extraordinary landscape of Phang Nga Bay. James Bond's island - in "The Man with the Golden Gun" - is included in the program, as well as a fishing village, and in the afternoon we head for Phuket. Staying here is of no interest except for this boat ride.

Splendid. On board a motorized dugout canoe, for five hours, we travel through the mangroves, places once infested with crocodiles and snakes, which still look unwelcoming; they are large expanses of submerged land, and the trees have huge roots that tangle under the water. At low tide it is a striking sight. The whole valley where the bay meets is bristling with peaks or sheer mountains. And this fishing village is really incredible. It's like walking inside a city built on water. We only walk on boards 2 meters above the water, and all life here is organized for fishing. When there is no fishing, the men sleep, the women take care of the souvenirs, there is a school, a mosque... it is the most picturesque village I have ever visited!
Unfortunately my companion, Ute-the-brave, is leaving me, she has only two weeks left before leaving and she wants to spend them on a quiet island.

Visit of the James Bond island, wow, the postcard on sunset...
This rock is the great curiosity of the area, and the island is
swarming with sellers of trinkets and souvenirs who have a lot to
do.

Back to Phang Nga Bay at 2pm for dinner and the first bus to
Phuket.
That's it. I am there. Low-end hotel but still expensive.
I am in Phuket. Bank, post office, and the ticket for Koh Pee Pee
tomorrow.

The day after tomorrow morning: horribly long because I have to
wait 14 hours to take the boat.
Phuket, I will remember it. It is ugly and there is nothing. In fact,
only its beaches are interesting. Well, ok, they are beautiful, I
must say...
I go to the post office for nothing ! Nobody thinks about me,
hello my social life... I phone Geneva, everything is fine at home.

Then, hop! In the boat. Two hours of sailing. Arrival under a
monstrous storm. I am soaked because I spent the crossing on
the outside deck. The sky is heavy, magnificently black, with grey
and white streaks and lightning. Good morning welcome...

On the other hand, it's so beautiful! It looks like an island of
pirates, simple, hyper-tropical because it is lined with palm trees,
a real beauty! I'm at the port and take a *long-tail* boat to go to
Long Beach, five minutes away, where the guidebook says the
cheap bungalows are.
It's nice. The water is incredibly clear! And what fish seen since
the boat!

Splendid beach, rather broad, of the bungalows out of wooden and an immense Thai house which is used as restaurant and reception. A lot of young people. It is cool.

I ask permission to put posters for massages in strategic places in the restaurant and on the line of bungalows, we'll see if it bites ...

23. The dream island : Koh Pee Pee

First alarm clock on the island. 5:30 am, the alarm clock rings.
Yes, don't lose the good habits!
Tai-chi and yoga on the beach.
Ouaahhhh ! What a wonder... What a pity I can't see the sunrise,
it is hidden by the island in front. Mountains hide it.
The place is splendid. It is soft. I really realize that I'm on an
island. Sometimes it's not obvious, but here it's obvious, I know
I'm lost on a piece of land somewhere...
The silence is broken by the ultra-noisy boats that come and go
between the village and this beach. Of course, these are the free
exhausts of puncture-proof diesel engines and champions of
black smoke. They are at more than 100 decibels per boat, and on
the water... the noise ricochets endlessly...

The bungalows are cool, made of wood and bamboo. Sober,
nothing too much, the toilets are a hole in which I pour the water
to evacuate the waste. The showers are outside, also made of
wood, old wood full of holes. Hum... I feel that there will be
some staring... sorry, I like the game too much...

The corals, the fish, it's hardly believable! And I'm not getting
carried away by saying this. The pulse at 50, I repeat, it's

incredible! I move forward three meters into the water and already the first fish are coming. It's great. They say to me, "Hey, hi there! After five minutes without moving, there are fifty of them circling me! And the colors! Yellow, blue, bright grey, I can't believe my eyes. I am a child, I am swimming in happiness. Immediately, I run to rent a mask and a snorkel and I go back into a meter of water. The water is so clear. I take pictures of the fish around my foot, because no one will believe me...
This time I squat down with the mask, without moving. It's a dream! They are in three dimensions. And they look at me, they are all around me watching me with their little eyes. I laugh, I'm happy. And it makes a funny noise, laughing with a tuba in my mouth!
When I move my hand forward, some of them brush against it to play. I can touch one or two of them. It's exciting, exhilarating, I become a child again.

Later, I go for a drink at the local restaurant, still drunk with joy, and I discuss massages with a waitress. The chef is interested. He doesn't believe the price. 100 baths for two hours, that's impossible! But yes, with the Phil, it is possible! Appointment is made for 12 hours.
I give him a great massage for two and a half hours. I'm exhausted because he's so heavy.
He is so happy that he gives me two 100 baths notes. I only take one as agreed. It will be a good business card. Afterwards, on the beach, I give several photocopies to some of the women I had seen before.
As a result, at the end of the afternoon, a group of four women come to my bungalow. One of them wants a massage. She's in her fifties and must have back problems. Tomorrow, 5pm, it's on. And that will keep me busy.
My social life is exploding! ☺

Today is Wednesday, a day of travel, communication and meetings. A day ruled by Mercury.
Indeed, while I am having breakfast, I see again the Hungarian mammas I saw the day before and to whom I have to give a massage at the end of the afternoon. One of them wants her massage now. Ok...
Finish the coffee first, and let's go. Gotta be flexible!
Just don't burp her...

It's going well. About 2 hours and 15 minutes, she is happy.
I'm now getting to know a little bit about how people are after massages: they are fast, awake, full of energy. And it doesn't fail!
Besides, she doesn't speak a word of English, and her daughter has to stay by her side to translate when I ask her to relax or turn on her side.

I then leave for the village by a small path along the jungle. 20 minutes. Barefoot and wearing my flip-flops on my back inside my cotton pants. I already love this life...
When I get there it's horrible. It's ugly, the prices are out of themselves and the people are not friendly. As by chance, it's full of Chinese tourists...
They annoy me these people, always together, stupidly grouped like sheep, loving organized trips where they are dragged to get their money, and they seem to like it, the poor...
The beach of the port is ugly, it seems to be for rich people *(the bungalows are very expensive)* who have no taste.
I quickly come back to my little quiet place and this beautiful sandy beach. The dream!
Loooonnng afternoon where I'm a bit bored.

The evenings are short, there's nothing to do, so I eat and then... well, not much. Anyway, in the water all day under the sun, in the evening I'm quite tired.

Today, in addition to the mask and snorkel, I rented fins. So I can go further, deeper. I love it! Respect for the beauty of the corals. They look like giant flowers, or mushrooms, or broken wood, there's everything.
And I see a shark, my first! Small, maybe a meter, a young one probably. And I feel ancestral and visceral fears rising in me. The water, with all that it represents, my intra-uterine life with the emotions and feelings of my mother when I was in her womb. The anguish of finding myself in a world that is not mine, facing monsters that make us all shudder, maintaining so many legends and who are perfectly adapted to this environment. The absolute masters.

Everyone is talking about two sharks here. The small one I saw, and another one that's about two meters long but apparently runs away as soon as it sees a diver. Maybe I'll see it tomorrow.
I'm still staying here as I've rented the equipment for two days and I might go on a dive-tour-the-island-and-bamboo-tour.

Back in the water. I'm trying to play it super-pro, like world champion freediving. I try to be as calm and humble as possible, as you have to be when you go into the sea, because it's another world.
And I see them! And my heart stops! All life stops. I am only a piece of wood.
First one. Then two, together, bigger, maybe 1.5 meters, swimming slowly.
Perfectly adapted to their environment. Splendid creatures. The Formula 1 of the sea.
It must be said that this morning the water is low, the bottom, in some places, does not exceed four or five meters, and the sharks turn here. Among a multitude of fish, alone or in schools.
Sometimes I see up to 200 fish in a group, swimming against the current, waiting for nutrients from the sea.

And if I do the same, in the direction of the current, then I become a big fish that swims like them. And from the morning sun I can see its rays all dipping at the same angle, like blinds letting in the light.
The visibility is good, up to at least 30 meters ahead, horizontally. After that I can see shadows, and when fishes pass in front of the light, and I know that there are sharks around, my imagination goes wild and I think I can see their shapes and shadows everywhere!
So control my breathing, calm down and trust in the beauty of life, and see objectively that sharks are just big fish perfectly adapted to their environment.

This does not prevent me from leaving the beach with a wooden stick of about 1.5 meters long, like a broomstick, and I firmly clung to it to protect myself as I saw the monsters turn a few meters away from me to continue their way, then disappear into the land of shadows ...
The nearest one passes calmly about 2 meters from me.
My fingers are embedded in the wooden handle, heart at 180 beats...

Back on the beach, my heart is still
beating with excitement and admiration.

Humans are definitely simpletons when they don't know.
Yes, because it's all there. With knowledge, fears disappear.
Later, when I learned what sharks are, how they live, feed and
reproduce, and especially why and how they can be interested in us,
well, all my fears disappeared and I had nothing but love and
admiration for them when I saw them evolve, or even reproduce
among themselves.

I even kissed one on its snout while it was sleeping.
I know, it sounds a bit flamboyant, but you know me, I'm not a liar.
It was a leopard shark, one of my favorites, and I saw it at a depth of
about 12 meters, resting on the sand. It was about six feet tall,
beautiful, and not moving. Usually you can get pretty close, no more
than 3 meters, and land next to them on the sand, but soon the
Lorenzini bulbs - present on the front of their heads - detect an
abnormal agitation or vibration in the water, and they go off
peacefully, with crazy grace, propelled by their long tails... You
can't help but love them.
But this one must have been sleeping deeper. So I landed gently on
the sand, like a special space shuttle would, very slowly, about 3
meters away from him. I knew it would all come down to this, I had
to approach as slowly as possible, holding my breath, not moving
the water, no vibrations...
I took a deep breath, the longest possible, forcing myself to stay in
contact with the ground because my lungs would inevitably rise. I
could then approach the beast by containing my breathing, very
slowly, inch by inch, until I was so close.... It was terrifying and
exhilarating at the same time.
Then I slowly
removed the regulator from my mouth, not letting any bubbles or
vibrations escape into the water, and I stepped forward to place a
kiss on its snout.
Koh Lanta, "shark kissing challenge" won.
I then pulled back, slowly, and 3 meters away from him, I put my
regulator back in my mouth, on the verge of apoplexy, to finally take
a huge breath...
I had kissed my shark.
Who can say the same? This moment was captured on film by my
photographer friend who was with me.

So sharks are not dangerous, only 5 species out of 140 could - and I mean "could" - be "interested" in you, and even then, only if you do the wrong thing. Like swimming like someone who is afraid and will therefore emit the vibrations of a fish in danger or sick, an easy prey in the wild for any predator that prefers to save its energy to feed. Finally, isn't this what happens in the great plains of the Serengeti, with the big cats, for example? Nature is well done, predators first go after the weakest, easiest to eat. For sharks, it's the same.
So swim quietly, don't excite them with rapid and disorderly movements, and there will be little chance that one of them will be interested in you.

Knowledge, friends, is what frees us from irrational fears and anxieties.

I feel great today.
Yesterday I was a bit depressed and agitated, but everything went away with the sharks, as if after an orgasm...
In the afternoon I went back and saw two of them again. They are grey with black fins. I will learn that they are called blacktips. Basic. I meet a lot of people. There's a lot of movement on the island and the longtail boats are always bringing their tourists, morning and afternoon. Most of the life is spent at the beach restaurant, which must be at least 200 meters long, covered with straw and bamboo. Great view on the sea and the two islands in front, about 1 km away. Some stay one day, others one week or more. Many French and Swedish people. I avoid talking to the French. I'm not here for that and I'm not really interested in the French mentality.

Nice Sunday today ! The air is light, I'm going for a walk, a little air will do me good.

And what a wonderful day I'm having!

There are times when we have like an aura around us, people like us, we have the "tchatche", we are good. And right now, this is exactly my mood. On the boat that takes us around, I am surrounded by pretty girls, pretty landscapes... but what a nice day!

I see a sea serpent, streaked with blue and black, splendid, swimming on the surface with an elegant sensuality, beautiful islands. We eat on a beach where two families of monkeys live; the male comes to see who are these inquisitors who come to disturb the quietude of his domain, and then returns to his picking, while I go to see who is this animal...

It is fantastic to see them evolve in their element, totally free. I feel life, freedom and joy flowing through my veins.

I also meet, during the two snorkeling sessions, a big octopus, about a meter in diameter, with all its tentacles spread out and, when I want to tease it with my snorkel as a stick, it clings to it with its suction cups and I have a hard time getting it to leave.

Back around 4pm. There's a note on my door for a massage at 7pm.

Rest, meditation.

That's the time, I'm going. I got the number of the bungalow. It's some kind of Swedish Viking, six feet tall, 200 pounds! Ouch, this is not going to be a cakewalk! Too big to do the massage on the bed, we have to go to the beach. This will be the last time I do this!

Sand everywhere, my knees hurt from the sand, the darkness makes me sleepy and most of all, the guy, completely relaxed as per my instructions, sometimes impossible to lift or move!

I hurt my back!

Afterwards, the guy super happy, we drink a drink together, I am washed! More than two and a half hours. And even then, I hurried and skipped some positions. But considering the length of the segments, there was too much work. His toes, for example, felt like fingers!

The girls: there's the little blonde, Swedish, cute as a button, she's leaving tomorrow. There's the Romanian girl, blonde, sexy, young *(17)*, she wants a massage tonight at 6pm. There's also this English girl, fantastic, travelling for 2 years, who spent 3 years in Japan for work, mysterious, happy, a radiant aura around her. Hummm, I love this place...

Unfortunately, everything is ephemeral, impermanent. In a few days, everyone will be dispersed again. It's hard not to get attached.
Impossible even, fate will show me!
Because the next day, chance tells me that they all leave at the same time the next day. Oops, damn it. Sadness.
But during the day, the beautiful Romanian doll comes to me because she wants a massage. Great! And beautiful! Imagine a dream creature asking you to touch her, to massage her for two hours. A totally fabulous, firm, deliciously hilly body of a young woman left half-naked in front of you. It is sometimes difficult to concentrate, especially when the little one, lying on her back with her eyes closed, puts her thong back in place, showing me her beautiful apricot perfectly. But how do you want me to work then?
Well, I do my job with delight, sometimes my massage pants a little too tight I must say, my best massage since I left the monastery. She loved it. She wants to come back...

My brain and my senses need to explode, I'm working on it...

Meanwhile, I befriend Mary, the Zimbabwean-born Englishwoman, blonde, tall, 33, who has spent her last years

travelling. She is very sweet, wise and has a smile that speaks volumes about her knowledge of life and her humility. Everything I like.
We go diving together. When I see her snorkeling beside me, doing acrobatic figs in the water, her body moving like a dolphin, I realize how sensual she is and how much I want to know her more.

Let's not forget that I left, in principle, to go and find my wife, the one who would become my wife. And a woman who gives me butterflies in the stomach, that's not common. I think I'm going to take a serious interest in her!

6pm: the massage. The young Romanian girl comes back. Little icing on my cake... The girl is dressed sexy. She has a white body, not a bit of fat, a firm and perfumed skin, supple limbs. A delight, a treat, the consecration, the dream of every masseur. I enjoy myself for two and a half hours, she falls asleep at the end when I massage her face, and can't believe my work. But that's normal, I got off so much that I put all my love and adoration of her body into every move I made. A real fantasy!
I think she's looking at me lovingly, her eyes half-closed and full of bliss, calling out to me softly for passion... I
have to control myself to limit my erections and not rub myself too much against her, some positions are really borderline, like legs totally spread, foot next to her sex for the extension of the inner thigh muscle, my toes at half a centimeter from the mini-string cover... Damn!
That would be... too sexual!
Next time I'll ask her to get naked.
A little bird tells me she will.

Like I said, I love to play...

I eat with Mary. We talk, she's leaving tomorrow.
In three minutes I know I'm going with her.
She has to go to the border for a two-week visa, and then to a
national park. So we can spend four or five days together. Okay,
the decision is made.
She is surprised... and delighted.
We sleep together in her bungalow. No sex, lots of tenderness. I
know that's a sign, too, from my side...

Tuesday: 5:30 a.m., wake up, pack my bag, sort out some details,
and at 9:00 a.m. we get ready to leave the island after breakfast. I
could have stayed another week because nothing, absolutely
nothing, displeased me on this beach, on this island.
But I think that I can give and receive so much with Mary that I
am leaving.

Those teasing Gods sent me the beautiful little Polish girl anyway,
right in front of my bungalow as I was leaving, she wants more,
and young and fresh as she is, I'm sure she too will want to play
more precisely this delicious game of refined sensuality leading to
the delights of the flesh.
Pfffff.... Sometimes I pester outright against these mischievous
Gods who play horribly with me... They beg me in a very
unpleasant way sometimes. Throw a shell at them!

This island is the most beautiful of all those I have seen. A real
postcard. I know I want to live there, I could stay there a long
time. It has everything I love. I walk barefoot, the people are
simple, fishermen are used to tourists. Rough, ok, but after some

exchanges, their smiles become natural. Lots of restaurants to fill me up with good things, girls coming all the time, discos in the evening to have fun, and accommodation is not expensive, in front of a sublime sea.

Here in Koh Pee Pee, everything is positive in my mind. For sure, I will come back. The sharks, the calm, the freshness of the arrivals and departures that bring the renewal of the travelers, the massages, the great people I met. It's good to leave with good memories.

I didn't know yet that I would come back later, to stay there for a year and a half working as a diving teacher! The most beautiful years of my life...
And this young girl from the East will haunt my fantasies for many years, and frequent erotic dreams in the morning...

Here I am, on Wednesday, in a Chinese hotel in Hat Yai, the second largest city in Thailand because it is a few kilometers from the Malaysian border. It is a city of exchanges.
Mary has her visa. We spent a second night against each other, without having made love yet. A sign, for those who know me, that something deep is being built. Our relationship is intense and deep. Like we've known each other for a long time, if you know what I mean... karmas, past lives, would you knock on my door?

Hat Yai to Pak Bara, a small fishing village, to take the boat to the island of Koh Something *(I do not remember)*. Few bungalows, even fewer tourists, a few travelers in tents, it is clear that there is no room for everyone here. We are hosted by a guy who lives six months a year here, and who built himself an incredible wooden house. He makes us feel very welcome. In the evening, some locals arrive, one with grilled fish, the other with a plate of rice. Everyone smokes, except me. It's really a beautiful conviviality.

We spent an hour and a half against each other, in 50 cm of warm water, on the beach, to relax. An extraordinary moment of sensuality, greed, romance and desire. Mary spends the whole night chatting with the locals, she is really passionate about communication.
And I, of course, stupid animal, not seeing her in the morning by my side, I start to imagine incredible stories and I make a stupid scene of jealousy. Ridiculous, of course. It's been a long time. No big deal...

We leave the island to return to the port of departure. An hour and a half by boat, to immediately jump on another one, bound for another less populated and quite far away island, Koh Lipe. That's why we chose it. Too remote, no tourist should go there. A piece of the world with a lover. The dream.

Indeed, it will take about 5 hours 30 by boat to get there! And it is expensive. I understand that there are few tourists who come to this national park. There, we feel that we are on a deserted island or almost, isolated, lost in the middle of the ocean. I love it.

It's a full moon. AT 6 p.m. it's still light, the sky is zebra-shaped with pink and orange, and the moon is already shining. So much for the fantastic colors that surround us. It's intensely sweet and enjoyable.

The neurons are sure to be popping.

Our bungalow is in the only fishing village on the island, there must be only four, and I don't see any tourists. Yes!

Children, mothers, some fishermen, it breathes with great simplicity and authenticity!

I feel good with Mary. And so is she. It's not a dream in fact, it's simply a woman I could marry. I know that in my bones. I'm not saying this on a whim, I think she's fantastic.

I feel very humbled by her because of all she has done. So not macho at all. Our beginning of relationship is balanced and unashamed.

After a lot of "sex" talk on the boat to get here, we finally make love once we get to the bungalow.

It's dark, we light a couple of candles, incense sticks to keep the bugs away, and start warming up. Oh sure, the temperature rose quickly! Only we got so hot that the bungalow caught fire! No shit! Well, just some of her clothes next to the candle, which caught fire. I immediately jumped on it, put out the fire with my hands and burned three fingers. Not too bad.

When we talk about it afterwards, we laugh about it.

And since then we have not stopped playing erotic games, making love, so that the box of condoms did not last long!

This morning we went to discover the village of the "Gypsie Sea", the Gypsies of the Sea, in the hope of buying condoms. Can you believe it? We were probably the only tourists in the year to land on this floating village, not necessarily to discover the harmony of this way of life, but more pragmatically to find condoms! ☺ Luckily there is a health clinic here, they gave me ten free ones. I leave it to your imagination on how I made myself understood to ask for condoms from a Thai woman who does not speak English...

You meet people who come here regularly, I can see why.
This is the island of paradise.
The colors, the village, everything is so simple, so harmonious and quiet... what more could you want?

The new couple.
This is the Holy Grail for me! It's my life's mission to achieve it. Well, it's also the hardest in my opinion. That's why I've been married three times (three weddings and a funeral) and I still believe in it. Until the end. And always more finely...

Since humanity entered the Aquarian age, around the 60s, there have been revolutions. That of women, May 68, the various genders claiming their rights and words, and later on, around the year 2000, the first dating sites appeared. And since then, there have never been so many. Why? It's very simple: the energies in place on Earth push us to complete ourselves, to become more and more complete. Full of ourselves, of our own energy, and no longer that of the other...

This is where the understanding must become fine, obvious.

As a child, I always saw couples loving each other, and then hating each other, only to love each other again, to break up again, and so on.
I saw couples who were together only to vampire each other energetically, to feed off each other. Power relationships, harmful or toxic, that nourished one while impoverishing the other. Or couples unable to separate, who only stayed together to protect their

family... So they ate each other's noses all day long in relationships that are not of the order of love and benevolence.

Since the 2000s, the energies in place have pushed people, young or old, to internalize their needs. They then discover that they actually need the other person less than they think, and that they are not so bad alone.
From then on, dating sites naturally find their public and explode. There have never been so many singles in the big cities as there are now.
And people are waiting...
For what? No one knows, and everyone is waiting...

In fact, the Aquarian Age pushes us to complete ourselves, to fill ourselves perfectly with our Yin and Yang.
So I "man" must complete my Yin part, my feminine, my sensitivity, my softness, take the time to do, and especially to be. And you "woman", you must complete your being with this Yang part which is the masculinity, the fact of taking a decision and to stick to it, to have more rigor and discipline in your life, not to go back in doubt, to learn tenacity, to know how to undertake alone, to build your life like a builder...
The Yin, the Yang, everything starts to make sense, no?
When I have reconciled with my Yin, I will no longer need my partner's to feel complete.
When my partner has refilled her own Yang, she won't have to suck on mine to feel good.
We will no longer need to destroy ourselves by eating our energies, we will be nourished by the other's, do you understand?
Thus the new couples will be able to find each other, to form themselves, to apprehend together, as complete beings, the future and the possibilities of evolution as two.
The couple is an entity in itself, independent of the two characters. There is the man, the woman, and the couple.

A fusion of three energy fields.
Sexuality will also change.
This has already begun since we see new sexualities emerging, such as the "no sex" who claim not to need it to live fulfilled, the threesomes, the homos who can now marry.
With the new couple, sexuality is more subtle, less bestial. It is no longer a question of copulating to have pleasure but of evolving together towards something unknown and much more nourishing than a simple orgasm.
Kundalini, when you open yourself to us...

Personally, I consider that the woman is a key for me.
The key that will allow me to dive into her bosom, to swim in her inner lake, to recharge my batteries, to find peace, to push myself to practice occupations to "be" rather than to "do", to be myself and to improve myself, because damn it, I'm still a basic bumbling man for whom a beer in one hand and the TV remote control in the other are enough to spend a good afternoon.
One last absolutely essential condition to create this new couple: we have to talk, talk and talk some more.
Talk, talk, talk. All the time.
Putting words to our ailments.
Talk about sex, talk about the awkwardness between us, talk about what's sticking...
Only talking can unblock situations. A few words can leave room for the sun and chase away the clouds.

I'm not lying to myself, I know that I need a woman to develop my internal life, my intimate life. Otherwise I can be lazy, and like everyone else, I like that...

24. Adam and Eve in Paradise

Third day of pure happiness.
Yesterday we explored the corals together. What a joy to be with her in mask and snorkel. She is my little mermaid, so graceful in the water, so voluptuous with her dream body.

Yesterday, the shock! Talking with her, about what she did before, I realize an essential fact.
When I was preparing my trips, I was a rookie and I was looking for easy travel, countries with developed tourism, in short "the good life". Now that I'm a little less of a virgin, I realize that if there is one continent that can bring me a lot, it will undoubtedly be Asia. Australia and America will be for fun, except maybe South America. But spiritually speaking, I won't have much to gain from it. So if I go ahead with what was initially planned, I'll come back to Asia in about five years, just enough time to finish this trip, get a job for a year or two, and go back.
To live Asia, in my opinion, you need to have a strong mind, if possible young too, to be very adaptable to the sweet mess around. I deduce that I have to do it now.

So I'm thinking of a different journey. A different journey. For the sequel.

God, it's just that the people we meet along the way always have a message to bring and it's never for nothing. An encounter can change our path, alter the trajectory of our destiny, or simply help us to reflect.

It's very exciting for me to have to rethink a route in these countries I never imagined going to. China, for example!

A route is taking shape in my head. It's not very difficult because Mary is going north and she inspired me. I would like to spend more time with her. She brings me a lot, I've never met such a person. She has no limits, no fears or apprehensions that are not justified; I feel small next to her and that's what keeps my ego low, almost non-existent; I have everything to learn from her. And it can only be good to leave my ego on the doorstep of her heart, having trampled and crushed it well beforehand...

I'm going to stop writing down my expenses every day, it's so "petty banker" and it doesn't really do anything for me anymore. I know how much I withdraw from the bank anyway, so I can do my calculations.

It's incredible how much she inspires me. I never stop talking to her about poetry, complimenting her in such a colorful way that she sees me as the epitome of the famous and envied "French lover", like Cyrano de Bergerac. The nose less long.

Every morning we get up before six. Meditation in front of the rising sun, yoga, stretching, both of us... it makes me crazy with joy.

We find a bigger bungalow. Not many people here anymore. These last two days were holidays in Thailand, and all the bungalows were full. For the first time, in the restaurant, the Thai people were tourists like us, on holiday or on a trip.

Yesterday was a full day of groping. I hadn't done that for a long time. I pinged from the bed to the hammock, from the hammock to the chair, occasionally a shower, before coming back to the starting point to begin a new cycle. 24 beats per minute all day, and 5 of tension.

I realize that I am living some of the most wonderful moments of my life. I am on an island 1,800 meters long and 500 meters wide, a hundred inhabitants, 15 tourists, breathtaking beaches, amazing colors between sunrise and sunset, the beauty of the sea and I am living an idyllic love story.
I'm really happy...
I must have done some nice things in another life to deserve this. But everything has a price of course...

When we go to the other side of the island, to the other beach, it's to rub against each other, talking in 50 cm of turquoise water at 28 degrees, when it's 40 in the shade. It is a lagoon. The sand is white, incredibly fine. There are lots of small translucent crabs looking at us with their funny eyes, raised a centimeter above their bodies.
Nobody. The beach is about 500 meters long and there is nobody there!
So, we make love...

We play, we rub ourselves...
Adam and Eve.

Last night we talked seriously.
It continues north. Burma, India, Nepal...
I'm interested.
We could go through Bangladesh to India, for instance.
Then she'll go back to Europe and do the opposite of mine.
After Nepal, I'm interested in Tibet, and by cutting China from
west to east, I can reach the Pacific coast to Hong Kong, and
then go down to Malaysia via the Philippines.
Wow, I'm really excited about this!
What dreams, what projects!

It's a beautiful journey, and if I hadn't met Mary, I wouldn't have
thought of it.
So we're going to go on a bit of a journey together. Cooooooll...
And, among other things, between two visa applications in
Bangkok, we'll both take the Aids test because we're fed up with
eating condoms, we want to make love in total freedom.

It's been windy for two days now, just after the full moon. The
sea is rougher and the tides are higher. The bay in front of us
empties completely when the tide is low. No more water! It's
incredible. All the underwater rocks, the corals, are visible. An
incredible sight. In one hour, when the tide comes back in,
everything is covered again.

It's great to see the place of children here in this authentic little
village. They are everywhere, and they behave like adults. I mean
they are free, they do what they want and, in the morning and

evening on the beach, it is a real pleasure to see them playing or chatting like grown-ups, drawing on the sand. Like this little three year old girl, in the water at low tide, all in her thoughts and stories, looking at the crabs and seaweed, while elsewhere any other child of her age would be calling her mother for fear of being left alone...

Many men carrying children in their arms, that too is a beautiful sight. They are considered the new generation of the island and they have their own place, they are not considered annoying, noisy, useless or inferior.

Every adult cares for the children of the island, talks to them and considers them their own.

Two more days.

I stop counting the days, I don't know what the date is today, and it doesn't matter.

We spend fantastic days on our paradise beach, we take pictures, do tai chi, sports, games, we snog in the water, the whole beach is the witness of our complicity, she is our mistress, she lets us love each other, and I think she enjoys it.

Such a beautiful beach can only be seen through the eyes of those who love each other.

Many crabs will remember her body, the sun reflecting in her hair, and the sand sticking in patches on her sensual forms...

Our moans too.

We live a very healthy life, and Mary is very happy. She tells me she feels fresh, clear, pure, brown *(tan)* and happy. She sings Irish ballads in the shower and plays tunes from her culture on her flute. She has total confidence in me. And that makes me feel good, it's been a long time since a girl gave herself to me, didn't confide in me completely. Why not?

The dialogue ! Of course...

I don't know why, but with her I can talk about everything, and with sincerity. Even intimate things like my libido, nothing is dirty with her. And mine is complex, varied and sometimes confusing...

Just great !

.

As you know, I went around the world with the firm intention of finding the one who would become my wife. That was the deepest reason for my departure, unconsciously...

It so happens that the one who later became my wife, my first wife and mother of my wonderful daughters, I knew her from before. I had already dated her.
When I tell you that the groups of souls generally all reincarnate in the same place, it is not for nothing...
But hey... it wasn't the time at that time.
So here's a nice lesson: when it's not the time... well, it's not the time, and that's it.

We met again two years after my departure, and as she was the one who wrote to me and answered most often to the mails I regularly sent to my friends in Geneva, she was the first one I saw when I came back to say hello to everyone, during the off-season in Thailand. And it was a good thing, because we immediately fell in love again at first sight.
It was then the right time! Bingo!
Thanks to this trip, we have written a lot to each other and we have created links that are invisible.

Two beautiful children, ten years of happiness, at the end of which I asked for a divorce, to find a more... unstable, surprising, unpredictable, unexpected life, full of unknowns.

Because I am like that, and I was fading away little by little...
But this did not affect our love, which will remain eternal, in the
ether (ether-nal).

A lot of wind these days, which makes the boat trip we wanted to
do with several people here impossible. Maybe tomorrow, on our
last day here in paradise...

Among all our common points, I forgot to mention the game.
We have invented secrets between us, we play several games,
backgammon, cards, dice, and when we reach a certain number
of games won, the winner has a magic card, a "joker", the "click"
that he can use at any time to realize his fantasy, and the other
will have to comply with it, imperatively, without any restraint.
Just to maintain a powerful intellectual excitement...
Enormous!
Our complicity is at its strongest.

Today, a boat tour. We visit some nearby islands on a motorboat,
see some beautiful corals, and laze around on a beach eating
coconuts. Our bodies are blooming, tanned, feline, muscular. But
mine is a bit tired: too much sun, a lot of sex, my shoulders are
sore and so is my back.
But how good it is to feel at the top!

Have you ever imagined, or conceptualized the fact that when we
make love, the man gives, and the woman receives. At least that's
how I see it. At least when it's a true exchange of love. The man

gives energy back to the woman by re-inflating her, as one might do with an inner tube. Ok, I know, the image is not very flattering, but it is a fact that I have noticed very often. At the end of the exchange of love, the man is very often exhausted, and the woman in great shape. The yang man has given a maximum of energy to the woman, who is recharged. The man is exhausted and happy, his thighs often in compote. The woman often wants more, because she is not exhausted...
I like to believe in these "yin and yang" energies that are replenished by our mixtures.

25. Krabi, Bangkok, and goodbye Thailand

Friday 4 March: back to civilisation, then Hat Yai.
In the guesthouse... I am sad.
Again noise, radios, televisions, nuisances and consumerism,
whereas on our island we had nothing and needed nothing.
Tense people, stressful atmosphere, damn, we were so good
there!
We left this morning at 9am, after a last tai chi on the beach,
followed by a hearty breakfast that we did not return on the boat.
5 hours of boat for the 50 km that separate us from the mainland.
I must say, my heart was in my throat.
There is one plane a week from Bangkok to Burma, a country
that is completely closed to tourism for the moment, and that
grants a maximum of two weeks of visa to travelers who want to
visit it.
Mary has some things to do before she can go, like applying for a
new passport, hers being full, and going to see a dentist, so she
calculated that she had to leave now. End of paradise!
As for me, I have to go through Krabi to pick up the mail that I
hope will be plentiful, and stay for two or three days while she
starts to sort out her affairs in Bangkok. We'll meet there.
In the meantime, we are in Hat Yai and the first good thing about

civilization is the food, as there is milk and cakes again and all the good things we were deprived of for nine days.

I want to force myself to live with the same tranquility as before, just so I don't start running around unnecessarily...

Not to get caught up in the System and its stressful race.

Now that I feel more balanced and we both feel great, we'll continue like this. We are both well aware of that.

Saturday: while she goes to the border to try to get two more weeks, I go shopping. A cheap extra-flat calculator and, passing a music store, I go in and come out five minutes later with a harmonica and a book on how to become a tenor, and a flute.

I have a lot of time on my hands, and I've always wanted to play an instrument, so...

I've kept some sand from our magical island. This sand is the finest I've ever touched, it's pure silk. The whole beach was silk, and the neurons flickered with excitement as we walked on it barefoot.

A few days later : I start to play the harmonica thanks to the Thai book *(where everything is written in Thai)* which allows me to create little tunes. Well, when I say play... for the moment I blow in it, and the birds run away !

I haven't attacked the flute yet. Mary told me she will teach me.

Sunday: we split up this morning, I leave for Krabi, and she for Bangkok. We'll meet again in four days if all goes well.

Painful trip in a minibus, 5 hours and a half of sardine, in an oil I would have done without ...

Then long-tail boat to the beaches which are three, enclosing a piece of land, a peninsula with rocky peaks and impressive peaks, just at the ends of the beaches.

I expected better. Krabi, it's hyper touristy, I find a bit the atmosphere of Koh Samui.

Many guesthouses along the beach, menus for westerners, pizzas, spaghetti carbonara, cheeseburgers.
Ok, I'm fine with that, just don't stay too long!

Bad news on the phone today, my credit card is no longer valid. This means that Visa will have to send me a new one, it will take some time, and the problem is that after Bangkok, I don't go to very developed countries and safe enough to receive a credit card without any signature!
Tomorrow, I'm going to get the letter explaining all this at the post office in Krabi, and I'll see what the solution will be.

Great, I have the letter and it's for the Swiss Visa card I don't use. False alarm then.

Letter from my mother, phoned my sister, it feels good!

Discovery of the surroundings of the beaches and the mountains. Sneakers and elastic band on my feet to prevent a sprain, I improvise myself as a climber. It's great, it's so steep that there are ropes to help the ascent. At the top, we have to go back down in the middle of the mountain because there is an inner lake. The descent towards the lagoon is even more vertiginous. It is by abseiling that it is done. Very wild, the vegetation is dense, there are gigantic trees whose trunk is at least four meters in circumference! The humidity is incredible, impossible to dry my t-shirt even when I stop. Inside the mountain, in the inner lagoon, we are in prehistory. Nothing seems to have changed since then. Unfortunately there is not much water left. Exhausting climb up and down on the beach. Lots of monkeys here, it's great! Besides, they look so human, I feel like talking to goblins, or dwarfs...

In the afternoon I see a big jellyfish, enormous, floating three

meters below the surface in deep water, surrounded by small yellow fish that protect themselves from the graceful and slow movements of its paralyzing carapace, this transparent bubble that contracts spasmodically taking all its little world to get lost in the big blue. It's more beautiful than any TV documentary!
Not to mention the drifting school of thousands of jellyfish, small ones this time, ready to ensnare me...
It's true that every touch or rubbing with these jellyfish causes irritation or burns. I've experienced it myself.
It's raining cats and dogs tonight.

It's crazy, it's always the same. Nothing for weeks, and everything happens at once! Hey, girls...

I meet here an American girl of the same age as Mary, beautiful, nice and I could like her. She is alone and it would be a fantastic opportunity. But here I am, I prefer to continue my relationship with Mary, with a pure heart, and be able to look her in the eye when I meet her on Thursday in Bangkok.
Aaahhh, damn, if I didn't have so many qualms...
Random brain, please go back upstairs!

Everyone goes to bed separately.
The next day the weather is stormy.
Like every morning, I wake up to the crowing of the rooster, a big jerk, maybe the biggest I've ever seen, who takes great pleasure in crowing in the morning right under my window. If I had rocks in my bungalow, I'd throw them at him!
And yet, God knows I love animals. But perhaps he is getting even, for when I was playing the harmonica in my bungalow, he came to me, surrounded by his chickens and with his crest proudly raised, and tried to intimidate the one who dared to make noise rather than music on his estate.

I'm happy to leave. I'm starting to feel the need to change countries.
I've been in Thailand for almost four months now, and for a first time in Asia, it's already good. Mostly I feel the need for more excitement than just moving, walking, taking a bus or a boat.
I need a new culture, a new currency, new faces and a new location on the globe.

One more week in Bangkok, just to settle some administrative formalities, to do the AIDS test as Mary will do for our sexual tranquility, to get new vaccines if necessary, visas for Burma, Bangladesh, and Nepal, some purchases such as photo films which are very expensive in those countries, to exchange or sell the books I read as well as the guidebooks which are no longer useful, to send by mail various things to my mother, that's a little bit what will make up the program of this week in Bangkok.
And to take care of Mary...

The storm is rumbling here in Krabi. Still on the beaches, I wait for it to calm down so I can take a boat to the city.
It's amazing how different the air smells when it rains. And I have to say that my sense of smell has improved a lot since I stopped smoking and started meditating.

I leave in the rain. I'm alone in the motorboat with the fisherman. The sea is rough and every time the bow splits the wave, the wind throws either spray over the boat or buckets of salt water. He was already soaked from the start as he was not covered by a small tarpaulin. After ten minutes I'm as wet as he is, but happy. I run my tongue over my lips to collect the salt water, it drips down my face. The clouds in the sky are unbelievably dense, everywhere on the horizon, they are grey or black, gaps of blue sky, dark curtains of rain falling not far away. It's Dantesque in its power!

Bus to Bangkok, fifteen hours of travel.

My ass hurts, and my knees because the seats are too small for me. Anyway, let's go...

Appointment with Mary.

She is there, great! And great. Big smile. Very happy to see me again.

We spend the day taking her things to change Guesthouse. We found a superb room, all in wood, next to Khao San road, the travelers' district.

We visit a market like I've never seen before. An incredible jumble of stalls where the butcher's shop is next to the fishmonger's, between two stalls of fruits and clothes. I've never seen anything like it before. Meat, offal, whole beef carcasses are displayed in broad daylight, mutton tripe, cow's stomachs are next to fish and shellfish. The smell is disgusting, I want to vomit. Just next to the tripe and blood on the floor, a pretty flower stall...

Again, the left side of the brain, the sweet Asian mess...

Thais use more the left side of their brain, like almost all Asians I think, and it's their creativity, the illogical, the imaginary, the immaterial, the abstract, the opposite of us westerners who use rather our right side, the one of order, logic, calculations, programming of our lives. This is why books and guides warn us not to ask ourselves too many questions because they live and think differently from us.

The proof once again with this market. Or the bus to get here, half of whose windshield was held up by tape and stickers, whose driver was driving with restricted visibility. Unimaginable for us! I fucking love it!

Evening full of tenderness and love with Mary, and I eat the best ice cream of my life. On her warm body.

Intense, burning with sensuality.

Screaming. Wild night.

The next day: we have to take care of our visas.
Up at seven o'clock, we make a date at the Bangladeshi embassy.
Laughs…

Reunion with the crazy life of Bangkok and its excess.

I wait at the bus stop . In all those which pass, people sleep.
Proof of the length of the journeys. And suffocation arrives. I
can't tell if it's heat clouds from the sun or exhaust fumes, but
hot, suffocating mists envelop me and half suffocate me. It's a
feeling of shame towards the earth, guilt towards nature, and
helplessness when I see these vehicles, big or small, ejecting such
toxic black clouds as they accelerate. People know this, but how
do they get to work and earn a living? They have to drive these
beat-up cars that sometimes run out of gas, and that goes beyond
any ecological consideration. So they put a scarf over their nose,
some use a gas mask like in operating theatres, they make do.
Man adapts...
The city is so big, everywhere the streets are jammed, there is no
center, it's a mess everywhere! It took me an hour to get to the
embassy, a point 15 cm away on the map. No problem. We were
a bit lucky because it should have been closed. We got our visas
and above all a fantastic first contact with the first Bangladeshi
people.
They were pleasantly surprised that we wanted to travel and
transit through their country. Few tourists do it, it's a country off
the tourist routes and the people at the consulate give us a good
welcome.
Moreover, we will take a road that nobody uses to go to Nepal.
Straight north to cross India, towards Darjeeling *(the tea)* and
arrive in Nepal.

"This is a road for adventurers," the ambassador tells us. Wow, very exciting! Mary is really great
for this because she has so much strength in her that she is not afraid to venture off the beaten track.
After Bangladesh, we go to the Nepalese consulate.
Okay, it's just five times more expensive.
We'll get the passports on Monday.
Then I go to the hospital and ask for a blood test for HIV. Result on Wednesday.
Quiet fucks for soon.

At night, everyone in the showbiz street is oozing, greasy and irritable. I feel the same tension. Even between Mary and me. Fatigue, stress, heat and pollution.
What a cocktail! Not great for harmony...
After a night on our own, in the morning we talk for an hour and it gets better. Many things come out. It's good, it had to be, and... an hour later, the room is upside down, the senses under the blood, something like that!
Love...

It's good that it's Saturday today, no paperwork to do in town.
Just take time to read, write, play...

Monday, March 14: The weekend passed like a flash. That's good. Yesterday I slept at least six hours during the day. A real Sunday. Anyway, as soon as we get out we are enveloped in the heat and the exhaust fumes. Added to that, the crowd of tourists and travelers, and the unkind locals, we are still better off in our wooden room, under the fan, each of us dealing with our administrative concerns, writing, thinking and tidying.
All our visas are here, tomorrow we still have to go to the hospital, a last shindig in Bangkok, and we can leave with a happy

heart.

Tuesday: HIV result from the hospital. Negative of course. Yeeaaahh... it's gonna be a sausage fest, a panty fest!

Big storm yesterday. It's good to hear the rain and smell it afterwards.
And at the same time, like a law of nature, there's also a storm between Mary and me. A trifle. Sobbing, reconciliation, tenderness, cuddly night. The routine of a couple, you know.
Mary and I talk a lot, about everything, and that's good because I discover a lot of hidden truths in myself. In particular, I'm not far from being a vegetarian; I'm not yet a vegetarian because of the beef I like, even though it's inedible here. The other day, even a cat left two teeth on the floor! So, if beef is inedible and I don't eat pork at all, then that leaves chicken. But you have to see how they are raised and in what conditions they evolve; it's pretty unhealthy, and I could do without it.
I wonder why I still eat meat... damn the blinders I still wear!

Wednesday: I am now writing in a very weak state. Last night we had decided on a last party in Bangkok. More like a last party, but a first time in Bangkok.
And bad luck, I drink two beers and start to feel bad. Impossible to explain why to Mary. We go to the city, to visit Patpong *(which is in fact the name of the billionaire who owns the whole street)*; it's the street of bars, go-go girls and sex shows. But I'm in trouble. An hour later, before entering a disco, I throw up my chocolate ice cream eaten before the beer. I think the banana split was too much and doesn't go well with hops... We stay two hours in the club, Mary wants to dance, it's a European club with a lot of Thai people. Back to the guesthouse, I will only get out of bed today at eleven o'clock, not feeling well. I could not visit the national museum with Mary. Too bad...

Late afternoon, it's better. There's a monster storm. It's been so hot today that it's really happy that everyone is celebrating with joy the shovels, picks and halberds that are falling in a noise of the sky tearing apart.

We do the accounts with Mary. We settle everything and make the final arrangements.
Mary is on her 721st day of travel, and I am on my 167th.

What I read about Bangladesh in a travel guidebook makes me think that, compared to Thailand, we are in for a rough ride.
It is the second poorest country in the world!
It is one of the most populated too. 115 million souls!
It's going to be quite an experience!

Tomorrow, on the road to Burma.
I don't know much about this country, except that since yesterday, tourists can have a thirty day visa instead of two weeks.
So a country that is just opening up to tourism.

That's it, I'm done with Thailand, this Thursday at 11am, I go to the post office, to the bank, and I'm done.
At 4pm, the plane will take us to Burma, and then... but that's another story!

26. The Burmese: People with a pure heart

Destination Burma.
The plane leaves Bangkok more than an hour late.
This allows Mary and I to study for the first time the information provided by the various guidebooks on this country.
We soon fly over the big clouds that will burst in two hours over the megalopolis. Seen from above, they are magnificent. Cotton, shaving cream, charred snow, it's all so majestic. How can it all hold together in the atmosphere?

Like every time I'm on a plane to a new country, my whole body goes limp.
I feel like I'm going soft again, my spine is just a rubber tube. All the pressures fall away and dissipate. This lasts for a while. I become stunted in my seat.
Then comes the opposite effect. After the effect of total relaxation, I become aware that I am heading towards something new, and my brain, accepting this information, starts to distill the first questions. The currency? The language? Where to sleep? What to do when I arrive?

And here we go again for a new adventure... ·

Arrival without any problem in Rangoon, capital of Burma, also called Myanmar.

Tourists have to change $200 at such a low rate, charged by the government, that it just feels like we're giving our money to the military. But it's mandatory.
The state offers 6 jets *(local currency)* for 1 dollar, and on the street we are offered 100!
So I buy a bottle of whisky and a carton of 555 cigarettes *(recommended by the guide)* for $18
at the duty free shop, I can resell them for the equivalent of 2,000 jets and make a monstrous profit of $2! It's mainly to have cash because in this country we pay in dollars or in jets.
And for us, it's much better to pay in jets.

People are small, of the same height as the Thais *(by the way, do the Thais cut?)*, the faces are less wrinkled, less wrinkled at the level of the eyes, already more "Indian". Matte skin and above all, all the men wear the local "sarong", a cloth around the waist and legs, with a knot in front. A lot, a lot of courtesy and hospitality.
As soon as we arrived in front of the hotel, chosen at the airport and recommended by the local tourist office, we were harassed by black market vendors and dealers. First offers for whisky and cigarettes, and our dollars.
We throw our stuff in the room. Mary hasn't eaten anything all day, we're both a bit on edge, and we have to find some jets, as we only have official currency, which is different from the street currency. And to eat tonight, we need street money.
We find a guy who changes it for us and we eat on the sidewalk,

next to the hotel. Everybody is looking at us, there are no tourists. The looks are nice. We have a very decent dinner of stir-fried rice with garlic and vegetables that Mary took twice, tea, spring rolls, two slices of cake, all for less than a dollar!
It's crazy...
We realize that we really need to speak a few words of Burmese because very few people speak English.
Don't forget that this country is just starting to open up...<
It's only been a few months that the country accepts foreign visas...

First day.
Wake up. Things are not going well between Mary and me ! We are yelling at each other. Gently, respectfully. And the emotional pus drains out...
It's weird to yell at each other gently.
But our hearts are close, so why yell?
I don't think I'm writing this to defend myself, but she's making it hard for herself. She got tangled up this morning, and we got torn apart. And then came the essential questions: do we continue together?
I get up this morning, in my head I was going all the way to Nepal with her, and now we're wondering if we're continuing together.
Why are girls so complicated?
The big question for me now is: if we stop our story, what am I doing in this country? And what would I be doing in Bangladesh? I'm interested in these countries but to share the emotions with two people. But alone? To prove to myself what? That I can walk alone for long?

So if we split up, I go back to my original project?

This is the second time on this trip that I follow a girl and it doesn't work for me!
 Is this not a pattern that repeats itself?

The savior's cape.
Ahhh, the magnificent story of life and the invisible influences that influence us without our knowledge...
One might think that everything is linear, and a non-awakened human will certainly not be aware of the beauty and magnificence of the events on his way. The lived experiences are very often underhand, tenuous and finely placed there for a deep understanding of our beings. But this one often comes after the events are lived...

Let me tell you about one:
My second marriage was to a young woman 16 years younger than me. With a 2 year old baby. Since the time I asked the Gods to send me a beautiful blonde to amuse me - I had only had brunettes until then - here they were sending me a perfect Swedish girl!
Not content with playing with me, the Gods took me at my word and gave me the blondest of blondes.
Ah, but they are teasing!
So I hook up with a beautiful blonde and her baby, everything goes well and... I marry her.
Why do things by halves?
What I didn't know was that I had a pattern firmly embedded in me, and that this new woman would allow me to realize it first, and then get rid of it.
The sacrosanct pattern of the savior.
I wore the invisible cape of the savior on my shoulders since I was a child.

*The child that I was once, always set out to save his mother, this
mother so badly off who spent her time complaining and suffering,
necessarily the little guy that I was promised to "save mom at all
costs".*
*So, without realizing it, all the women in distress that I met on my
way were pretexts for this hidden mission, and reinforced my well-
established pattern of the savior.*
*This young Swedish woman who was cleaning houses for a living,
alone with her child...*
*The Gods deemed this situation absolutely perfect, and tested me to
see if I would blindly jump into this relationship or reconsider their
offer, and open my eyes to this invisible cloak on my shoulders.*
Well, I went for it, like the good fat guy I was back then.

*Nine months later, I kicked her out of our house, again, because she
was still drunk at 5:00 p.m. when I picked up the kids from school.*

*Separation, divorce application. The "blind drunk" package, if you
will!*

Our marriage lasted nine months in all.
A gestation in fact...

*The time for me to realize that the time had come to free myself from
this pattern, this invisible cloak that made me the savior of these
ladies.*
*I have since imperceptibly removed these energies from my body so
that they no longer assail me.*

The days spent together in Koh Lipe had been fantastic, my
weakness was to want it to continue.
But is it really a weakness?
Should I have gone on with my life without a care in the world

and without flexibility, being inflexible?

I don't know, I find it hard to understand, and she doesn't want us to continue together as friends, which I understand even less. She has created this situation because she is dissatisfied.

With what and why?

I didn't touch her much these last few days in Bangkok because she spent her days in her papers, organizing, disorganizing and then reorganizing, filing, sorting and finally putting even more mess in her things. In short, not very exciting for me. But I get by.

So she deduces that if I don't make love to her anymore, something serious is going on. And yet, there is nothing!

The art of complicating life, by Mary...

Anyway, we part ways. I take the train to Mandalay in the north of the country, a thirteen hour drive, and maybe we'll see each other there.

I leave her an address, so we can leave on good terms, if that's what she really wants.

We meet just before we leave, at the hotel.

I write her a letter.

She's very nice. I don't understand anything anymore.

It's really complicated, a woman!

Did she have her period? Was it a full moon?

I don't know...

I go to the station and hail a rickshaw, a three-wheeled bicycle. The poor little old man is having a hard time on a hill, so I get off and we walk together. Big clean streets. There are only a few cars, they are luxury goods, which gives an impression of calm, and the air, despite the great heat (35 °), is light.

Especially after Bangkok, it feels good!

The day falls, the sunset is magnificent and, added to that, the freshness of the evening and the magic of discovering these streets in the rickshaw, I feel puffs of euphoria and joy.
Quickly passed, because when I arrived at the station, thousands of people are waiting, sitting or standing, for the opening of the gates to the platforms.
They finally open, and it's the rush.
I am caught in the mass movement, and it is my weight, with my backpack and my long legs, that saves me.
Some people are laughing, others are shouting. It's impressive!
On the platform, I have the impression for a second that my little reservation will be quite ridiculous if everyone rushes to my place. What could I do?
My apprehension dissipates when the train arrives.
It hasn't stopped yet and I throw my bag and jump in, then walk around to find my seat. No problem, I find it.
Everywhere and all the time, people look at my shoes and my pants. Young people in the country who wear trousers are considered revolutionary! This is the first time I have been stared at by so many people.
It makes me a little uncomfortable when I pay attention.

I was able to trade the bottle of whiskey and the cigarettes on the black market at a good price. Everyone does the black market here. So it made me laugh when the employee of the state-owned Tourist Office, through which every visitor has to make hotel or train reservations - so that the state keeps control - offered to buy my dollars.
Important point: be careful with the pictures! At the train station,

for example, I wanted to take some, I thought about it, but the stations are important strategic points, like the bridges. The local guards wanted to confiscate my camera. So few or no pictures...

I spend all night tossing and turning in my seat. Some sleep on the floor. From time to time, I see a mouse looking for food. In the morning, the red star blazes above the horizon and the landscape is revealed. Flat. Completely flat. This is an agricultural country, the land is dry and early in the morning the farmers water their plots of land. Many of them ride on their carts pulled by oxen. There are many stops in the train stations where children offer water in transparent plastic bags or fruit through the windows. They are beautiful and are surprised to see a foreigner's face. I wave to them, we have fun.
The train passes, or rather skirts, a column of people begging or gesturing to the people in the train. The first tickets fly. I do the same. What a strange feeling to throw money out the window at children and women carrying their babies in their arms!
I later learn that the state has cut off the water here and people need money to buy it. That's why the train is braking and people are giving away tickets. Or maybe it's not the state's fault, but they're still running out of water.

It's amazing how poverty feeds me.
So many lessons...

Arrived in Mandalay at eleven o'clock in the morning after 16 hours of train! No kidding, it was going at 30 km/h!
I spent this trip between sleep and wake, like a sleepwalker. The heat, the shaking, nothing like that to make me soft.
Finally, here I am. A rickshaw driver addresses me, he is nice,

speaks good English and takes me to an expensive guesthouse *(6 $)*. Then, he stops me in a place to eat, in the market, then in another one so that I buy a sarong like all the men here, and return to the hotel to sleep.

The people: absolutely no aggression.

Some people wave at me in the street without me even moving. They are curious, but do not come towards me.

They are Buddhists. Muslims would come to me. The children are very funny and as soon as I smile at them, their faces light up and their eyes crinkle; they smile easily. There is no sense of harshness in this country. A journalist I met on the train told me that everyone eats. It's a poor country because it's badly run, and there's a huge black market for everything. So it's money that the state doesn't see. Hence the imbalance. The women and children all have a cream on their face to protect them from the sun, and it makes two big round spots on their cheeks. It's a mixture of flour and local perfumes with flowers, it smells good and they slather it on their faces rather roughly.

It's supposedly aesthetic and makes the women look beautiful, but I see them as clowns. But I'm getting used to it.

You can feel everywhere that this country has kept all its culture and tradition intact for the moment.

No inscriptions or advertisements for foreign products.

After the nap, I go for a walk.

A guy accosts me and offers me a ride. He is a rickshaw driver. I feel that he does not talk about business, he is cordial and seems honest. He takes me to his place, makes me read a guestbook where everyone has written their comments on the tours he organizes. Then he takes me on his bike, which is brand new, and he is proud of it. I have tea here, I eat there, he is with me all the time.

In the evening, there is no lighting in the streets, the candelabras are there but turned off, and everyone is on a bike. A few cars and, at nightfall, you can make out the silhouettes of the cyclists in the light of the rare car headlights. What a strange atmosphere! Streets of black silhouettes, shadows everywhere, subtle plays of light, it is disturbing...

I feel a purity in these people's relationships, in their spontaneous smiles. Nothing to do with Thailand where people are used to tourism. This morning, I shed a sudden tear when a man smiled at me so kindly in the street. We just passed each other. It touched me so much that I cried. We are not used to that in Europe. A man who smiles at another man must be homosexual. He has to be. Culture shock.

The driver, Wintin, teaches me to speak Burmese. Appointment is made for tomorrow.

Tonight, during dinner, some young boys are in the restaurant and curious smiles create sympathy. So much so that one of them spontaneously places a mosquito repellent spiral next to my legs while I eat. Such a thoughtful and unintentional gesture can only come from a pure heart. Emotion.

Another vision: that of this truck passing by, loaded with bundles of a thousand and one pieces of luggage, and tearing out the electric wires hanging in a bend because of the height of its load. I'm eating on a street corner in a stall, music, and nothing! No electricity. No one gets upset.

Typical Burmese food: fish or chicken curry. With five or six bowls containing different dishes, lentils, beans, various vegetable soup, plants, peanuts and rice. This is the national dish. Plus a bowl of chopped bamboo salad. I assure you that it is eaten and that it is good!

I buy a sarong, which is in fact a large fabric sewn to be folded on the front and closes like a skirt for three people! You put it on, hold the two sides with your hands and fold it over, one hand on the side and the other over the top, tying a knot in the front so that it holds. Very pleasant to wear.
It also allows you to do your business anywhere - even the big one - just by bending down, without anyone seeing anything. People do it, I see them sometimes in the fields. It's almost elegant...

First awakening in Mandalay, Sunday March 20.
After breakfast taken at the corner of the street, composed of Burmese tea with a lot of condensed sugar, a kind of banana pancake and a kind of big doughnut, I go to the Mya Mandala Hotel where I have an appointment with Mary. She's not here yet, so I take advantage of the pool, probably the only one in town. She arrives all smiles. Broken from the trip. We'll see each other at the Guesthouse.

Over dinner with my friend Ha Myint, he tells me how relationships are conducted here. A man who has his eye on a woman must first write her a letter to tell her that he is in love with her, and then another, and another, and another, and another, and another, and another, and another, and another, and another. Then they can date for three or four years, with the family always on their backs to watch them. Then comes the

wedding if everything goes well, and the first sexual intercourse.
He jokingly tells me that all the virgins in Asia are in Burma!
The woman is dependent on the man and obeys him perfectly.

Here comes the other rickshaw driver, so kind and courteous. He
has five children and lost his wife when she gave birth to twins. It
makes me sad when he shows me the pictures...

I'm starting to memorize the first words and numbers. This is
important. If the person in front of me sees that I am making an
effort, the contact is better. Here the contact is very easy, so it
goes even better.
 Everything, except the hotels, is even cheaper than in Thailand.
Riding a rickshaw costs nothing, a meal costs about half a dollar,
which is half the price of Thailand.
A policeman earns eight dollars a month.
A new rickshaw costs $100.

We visit the night market of the city, very colorful, lots of "hello",
some sweets and pens to the children who take our hands, and
we drink tea in some charming places. In one of these places, a
large family offers Mary a very nice fan.
Low tables, stools 20 cm from the ground to sit on, and Chinese
tea *(normal and without sugar) is* served for free. We take two
Burmese teas - the color is more red - and with lots of condensed
milk. Atmosphere as everywhere "hello-hello-mingalaba *(good
morning)*", frank and spontaneous smiles.
Big discussion with Mary about the facts of the last few days
and... reconciliation on the pillow.

A fresh start. I also have my share of responsibility. I don't treat

her as a "partner" and I make some decisions alone, without informing her when I should.
From now on it will be different.

27. The face of Myanmar

I went to visit a shoe shop where they make motorcycle boots, the same as in Europe, for $15 instead of the usual $200! There's really some business to be done...

I've got the shits this morning, I've emptied half my bowels! In liquid! Cash...

Visit of the Mandalay mountain, 1 600 steps and several monasteries and pagodas, one of which contains 709 small white chapels with a marble stele on which Buddhist texts are written. It is the largest open book in the world!
In the evening, we are invited by Wintin, our rickshaw driver, to eat traditional food at his place. Delicious! We eat in front of a dozen pairs of eyes, big and small, living in the house. All the girls envy Mary's pharaonic nose, compared to theirs which is flat and round! We go back home quite exhausted. Tomorrow, we move!

Tuesday: Today I'm in a warlike mood.
Don't know why. It's a day like that... Tuesday is a day ruled by Mars, God of War.

I feel like being aggressive towards all those people who look at me when I eat, I feel like scattering this crowd that gathers and observes us while talking in low voices when we choose a fabric at the market to make a shirt. Always these stressful situations that annoy me.

Normally these are the kind of days when nothing stands in my way in Europe, when I do things the way I want.

Here, it's not like that. I'm in a third world country. That's a lesson for me.

Fortunately, Mary calms me down. Sometimes I feel like the tiger inside me wants to come out and disperse the crowd watching us. I'm not used to being stared at so much, everywhere and all the time. I wish I had some peace. We are really giving of ourselves here. We give of ourselves. For free. Every day.

We take the local bus, which is a small van where 20 people pile up wherever they can, and we, privileged rich tourists, have taken a seat next to the driver for double the price, $1!

We drive for two hours through the surrounding countryside and start climbing into the mountains. The destination village is a small retreat station from the time of the British settlers. It is cooler and the village is quiet.

Mary had read in England *(so it's been over five years)* that a "cottage", a small castle renovated in the purest British style, is somewhere in this village. That's why we are here. We find the residence, which is now a classy hotel, the rooms being $30, so exclusively for tourists. "

PffffuuUUUuuuuiiitttt!" *(Admiring whistle)*. What a house! We have just walked half an hour carrying our bags, we are hungry and wet with perspiration when we enter the "castel", to address the reception.

Immediately, we felt like kings. Courteous welcome, friendly staff, we were shown to our room. It's a great place to stay! Huge, all in wood, fireplace, wooden floor blackened by the millions of steps that have worn it down over the last 100 years, and in the corner of the room *(80 m2),* a mezzanine-style outdoor area. Everything is superb. Mary is happy. We'll be fine here!

Outside, a well-kept park, lawn, majestic trees, birds, squirrels...

You should also know that not so long ago, the Burmese empire was colonized by the British. You can still see their "so British" traces everywhere. So obviously, in a country without TV, radio and press, information does not circulate quickly.

Most people think we are English and that they are still colonized. Which bothers me, because I'm always given the right seat, people seem to give way to me, are too humble, and I, the philanthropist, like to have in front of me one of my fellow men. I am not/no longer a conqueror, I certainly was a lot of that in my previous lives as a warrior. Now I strive for fairness, I no longer seek conflict or domination. Especially in poor countries. I usually go with humility, without showing that I have more than they do.

And I never forget that I too come from the earth, as the son of a farmer, and I will always respect the little people.

Typical British dinner, roast beef in sauce, with potatoes and vegetables.

Heavens, it's nearly 5 o'clock! I have to order my tea!

Tea time, my Lord!

Slept well, very good quality bedding, royal silence, and the little

295

birds in the morning. We are really treating ourselves to a
luxurious stay, Mr. Marquis!
The Duchess and I are going to walk around, show ourselves to
the subjects of our kingdom, and why not take a tithe...

At the market, obviously very colorful and lively, everyone stares
at us. I'm getting used to that. The particularity of this village is
the mode of transportation, which is the stagecoach. There are
plenty of them, beautifully painted, and pulled by horses of
course. It is the local taxi. Folklorico!
We spend the whole afternoon in a beautiful botanical garden
near a lake, a superb place 3 km outside the village, and for the
occasion we rent bikes. Mine hurts because the saddle goes into
my ass, and not being on the other side, it's unpleasant...
Very happy to go back to our beautiful second home, massages,
reading, tranquillos, bonitos, amorosos...

The next day, big day. Or rather, outdoor day. We go to see the
local waterfalls, take the bikes, and off we go. Only the bikes have
only one gear, mine is too small, I touch the handlebars with my
knees at each pedaling and the saddle comes to tease my
prostate...
Anyway, let's go! We ride for an hour to the next village. The
roads are lined with trees with beautiful flowers and all the people
we meet smile or honk.
Arrived at the village, we take a small road and ten minutes later,
here we are at the beginning of the stroll, because we have to
leave our bikes in a kind of carpark, and one shows us the road
which points towards the valley. And it goes downhill! Rocky
terrain. We walk for another hour, alone, wondering if the road is
the right one, and we finally reach a real wonder of nature: a 150

meters high waterfall and several pools created by the waterfall. We swim, walk around, and decide to go back following another path because we had seen some kids taking it. Obviously, we get lost, we climb like crazy to get to the top but we are well and truly lost! Fortunately, a farmer leads us on the right path. In the meantime, I burn my foot in ashes because they were burning the fields...

We arrive at the bikes exhausted and take the opposite way back, all uphill! I hurt my feet on the bike... Grrrr! I can't and don't want to go any further. We stop a truck that brings us and the bikes back to the hotel.

Fifteen minutes later, I sleep to wake up only the next morning. It must be said that I left the morning of this excursion with a nephritic colic and that my intestines are dancing the java. So the Phil is in a bad way!

My intestines have been upset for four or five days now...

We have the right to a superb thunderstorm with thunder and lightning and, in this manor, it's perfect!

We change our program by a hair's breadth, because we are well here and we stay a little longer; we will shorten the rest, since our visa is only for two weeks...

Incredible, the number of catholic and methodist churches in this small village. Made of red bricks, they are real miniature cathedrals.

Surprisingly here, because this is really where it's the most, but I think it extends to the rest of the country as well, are the sugar cane fields. Everywhere on the street corners you can drink freshly squeezed juice. All the bars have a kind of local press, a sort of metal workbench on which two large wheels spaced one centimeter apart are fitted, turning with a crank and cogged wheels. The person takes one or two sticks of sugar cane, and pushes them between the rollers. Immediately, the flesh of the wood is crushed and liquid comes out. Then the wood waste is folded in half, in four, until there is no more juice. It's amazing how much juice is locked up in those canes! It baffles me. When they squeeze the cane, they also slip in a lemon which is in turn squeezed out of the fibers and the liquid is collected directly into a glass without any other additives, and offered to the consumer. It's absolutely delicious, I love it!

A few words about Burma: a few years ago, in 1988, the government changed its policy and changed the names of several cities and the country as well. Previously this country was called Burma because the main race was the Burmese. Now the country is called "Myanmar" which means "gathering of the four peoples". Some people don't like to be called Burma anymore. Another name that will change on the world map in the next few years.

A little word about Buddhism here: all the children join at the age of twelve, shave their heads, and simply follow the five fundamental precepts of this religion. It is a healthy and easy life that they will follow for several years. They stay there as long as their parents wish, depending on their degree of piety. Their only preoccupation is to beg for food by passing restaurants or houses with their bowls in their hands, and it is always an honor for a family to be graced with their visit because they allow that family to be generous, this being done without any look. If there were a look, ego could take over, because begging for food with the eyes could cause the other protagonist to feel superior. So no looks between them.

The life of Buddha: Buddha was born in 566 BC, which means that all the calendars of Buddhist countries are currently dated in the year 2561, whereas we are in 1995. Buddha, the son of a king, was pampered and brought up with the greatest care until the age of 19. One day, leaving his palace, he saw old age, illness and death among his people. He, who had never known any pain, asked to go and live in the forest to find an answer to his questions. He lived there for six years in the strictest destitution and material detachment, and inflicted various hardships on himself (such as fasting for a month), thinking he would eventually find the truth. He did not die but his quest remained in vain until one day, after a meditation, he had a revelation and, during his enlightenment, wrote the basic precepts of his religion and the steps to follow to reach "nirvana", a state of happiness for man. This is the story of Buddha and why temples and pagodas all contain representations or statues in his image, revered by all.

We have to take the train back to Mandalay. The driver of the coach, thinking we were nice I guess, starts his horse in a frantic cavalcade but about 500 meters from the station, something hits my forearm on the windowsill. The tire came off and exploded! Bad luck... We end up walking.
As soon as we arrive at the station, we are taken aside by the station master who puts us in his office to make us wait. Or to put us aside from the people. Exactly as he would have done for English nobles in the last century... which I don't like, and didn't want.

The train arrives as scheduled. We were put into upper-class cars. Soldiers entered the other cars through the windows, there was a lot of shouting and exclamations. The train left half an hour late. Immediately afterwards, the daylight was fading and we found ourselves in the dark, without any light in the carriage. Some people next to us offer us candles, and we drive at 15 km/h for 4 hours, under a landscape lit only by the moon, until Mandalay. There are still things to live in one's life, and this is one of them!

Hotel. Different from the first time. It's Saturday.
In the morning, I go to the market to get my shirt I ordered two weeks ago and, in the middle of the market, I step in a gutter full of shit, garbage and blood, in short... all the shit of the market! Fucking shit! People are laughing, and I'm ashamed. One foot black with mud and the other normal, and nothing to wash myself. I go back to the hotel, a heavy bar on my forehead...
I'm a bit under pressure.
Everything is going too fast. We don't have much time and have to hurry. No time to feel things and events. This disturbs my rhythm.

Today, we're going to Mingun, a small town an hour and a half away by boat, and this evening we're coming back to take another boat. It goes fast, very fast. Too fast...

The boat is small, twenty people are sitting on the deck, or rather piled up, and we go up the river to the village of Mingun. Nice. Good atmosphere, no tourists. Groups of girls holding each other's waists or touching each other in a friendly way, mothers breastfeeding their babies, eyes that accept Mary and me.
An hour later, the sky darkens and in five minutes it's a storm.

Everyone takes shelter where they can, which is nowhere, and we take shelter under teak mats. Fortunately it doesn't last. We disembark under the returning sun. Here, a small quiet village, the few tourists can ride on ox carts that act as taxis. No roads, two restaurants, cows, goats, chickens and children everywhere!
We are assaulted by children, and we walk around with clusters of kids on our arms. Under their consecutive assaults, we bombard them with candy, a first salvo of grey pencils to discourage them, but that is not enough, the buggers come back to the charge. We have to fall back and drop some inflatable balloons bought the day before at the market. The counter-attack seemed to work and the enemy retreated. A few brave men remained and spent the rest of the day with us.

We then visit a very spectacular site as it is the largest construction since the pyramids, in this case a temple built with the help of 20,000 men, slaves, in 1800 and counting, by a king who thought he was the reincarnation of Buddha and wanted to build a pagoda in his image. It was not finished and only a third of it is visible, reaching fifty meters high, damaged by an earthquake.
This village, with its children, is one of the most spiritual and charming moments so far!

We have a few days left in this lovely country, but Mary and I are having a hard time.
We're getting into it unnecessarily - from my point of view - and then we don't talk for hours, each of us grumbling our frustration in our corner, and these sequences are heavy. I'm questioning myself and my relationship.

She's busting my chops when I'm doing everything to please her. It's not fair. Between her rules, the hassles caused by her disordered brain and mental turmoil, the unspoken words and heavy looks, it's starting to weigh on me and it's not what I need. I sometimes fall asleep next to her replaying patterns for hours in which we talk to each other or yell at each other... it gets tiring in my own sleepiness.

So I wake up in a bad mood, having slept badly and a bit tired. Mary, could this be the end between us?

The next day, a big discussion at the café. The words are cold, studied, it seems that it's not only me who ate anger all night.

I have the nice guy with a girl syndrome, because my mom suffered too much when I was little. As a little boy, all I saw was a tired, sad mother who was always in need of something, mainly love. A frantic demand for that something that wasn't coming, and decay aided by medication to try to hold on. The System calls it "depression".

Added to that, one or two suicide attempts with drugs, plus a few trips to the hospital because she wanted to test her legs under a car or to see if her body could resist the 180 kg of a motorcycle launched at 60 km/h, and here I am, getting into the habit of going to the hospital and spending time with mom's hand in mine.

So of course, as an adult, I still take care of my partner in crime, and the famous "savior's cape" has settled on my shoulders. A woman in distress, and Phil comes running... A woman cries, Phil is there to comfort her. Another woman with a small child is cleaning the house for a living, no problem, I marry her.

So Mary thinks I'm a bit discreet with her, not attentive enough, or distracted, etc. Yep, it's kind of normal because I'm not attracted to her like I was in the beginning. I need more sensuality and less I'm-too-small-headed-in-my-storage-because-I'm-bordered, more darling-if-we-were-funny-with-our-bodies-this-night?

I'm bored with her, that's what.

So, from cause to effect, so is she.

We decide to leave each other.

It's over.

I'm sad.

...

The first fifteen minutes.

The time it takes for my fearsome and powerful hunter's brain to see the possibility of being able to look at chicks in the street again without forbidding myself, to be able to touch another body again, to feel the freedom in me again, and... Everything is fine, no spleen or blues.

I want to drink, to get drunk on life and my new found freedom. Which I do that evening, just to prove Mary right, who sometimes wonders who this strange guy is next to her, she so-British-pinched-ass. Now she'll be able to tell herself that she was right to leave me, that I'm not reasonable...

Clearly, this word is not for me!

Boom... bang, cash that right in! That's pretty hard-hitting!
How to explain this reversal, this ubiquitous turn of events? How

could I, who dreamed of meeting the ultimate love, pure and devoted, like the knight kneeling down to dedicate and commit his life to his sweetheart, find myself lighthearted and intoxicated by my new freedom, when at last I had experienced the very essence of my quest?

What is wrong with you, Phil?

All these paradoxes that make up your personality, that still play tricks on you? Sometimes I don't understand you anymore...

Well, it's true, this English woman wasn't really culturally compatible with your mountain values...

Perhaps.

Are you sure about that? Or is it the temperamental kid who wants to play and then get his precious freedom back?

Also possible...

Because the guy who gets over such a breakup so quickly, either didn't fall in love, or will have played the comedy.

But no, in fact, the explanation is different.
Everything is not so simple.

On the road, the people we meet are free and in search of their truth. We meet, we share, we exchange messages, and the course of our long quiet rivers takes us further and further away.

This powerfully loved woman will have been so for the time of our romance. And everything has an end.
I idolized her at first.
How could I have done otherwise?
A woman who has been travelling alone for 18 months, gentle, strong, beautiful, feminine, spiritual, with a dream body.
A mermaid on my way...
Of course, I, the freshwater sailor, fall under her charms, sensitive as I am, and I fall in love.

But of what, exactly?
*I was admiring, yes. I was lonely, yes. I found myself proud to be
with her. I've always wanted a beautiful woman by my side, it fulfills
me and makes me puff out my chest like a rooster. And our sexuality,
our games, the slow way our bodies joined, all of that lifted our
relationship high.*
But after the first few weeks, the magic gradually faded.
*Probably this woman was meant to remain a mermaid in my heart,
almost unreal, unattainable, too ethereal for a guy like me, at the
time.*
Too mature too. I wasn't ready for her, I think, looking back.
*Too much of a "mad dog", eager for pleasure and freedom, I must
have lacked the natural English phlegm, like "Dare I ask you,
Charles-Henri, to fuck me intensely tonight, taking me like a maid
you would rape?".*
She must have sensed this, and stopped trying.
*And our relations went downhill, until the last explanation, calm,
cold, and composed, in the purest aspect of the London bourgeoisie.
Goodbye, Mary.*

I never heard from her again.

*Thank you to life for giving me the ability to not get stuck in old
memories, to not live in the past, to not be depressed like my mother,
and to always be able to get back up to continue on my path.*
There are still memories.
Thankfully.
They can never be taken away from me.

*And that's also why travel is so important to me; I'll be a little old
man with an indelible smile in a while...*

Last night in Myanmar, I asked my favorite bike driver to find me some beers, a dozen for him and for me. But he won't drink, he can't and is not free to do what he wants.
I uncork them one after the other, alone in my hotel room, still full of our discussions and the sometimes cruel words.
Mary has left, taking her things, she continues on her way to India.

I'm drowning tonight... Gobble-gobble of local beers.

The next morning, I wake up in the coal tar.
I pack all my stuff in an artistic and visual blur, and head for the capital to take a plane to Dhaka, capital of Bangladesh.

I don't really know what I'm going to do there, I'm supposed to cross it by foot... My steps guide me there, so...

What next?

Well, Bangladesh crossed on foot, three months of pure
nightmare, I still wonder today, 30 years later, what could have
gone through my head to have made such a plan, and to have
done it...
Not glop the guy !

Then came Nepal, a few months in this mountainous country
where, of course, I did a fantastic 320 km trek around the
Annapurna's, with a 25 kg backpack, with warm clothes rented
for the occasion in Kathmandu, sometimes in difficulty,
sometimes in ecstasy, and always in humor, and in love with the
human being... And with the woman I met there

Then direction India, New Delhi and purchase of a legendary
bike! For me, who has spent my life on two wheels since the day
I turned 18, this was a blessed moment. The purchase of a pure
vintage beauty for my little princely ass. A 350cc Royal Enfield.
Except that in India, they see it coming from far away the little
dreamy westerner, and once again I'm well fooled.
But anyway, it will take me to the Himalayan foothills, to the

Buddhist community settled there after the Dalai Lama's escape a year ago, to be treated by a lama-doctor with a big yak head, who prescribes me herbs from the high Tibetan mountains, and heals me from the dysentery that has been infesting my guts for three weeks.

And finally, the return to Thailand where I become a diving teacher, with a thousand and one drinks and setbacks, the show-off with the instructor's big watch on my wrist, the girls who fall alone into my bed, the return to stupor and lust, but under water this time.

Then my wedding, still underwater, to do it right, with priest, photographer and witnesses.

Then my departure from Asia - my wife having become pregnant and having decided to follow her fears of giving birth over there - for the crossing of the Indian Ocean on an old 18-meter wooden boat, with its share of pukes, surprises and guaranteed emotions, for the return to Europe.

Another book.

The next one, **Absurd meaning of Life (without Whiskey)**, written in September 2022.

I love you, take good care of yourself!

Acknowledgements

Thanks to my friend Jean Louis Floch for his precious help in the correction of this book, which will have made it go from a dusty road book to something readable by all.

Thank you to all those I have met on the road who have allowed me to grow, through the heart or through human experience of our emotions and imperfection.

Thank you to the women I met and sometimes loved, who will sometimes have sponged off the emotional overflow due to such a journey.

Thank you to my angels, the Gods, Amélie and the Universe for allowing me to always have faith in myself, despite my daily doubts and my purely human apprehensions.

And thank you to my daughters who continue to guide me and help me become an ever more connected and luminous human.